Total Diplomacy
The Art of Winning RISK®

About the Author

Ehsan Honary received his Ph.D. in Robotics from the University of West of England (Bristol) and his M.Sc. in Artificial Intelligence from the University of Edinburgh. His interests are in autonomy, collective robotics, and software engineering. He has published many papers in his field. Ehsan was first introduced to Risk in 1990 and has been playing it ever since, given any opportunity! Despite his interests in other 'serious' disciplines, he has always managed to convince his family and friends that spending time playing Risk has many benefits. He is an active member of the Risk gaming community.

He also investigates games technology and expresses his artistic mind using 3D graphics and animations. He lives in Bristol (UK) with his wife.

Total Diplomacy
The Art of Winning RISK®

Ehsan Honary

A CIP catalogue record for this book is available from the British Library.

Library of Congress Control Number: 2007901326

Published by BookSurge, LLC

ISBN-10: 1-4196-6193-0

ISBN-13: 978-1-4196-6193-8

Cover Design: Ehsan Honary

Risk Map Art: Sara Honary

V-A.1

Book's website: www.totaldiplomacy.com

SF0716EM

To

My wonderful wife, Matin,

for her great company and compassion,

and to my parents for their patience and support

"A person who never made a mistake never tried anything new."

Albert Einstein

Contents

Map | xiii

The Risk Board Game

Preface

"I hear and I forget, I see and I remember, I do and I understand."

Old Aphorism

To gain experience and intuition, we need to practice. Practicing must be adventurous so that we can learn new concepts and experience new circumstances. However, being adventurous comes at a cost. If something goes wrong, we may end up paying a price; a price we may not be prepared to pay.

Is there a way to gain experience, without being exposed to the risk of undertaking such adventures? It turns out that there is indeed a way. *Simulated experiences* can put you in the right circumstances; while at the same time remove the potential risk and damage you may endure as a result of making bad decisions.

Simulated experience is big business. Everywhere you look; there is a hint that people are involved in a form of simulated training that lets them become better survival machines in the jungle. Of all the skills one can learn that improve life, there is one that stands out significantly from the rest: how to effectively *interact* with others. Effective interaction is the art of getting the most and losing the least in any given situation.

Hence, effective interaction encompasses a large number of fields such as psychology, diplomacy, politics, communication skills, effective body language, negotiation skills, and many others. To become a better survival machine, one has to seek to master all of these disciplines. This is when simulated experiences come to the rescue. If these experiences are made to be entertaining, they have a better chance of being used by people. Games provide one of the best forms of simulated experiences.

Putting games and effective interaction together leads to strategy games where players need to interact with each other. The best games are those that force players to interact just as they would in real life. For example, chess is one of the best strategy games ever. However, it does not expose the player to a variety of psychological issues. It is played between only two people, which ignores a whole number of issues when multiple players engage in a single game. It also ignores the concept of chance, which is a fact of life and the sooner one can get used to it, the better. The whole point behind using such games is to raise issues. Once a player recognises that he is weak in a particular skill, he can focus on that specific skill to improve his survival capability.

This book intends to raise issues when you play games. The best way to learn is by example. One of the best games for this purpose, as you will see in Chapter 1, is Risk[®1] and its variants. The intention in this book is not only to show you how to play these games better, but also to show you how you can apply your acquired skills to the real world.

To make this book a reality, I had to go through several stages of research. Apart from playing these games repeatedly (as difficult as this may sound!), I attempted to collate common strategies and techniques that experienced players use.

These strategies were placed on my dedicated website and were discussed by fans from around the world on the forums.

Various scenarios and situations were discussed and voted on. The intention was to collect the global opinion on the best tactics and strategies to use in Risk and to raise issues. For example, invariably a Risk player may ask the community in which he has been marked as the best player why everyone

---

[1] Risk® is a registered trademark of Hasbro.

wants to gang up on him. What should he do? Not only is this a strategic problem, but it is also a psychological one.

Forums and website are a great means of sharing your opinion and getting others to comment on them. However, after a while, you may end up with a collection of tips with no coherent and logical connection. How many times have you read a forum, only to realise that the tread contains a lot of noise and redundant information that has nothing to do with what you are searching for? In addition, they are hardly ever put into context with other related topics.

Many people are not familiar with psychological and negotiation skills discussed in the scientific world. There seems to be a need to collect all of this and place them in a book. There seems to be a need for the *bigger picture*.

This book intends to become the primary source of information on the tactics and strategies used in Risk, while simultaneously a resource for those who intend to use these skills in real life and benefit from all those hours spent playing games.

This book is by no mean limited to understanding only Risk. Almost all of the concepts discussed here are applicable to the majority of multiplayer strategy games. Many strategy games, including online variants, have inherited features of Risk and players can directly benefit from this book. The variants may have different maps and slightly different rules. The main strategies, however, remain the same. Debates are more common while playing board games. This requires skills in diplomacy and politics. Online games are more strategic and tactical, although diplomacy is used *passively*. For example, due to anonymity, swear words are used more often to intimidate other players. Remember, as long as you are dealing with humans, you will be subject to all of the psychological issues associated with competition over limited resources and the need to win. This book aims to explore these strategic issues without limiting the concepts to a particular game or rule set. Nevertheless, it is always easier to explain complex concepts by use of examples. The classic Risk is a game with which most people are familiar. Hence, it forms the basis of the scenarios and examples given in this book.

The book has a dedicated website at www.totaldiplomacy.com. Please visit the site and join the community for further discussions on strategies and insights into human psychology.

I greatly enjoyed preparing this book and learnt a great a deal in the process. I hope I have gathered enough to keep you engaged for the entire book and I hope you will enjoy reading and learning these concepts as much as I did writing them.

1 Why Risk?

"Every matter requires prior knowledge."

Sun Tzu

In everyday life, everyone needs to negotiate, make deals, take important decisions, understand other people's decisions and know how to look at the bigger picture.

However, many skills are difficult to come by. As the saying is, *you learn by doing*. It is not always easy to practice new skills by doing them in real life because you may not have enough opportunity to use them. For example, it is vital to know how to negotiate when you want to buy a car or a house. But let's face it, how many times would you buy a house in a lifetime? Most people only buy one house if at all. However, the agent you negotiate with buys and sells every day. Who do you think has the upper hand? Hence, there is no doubt that you need to practice. The question is; where would you go?

Once you know how to negotiate, you can become much more effective at it no matter what you are negotiating. Buying a house, making a business contract or even asking your dad to borrow the car would all use the same basic negotiation principle: that you need to know where you are and how valuable *something* is to you and to the other party. Once you have mastered this skill, you can use it anywhere.

The best method of practicing such skills is in an abstract environment where you have total control over certain aspects of the problem domain and you can focus on the specific skills under question. Where would you find such an abstract environment? Your best bet is to find a tool that is capable of teaching you many skills, while at the same time is fun to use. In addition, it should not feel like a complete waste of time.

Enter strategy: From the beginning of time, people have been involved in making strategic decisions. Equally, people have also been involved in strategic games since anyone can remember. People like to engage over abstract strategic puzzles and games for entertainment. They also valued games as educational tools. Strategic games helped them to focus their minds and enhance their problem-solving skills. There has been an explosion in the variety of these kind of games.

Fast forward to today: You now have a large number of strategic games at your disposal. There is a vast industry involved in the creation and promotion of any type of game imaginable. People spend a large amount of time simply playing games.

Then, Risk arrived. The world conquest game integrated both chance and logic in one package. Risk, as opposed to chess, did not require the player to think of perfect moves. At any point in the game, a player has a large number of winning options that he[2] can follow. Even a new player can win against more experienced players. The concept of chance is embedded into the game, and as the name suggests, players may need to take risks to win.

Risk has been a very successful strategy game. The success of this game largely depends on its flexibility. Since you have to deal with other players over a well-defined goal, you are pushed to negotiate with them continuously. You need to understand their position, where they are, where they are heading, whether they are friends or foes, if they listen to you or want you to listen to them, and so on and so forth. These issues all directly relate to real-life situations as well. In fact, this is why a new player feels right at home when playing for the first time. As soon as you know the basic rules of the game, you can start using your entire *life knowledge* to compete with

---

[2] In this book, for consistency, 'he' is used when a player is referenced.

other players over the resources provided in the game, and compete to win.

In short, Risk is a great game to use to fine-tune your tactical, strategical and diplomatical skills.

However, new games enter the market every day. It is entirely possible to initiate the design of yet another game specifically to improve a set of skills. Then again, one does not want to reinvent the wheel. Risk is already one of the most successful and popular strategy games of all time. It is only rational to use a game that a large number of people have been exposed to in their childhood. By using Risk as opposed to a new game, you would at least have a good chance of finding other eager players to play with.

1.1 Real Life Risking!

> *"Live as if you were to die tomorrow. Learn as if you were to live forever."*
>
> *Gandhi*

In this day and age, we always experience a lack of *time*. Everyone wants to use their time as effectively as possible. As many know, the best way to achieve this is by multitasking: doing many tasks at once. However, this is easier said than done. Playing Risk is entertaining, and simultaneously it teaches a number of lessons. For example, you will learn how to deal with people effectively, how to control your resources, how to fight for what you want and manage risk.

This book attempts to address two domains: it shows you how to win at Risk and it illustrates the finer concepts and skills required to deal with people. The idea is to use Risk as a training tool for skills otherwise challenging to master in real life.

You can map your real-life understanding of competition over global resources to Risk. By being familiar with the concept behind the game, you can focus on the actual skills in a more systematic way. Once you have mastered the dynamics of a particular situation, such as dealing with conflict escalation or understanding prisoners' dilemma, you can move away from the abstract environment of the game and apply your findings to the real world.

Risk, like any other game, has a set of well-defined rules and a specified goal. All you have to do is to conquer the world and win the game. If you cannot achieve this consistently, you obviously are not as good as other players, and you can keep practicing until you become better. This is in fact a simple, albeit harsh, measure of performance, but one that can easily be understood. In short, if you lose, keep working on your skills until you win. Practice makes perfect. You cannot blame someone else. If you lose consistently, you cannot blame it on luck either.

There is an analogy between Risk and real life. Each turn in Risk is like a day. Other players are your immediate competitors. You all compete for resources. Everyone has a common goal, which is to have more resources (time or money) and eventually ultimate power. Sometimes you are pushed into a direct conflict with your competitors over resources. For example, you may find yourself competing for the best office room in the company against your colleagues. Usually you cannot take the room by force (well, that is the norm). You need to use your diplomatical skills to acquire the room. Diplomatic solutions tend to cost less. People who use such solutions seem to become more successful in life. Just the same, players who tend to use diplomacy extensively in Risk, tend to win consistently.

The following list illustrates a number of benefits of using Risk as a training tool:

- Risk imposes limited resources, just as resources in the real world are limited. Competition for assets is always at the centre of any strategic decision making.

- Unlike real-time games, there is no time pressure in Risk. This means that you can analyse your moves in greater detail. You can pause the game and think about a move as if playing chess. However, the concept of time is present in the game. You can time your attacks and carry them out in the *right* turn.

- There is a clear objective in the game that simplifies the goal-seeking behaviour. You know exactly what you want, and you also know others' overall goal. All you have to figure out is the means and not the end. This simplifies the problem and lets you analyse your actions more systematically.

- Chance is integrated into the game in a clear way. As the name implies, it has an important role in the game, but this is not a game of chance. Consistent winners in Risk always feel that they won as a result of cunning strategies while being lucky at the right time. Amazingly enough, this is what most successful people feel about normal life too.

You can use Risk as a training tool to understand politics, art of selling, decision making, applied psychology, economics, etc., all in one activity.

Playing Risk and reading this book is similar to exercising. Everyone needs to exercise the art of debate, strategy and survival. While playing sports, or when in a gym, you focus on different muscle groups, work on your cardiovascular or perform bodybuilding activities. Similarly, in Risk, you work on your ability to convince people, to talk diplomatically, and to achieve the most with least effort. In short, you systematically train yourself in a controlled manner to know how to compete on many levels simultaneously.

As another example, suppose you meet your boss to explain a situation. Your colleagues may strive to interfere, provide their own inputs and upset the flow of the conversation. You will find many similar situations in Risk, as other players attempt to interfere with your plans. Playing Risk will prepare you for the real thing. You will no longer feel: "I could have said X instead...". This is equivalent of exercising with the aim of increasing your agility. When talking, you also need quick reactions. You can improve your agility by working on your skills. It is always better to practice in a controlled environment to minimise damage to your real life. After all, you do not want to upset any friends, family or colleagues by using your newly learnt skills on them. In a game, anyone can get away with their approach, because, after all, *it is only a game*.

What is interesting about playing Risk is that you can improve the way you handle people. It is well known that being able to influence people and get on well with them is perhaps one of the most valuable skills a person can have. There are many techniques that can be used to further your influence and likeability. You learn by doing, and in order to learn, you need to be in the right circumstances so that you can use your newly acquired skills. The Risk game puts you artificially into these situations, where you can analyse and understand the nature of human interactions. In about four or five hours you can systematically cover a wide range of techniques. It is a great opportunity to get entertained and to interact with your friends and family over a game, while also practicing your *interactive human skills*.

As you read this book, you will realise that the contents serve the same two purposes:

- One is to tell you how to win the game. This should be enough to get you win over your cousin.

- The other is to tell you how you can improve your social and diplomatical skills, understand the underlying phenomenon and appreciate why something works the way it does.

In addition everyone needs to know how to handle those who may use immoral techniques. Niccolo Machiavelli, whose name is synonymous with using cunning tactics and strategies to overcome one's enemies, states that,

> *"Any man who tries to be good all the time is bound to come to ruin among the great number who are not good. Hence a prince who wants to keep his authority must learn how not to be good, and use that knowledge, or refrain from using it, as necessity requires."*

The above assertion in Machiavelli's famous book, *Prince*, shows why it is critical to *know* the techniques of the dark side, as there is always a chance that you may be confronted with one who uses them.

The world can be like a wild jungle with many wolves inside. One has to be cautious and protective of his possessions.

Otherwise, all will be lost in a short time, without even realising where it has all gone wrong. Survival relies on two skills: intuition and experience. They are both related and, overtime, reinforce each other.

You need to know how deception works so that you can recognize when someone is deceiving you. Deception can be used in a simulated environment such as Risk in order to win the game.

The intention is not be deceptive in the real world. Instead, you want to use your knowledge to identify if someone has been deceptive and know the best way to deal with it.

As always, the best way to learn the details of a technique is to use it yourself. Experimenting in a harmless game is the best way to learn the skill while staying on the moral side.

Throughout this book, hopefully, you will come to appreciate the dynamics of strategic decision making and learn how to deal with people efficiently.

To be consistent, examples are provided solely for Risk when skills are explained. One can easily see that the main principles are also applicable to issues found in everyday situations. The main purpose of the book is to show how you can learn by experimenting with strategies in Risk and apply them to other domains.

1.2   What is Risk?

Risk is usually played using a Risk set with the cardboard map of the world. Nowadays, there are a large number of online and computer based Risks available too. As stated earlier, you are in charge of your armies, fighting over territories on a global map of the Earth with the goal of complete global conquest.

Initially, Risk may seem to have many complex and detailed rules. However, after a few turns, the game tends to become obvious and the rules become self-explanatory. There are as many different sets of rules and variations for Risk as there are countries on this planet! It is a matter of taste and past experience to choose a particular set of rules. Depending on the rule set, the game might last shorter or longer. For example, in *Mission Risk*, each player should only complete his own mission to win the game while stopping others to complete theirs.

In general, this book is independent of any specific set of rules or even maps. The strategies explained are applicable to any set. For consistency, global occupation on a classic Earth map is used as the main goal when examples or scenarios are presented.

It is assumed that the reader is already familiar with the classic set of rules and knows the basic principles of the game. You can use the Risk world map provided at the beginning of the book (Page xiii) as a reference.

2 The Three Layers

"The superior militarist foils enemies' plots; next best is to ruin their alliances; next after that is to attack their armed forces."

Sun Tzu

The activities of a Risk player can be divided into three distinct but parallel parts: *tactics & logistics*, *strategy* and *diplomacy*. A player needs to master all three to succeed consistently. The following shows this distinction:

- *Tactics* are methods used to get to a well-defined goal. The techniques used to carry out a battle and the manoeuvres required to achieve specific objectives are tactics. *Logistics* are the means to distribute resources to the frontlines or across the empire.

- *Strategy* is the overall plan.

- *Diplomacy* is any other means (moral or immoral) that helps to achieve the grand strategy. It usually means knowing how to engage with other people and get what you want.

The following Risk example shows the difference between the three layers. The overall goal is to win the game against other players.

- The strategy is to reduce other players' armies and undermine their ability to wage war against you or to weaken your position.

- Tactics are the methods of conquering a specific continent, or to getting hold of a strategic position and attempting to use it as a threat against another player.

- Diplomacy is to engage with another player and convince him to fight your enemy, so you do not have to do it yourself. It is the art of winning without the use of brute force.

These three layers are explained in detail in Chapters 4, 5 and 6. In addition to these three layers, you also need to know yourself. Equally, an important key is the psychological state of other players at any given time in the game. You need to exploit this to your advantage. Chapter 3 discusses your step-by-step thinking process, psychological profiling and associated concepts.

A successful politician needs to be a master of the *'art of debate'*. You need to be able to handle everything there is under the sun. Everyone out there seems to be dead set on getting you. In Risk, it is no different. Negotiation is an incredibly important skill. You need to know your opponent and their desires. You also need to know your desires and how to get what you want. Chapter 7 provides a large number of interconnected topics on this important skill. It will help you to master the art of dealing with people.

After reading these chapters, you will have covered a large number of concepts and skills. However, in order to successfully make decisions, you also need to understand the dynamics of the environment you are operating in. You need to know if there is anything statistically repetitive or predictable of which you can take advantage. Game theory provides a wealth of information on strategic situations and can systematically guide you in making the best decisions to succeed. It is as if a mathematician has come to your rescue to quantify your trade-off table. To put it another way, you will learn how to decide optimally. Chapter 8 explores these underlying dynamics.

Online games are becoming increasingly sophisticated and facilitate the discovery of other Risk players. Online Risk games, however, can be slightly different from the board game due to the nature of computer games combined with network gameplay. Chapter 9 explores these concepts. It also provides a number of *high-level walkthroughs* focusing on different aspects of the game

Chapter 10 provides a number of scenarios. These scenarios are designed as open questions where a number of options may exist. The reader is encouraged to solve each scenario and refer to given solutions for comparison. This chapter gives you the opportunity to learn by example.

In the end, a number of reference tables are provided. Here, you may find definition of concepts and a reference to where you can find them in the book.

While reading this book, remember that the outcome of a Risk game is set by who you are and the style you use to play. All the armies in the world cannot buy you victory if other players do not want you to win. Read on to discover how you can stop them doing just that by knowing who you are, who they are, and learning how to turn your weaknesses into strengths.

3 Temet Nosce

"When you know both yourself and others, you are never in danger; when you know yourself but not others, you have half a chance of winning; and when you know neither yourself nor others, you are in danger in every battle."

Sun Tzu

Albert Einstein had just administered an examination to an advanced class of Physics students. As he left the building, he was followed out by one of his teaching assistants.

"Excuse me, sir," said the shy assistant, not quite sure how to tell the great man about his blunder.

"Yes?" said Einstein.

"Um, eh, it's about the test you just handed out."

Einstein waited patiently. The student said, "I'm not sure that you realize it, but this is the same test you gave out last year. In fact, it's identical."

Einstein paused to think for a moment, then said, "Hmm, yes, it is the same test."

The teaching assistant was now very agitated: "What should we do, sir?"

A slow smile spread over Einstein's face. "I don't think we need to do anything. *The answers have changed.*"

And just as the answers change in Physics, so do the answers to your problems.

While to all appearances you may have the same tests given to you by life, consider the possibility that *the person* contemplating the problem might have changed. Time has passed; you have learned many things along the way.

Rather than forcing the same old solutions which did not work before, it might be time to try something else, something that emerges from the new person that you have become.

Similarly, in Risk, the problem might have stayed the same, but the answers can change. As a Risk player, you should always look for new ways and new strategies. The question stays the same: "How to conquer the world?" The answers, however, depend on you and your opponents. Knowing yourself and knowing them, over time, is the key to repetitive success.

This chapter explores the issues surrounding your mental state during the game. *Temet Nosce* is Latin for 'Know Yourself'. This is accepted as general wisdom, and it is for a good reason. If you lose control of yourself, you are at the mercy of others. If you lose control of others, you have no control at all and no chance of winning. In this chapter, you will learn how to work out the psychological profile of players, what type of opponents you may find in the game, and what you need to do against each category. Only then can you exploit this to your advantage.

First, you need to know what you want, what your plan is and how you want to get to your goal.

3.1 Mind Map

> *"There is nothing so powerful as an idea whose time has come ... and there is nothing so detrimental as someone who is still thinking old ideas."*
>
> ### Robert Kiyosaki in Rich Dad, Poor Dad

It is important to plan ahead even before the game starts. You have a limited amount of time during your turn, and any armies you can save up in advance is to your advantage. In addition, by thinking ahead, you will start to feel confident about the situation and know what you are doing.

The most successful players (or people for that matter) have a systematic thinking process that they apply to everything. In Risk, you need to think of a number of concepts every turn. This can be described with the *five P's rule*. This is a general thinking process that can be applied to everyday thinking as well. These are as follows:

- *Position*. Evaluate where you are in the game. *Know yourself*. Be honest with yourself and establish the facts. If you have made any mistakes, accept them and move on so you can find solutions for them.

- *Problem*. Capture the problem you are facing both in the short and long term. The short-term problems need immediate attention, while the long-term problems are related to your long-term strategy. In this phase you need to identify what it is you are trying to solve.

- *Possibilities*. Once you know your position and the problem, you can derive a number of options to pursue. You need to carry out a trade-off analysis and score various options based on their benefits. You need to look at risk factors for each option and know how you would deal with them. You should look at diplomacy solutions and how they may benefit you in the short or long term. You may need to sacrifice one thing to gain another.

- *Proposal*. Once you have evaluated your options, you can choose an option that best suites you. You need to carefully formulate your actions based on your objectives so that they can be followed. It is all too often that the thinking is correct, but the *delivery* is poor. Make sure you pay enough attention to detail so that all your hard work is not lost.

- *Price*. Every move has a cost. This cost can be *material* or *spiritual*. In Risk, the material cost can be:

  o   The number of armies involved in the invasion.

  o   The potential cost of losing a continent.

- o The cost of getting into a *'war of attrition'* with your neighbour.

The spiritual cost can be:

- o The political damage you may suffer as a result of initiating an invasion.

- o The impact of backstabbing on your image (in this game and future games).

- o How other players look at you as a *person*.

Figure 3-1 shows the five P's as a mind map. A mind map is an abstract representation of the concepts, or logical connection between the concepts you need to consider. The main mind map is broken into smaller more detailed parts for each 'P' shown in Figure 3-2 to Figure 3-6.

Figure 3-1. Mind map of a Risk player. You can follow the main five P's in clockwise order. The detail for each branch is then expanded in Figure 3-2 to Figure 3-6.

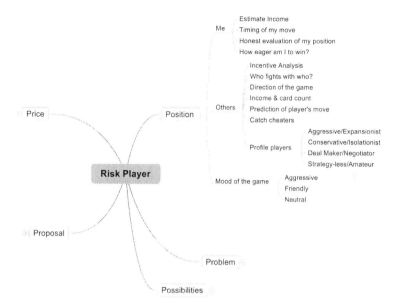

Figure 3-2. *Mind map for* Position.

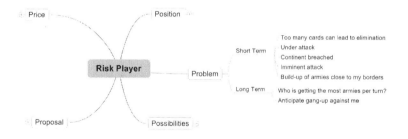

Figure 3-3. *Mind map for* Problem.

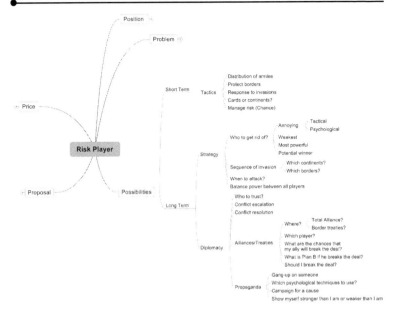

Figure 3-4. Mind map for Possibilities.

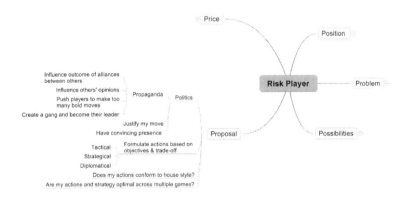

Figure 3-5. Mind map for Proposal.

Figure 3-6. Mind map for Price.

The mind map helps you to organise your thoughts into logical chunks. It helps you to expand on concepts where you think you might be weak or need further thought. Practicing a systematic number of steps such as the five P's will help you not to miss a step while taking your turn. You may know what you want to do and how to do it on paper, but when it comes to delivery, you tend to forget and fall back to *convenient old habits*. In order to break the cycle, you need to start from somewhere and force yourself into following a slightly different plan. The good news is that once you start repeating, the repetition process comes to your rescue. The more you repeat, the easier it gets until eventually, it is stored in your long-term memory.

Remember, while planning always devise a *Plan B*. This is a secondary plan in case Plan A (your original plan) fails. Your confidence will be a lot higher once you know that you have thought about your actions and you know what you will do if your original plan fails. You will feel in control of your actions, and hopefully the game.

3.2 Seven Beliefs

"Stick with it; as with everything else in life, at the end of the day it's how much you want it that will see you through."

Demis Hassabis

Now that you have worked out your mind map, you need to stick to it and *believe* that it will get you what you want. Those who believe they can win, never lose. Anthony Robins, a great author of many self-help books, has some fascinating ideas. He shows how one can systematically *program* oneself to become more efficient in life. His book, *Awaken the Giant Within*, is a must read for anyone who wants to give a kick to their lives.

Robbins suggests that you need to decrease your *limiting believes* and increase your *empowering believes* to improve your mental state.

- *Limiting beliefs* are beliefs that stop you from taking action, prevent you from growing, or lead you into a state of depression and the feeling of being unworthy and useless.

- *Empowering beliefs* are the ones that drive you to action, support growth and well-being.

The belief that you cannot fail is empowering, the belief that you are not in control of your destiny is limiting.

This is just as applicable to Risk as it is to anything else in life. Robbins thinks that you need to have the following *seven believes* in order to become invincible in life. They are indeed effective but simple rules. A great number of people have reported that following these rules deeply changed the way they perform and had an immense positive impact on their decision-making process. The seven beliefs are provided below along with Risk examples:

1. *Everything happens for a purpose and a reason, and it serves us.* In Risk: If you got invaded, look on the bright side. The invader may have stretched himself too much and soon might be taken out by someone else. He no longer would be your worry.

2. *There is no such thing as a failure. There are only results.* In Risk: Suppose you made a treaty with someone and later in the game, the treaty got broken. Do not look at it as a failure, instead look at it as a lesson learnt.

3. *Whatever happens, take responsibility.* In Risk: If you lost the game, do not blame it on other players. Do not presume that you would have won if your opponents had not done X. You are the common denominator in all of the actions taken in the game. If something has gone wrong, you should only blame yourself.

4. *It is not necessary to understand everything to be able to use everything.* In Risk: Just because you have not been playing the end game before, it does not mean you will not have a chance. Just because you could not understand a move someone made, it does not mean you cannot take advantage of it and exploit it. Even if you have not played against a new player, you can still win.

5. *People are your greatest resource.* In Risk: This is the most valuable belief you can have. Use other people to help you get what you want. Without others you will make it very difficult for yourself, if not impossible.

   a. If you want to make a difference, you need to interact with others. To gain power you need to share yours. If you do not share your power, no one will share their power with you. Without respect and appreciation for people, that is all people, you will not be able to build the network of dependencies that is needed to become successful.

   b. If you look at people as mere functions replaceable at your mood, you will eventually fail. To succeed you need others that support you and that are willing to go that extra mile with you.

6. *Work is play.* In Risk: Enjoy the game!

7. *There is no abiding success without commitment.* In Risk: Commit yourself to winning the game. If at any point in the game you give up winning, the chances are that you simply will not win. Be physically and mentally active in the game. Push yourself to the very end. If you need practice, work hard. Do your homework. After

all, there is no one better than yourself to push you forward. Be your own boss. Be a tough boss.

That is all you need. Just think about these every day. Memorise them and follow them by heart. You will get there in the end.

3.3   How to Profile Players?

"If you do not know the plan of your competitors, you cannot make informed alliances."

Sun Tzu

A ten-year-old boy who had lost his left arm in a car crash wanted to take up judo. His parents had their misgivings but found an old Japanese master who was willing to teach him.

For three months the sensei took the boy under his wing, but at the end, the boy realized that he had learnt only one move.

The sensei then announced that the boy was ready for his first tournament. To his surprise, the boy won his first two matches. The third match proved more difficult, but after some time, his opponent became impatient and charged. The boy used his one move to deflect the opponent and won the match.

Eventually, he reached the final. This time his opponent was bigger, stronger, and more experienced. For a while the boy was outmatched. The referee considered stopping the bout, but the sensei said: "No, let him continue."

Soon after the match resumed, his opponent dropped his guard. Instantly, the boy used his one move to pin him down. The boy won the match and the tournament and became the champion.

On the way home, the boy and his sensei reviewed every move in every match. After a bit of hesitation, the boy finally asked "Sensei, how did I win the tournament with only one move?"

"You won for two reasons," the sensei announced. "First, you've nearly mastered one of the most difficult throws in all of judo. And second, the only known defence for that move is for your opponent to grip your left arm."

Learn what you do well and master it, while simultaneously turning your weaknesses into strengths. Always understand your opponents and know what yours and their weaknesses are. Knowing your opponent is key in winning any game. Initially, you need to know the type of players you are playing against. Once you know who you are against, focus on the strong and weak points of each type. In the end, you need to know how to deal with each opponent. You can even go further and see how you can use one against the other. This section categorises all types of Risk players and shows you how you can use this information to your advantage.

3.3.1 *Aggressive/Expansionist*

What is it?

An expansionist player has a huge tendency to invade at the drop of a hat. He usually has it all planned out in his head and does not hesitate to attack if he has an opportunity.

How to spot?

An expansionist is usually very active in the game and tends to lead the invasions and initiate conflicts. He can be very annoying. In general, an aggressive player is a risk taker. Sometimes it pays off handsomely, and some other times it leads to disaster.

What is he good at?

He expands and takes chances. As a result, if there is an opportunity, such as eliminating another player, he is there sooner than anyone else.

What is his weakness?

He is temperamental and unpredictable. He can get himself into trouble by not thinking about all the aspects of a move. He may just invade for the sake of it.

How is he dealt with?

An aggressive player does not cooperate. Hence, you need to deal with him with force.

> *"When you meet a swordsman, draw your sword; do not recite poetry to one who is not a poet."*
>
> *A Cha'an Buddhist*

He is not usually interested in alliances and treaties, but equally he might not be active politically either. You can exploit this. Once you find such a player building up against you, prepare for long battles. Get rid of an aggressive player early in the game, or if you can, direct his aggression towards another player. Another way to destroy him is to gang up against him. Since he is an expansionist, he might have attacked more than one player. As a result, quite a few players may have incentives to join in. When the timing is right, set up a coalition and *solve this issue once and for all*. Since he is not usually politically active, he will be doomed.

3.3.2   *Conservative/Isolationist*

What is it?

A conservative player tends to perform his moves in a subtle way. He believes that by staying out of action, he will survive longer and have a higher probability of winning. He likes to build up slowly.

How to spot?

An isolationist player does not usually participate actively in attacking anyone. His favourite continent is Australia, followed by South America. A conservative player has the tendency to hesitate when he needs to take a risk. He prefers to stay in the comfort zone.

What is he good at?

He likes to stay out of trouble and usually does not create enemies for himself. If he is not blocking someone's path, the chances are that he will not get attacked. An isolationist intends to lose fewer armies so that he can use them to reinforce his defences.

What is his weakness?

An isolationist usually attempts to get himself physically isolated on the map. This isolation can get him stuck with nowhere in which to expand. For example, such a player residing in Australia has nowhere to go but Asia, which is a particularly difficult continent to conquer. He is not very active politically and as a result gets ignored most of the time when he wants to influence decisions. In addition, in negotiations one has to give something in return for something else. A conservative player may find it difficult to offer something as he only usually has his fortress.

How is he dealt with?

An isolationist player can be interested in alliances and treaties because he wants to strengthen some of his borders so he can be even more secure. Remember, all he wants is to build up slowly and steadily. As a result, he is always wary of attacks and long wars of attrition. Thus, if he is attacked, he usually has no choice but to get engaged, which means he is no longer an isolationist player. Get other players to notice him and suggest that he must be up to no good since he is building up, and if other players do not take care of him, he will become a big threat to everyone.

3.3.3 Dealmaker/Negotiator

What is it?

A negotiator is always interested in solving problems without using force. He can be tough to play against, especially if he is experienced.

How to spot?

A dealmaker usually comes knocking on your door offering you a deal. His deals are usually designed to benefit him, though ultimately he is always interested in making some sort of a deal. A deal is always better than no deal at all. If an agreement benefits both of you, so be it, so long as it benefits him.

What is he good at?

A dealmaker usually believes that those who have more deals will have a greater chance of succeeding in the game. Each deal that he makes lets him prevent useless expenditure of his armies, and over time he (and the other player who he has a deal with) can build up more armies. Since he fights less, he can end up with more armies towards the end of the game. He can count on those deals and use his extra resources to threaten someone else. A negotiator is a politically active player. A good negotiator can be very difficult to deal with. He may use an extensive amount of propaganda, which can have a huge impact on *world opinion*.

What is his weakness?

In Risk, a deal is only a verbal contract, which can always be broken. This is the biggest weakness of a negotiator, which can be *devastating* for someone who has counted on it so much.

How is he dealt with?

There are two ways of dealing with a negotiator: One is to make deals with him and follow them through; the other is to make deals but stab him in the back (That sounds like fun!). By taking the first option, you can both grow together and meet up later in the game for the big prize.

If you want to use the dark side of force, you can take advantage of his vulnerable position. He may have left a certain number of his borders thin as a result of a deal. Lightly defended borders can be extremely useful as an entrance to his empire.

If you suspect that you cannot trust him, breaking a deal earlier than him is an attractive solution. The only problem is that you need to consider the impact of this action on your image. A negotiator, who is a serial winner, would find it difficult to make a deal with other players. Even if he made a deal, breaking his deal is the best way to get rid of him. Overtime a good winning negotiator would not be trusted as much since players start to suspect that making a deal with him is not to their benefit.

3.3.4 Strategyless/Amateur

What is it?

An amateur is a new player in the game who does not have much experience. This category also covers those who are not sure what they want and just go with the flow, expecting a miracle.

How to spot?

An amateur is usually not very familiar with the dynamics of the game. He is usually undecided and hesitates every time he wants to make an important decision. He does not have a strategy and usually appears to act randomly.

What is he good at?

An amateur is an experimenter. He may randomly choose a move just for the sake of it. Sometimes he can get lucky, which means he can become a bigger threat than what he really is.

What is his weakness?

An amateur, by definition, does not know which move to make most of the time. He makes obvious mistakes. He is also vulnerable to exploitation. He may be convinced by others to follow a particular strategy only to discover later that it was more useful to his opponents than to him.

How is he dealt with?

The trick in dealing with an amateur is to see how much you can use him against others. Those who can get the amateurs to fight with their enemies are usually *invincible*. You should aim to get an amateur to fight on your side. Since he can benefit from your protection, he will be interested in listening to you. You need to keep him on your side for as long as you can. Watch out for an amateur who suddenly turns his back on you. If this happens, remove him as soon as you can.

3.3.5 The Line Up

"The man who doesn't want anything is invincible."

The categorisation presented above is a general way to describe the *behaviour* of a player more than his *personality*. In Risk, you can have many strategies. Apart from the *Amateur* category, you can always switch between isolationist, expansionist, or negotiator profiles. In general, players tend to adopt one flavour more than others.

The following compares each category against others and highlights the *view* each type has of other players.

Isolationist thinks of:

- *Isolationist:* Someone to meet at the end of the game.

- *Expansionist:* He is unpredictable and hard to negotiate with. I need to stay out of his way.

- *Negotiator:* He is good to deal with. Perhaps I can secure some of my borders with a treaty with him.

- *Amateur:* I hope he does not make a random invasion against me. Better persuade him to attack others.

Expansionist thinks of:

- *Isolationist:* Would I gain anything by attacking him? I do not have to worry about him. I will sort him out at the end of the game.

- *Expansionist:* It is either me or you. Let's have a fight.

- *Negotiator:* If he wants to have a deal, so be it. I can always break it later on. He makes all these deals and thinks he can win without fighting. He is so wrong.

- *Amateur:* Got to get his cards and remove him sooner rather than later.

Negotiator thinks of:

- *Isolationist:* He is probably not going to bother me. I will make a deal with him so he will not expand in my direction. He may even get stuck. Better allocate my armies for someone else.

- *Expansionist:* I need to watch out for him. He probably will not accept my deals. I need to somehow direct his menace to someone else. Perhaps I can get two expansionists to fight each other, so I can then go for the kill and get the cards.

- *Negotiator:* Let's make a deal. Those who make a deal have a lot more chance of winning. I shall meet up with him at the end of the game.

- *Amateur:* I need to tell him how important it is to make deals. I can offer him a deal to protect his borders. I doubt if he would stab me in the back and break my deal. This will put me in a very good position to compete with others. I can then guide him to fight my enemies.

Amateur against:

- *Isolationist:* At least there is someone who is not bothering me. I like to be in his position. He seems very secure and strong.

- *Expansionist:* This guy is going to kill me any second. Better stay out of his way.

- *Negotiator:* I think I can manage him. Not sure if he is trying to take advantage of me with his deals. Better think hard on this.

- *Amateur:* We are both in the same boat. I should at least do better than him.

Once you have figured out what players you are up against, the question is what to do about them. Which type should you deal with first? Should you remove a particular type at all costs? To analyse this, one can get inspired by human resource management techniques.

One of the systems suggested for managing employees of a company is the 20-70-10 rule or *rank-and-yank*. There have been a number of studies where researchers have found that of the 100% of employees, the following is true:

- 20% are efficient employees

- 70% are normal employees

- 10% are inefficient employees

The rule suggests that at the end of each year, the employer should fire the bottom 10% and hire fresh workforce in their place. On paper, this may increase a system's efficiency. After all, it is all about promoting the good stuff and getting rid of the bad stuff.

In Risk, you can be inspired by this rule. Your strategy could be to get rid of the *top* (the 20%) and the *bottom* (the 10%). The bottom should be easy since they make mistakes. Attempting to remove the top yourself can cost you dearly. A better solution is to get the *normals*, i.e. the other 70%, to do the job for you. Get *the normals* to fight with the top players in the game, weakening the strongest and themselves in the process. All you have to do is to enter the scene and steal the trophy!

It is beneficial to notice that the 20-70-10 firing rule was actually adopted by some companies (such as the ill-fated Enron in the U.S.). In the context of HR management, it turned out to have an inverse effect and did not really improve the efficiency. Since the process is iterative, over time the ratio of least efficient employees actually became less than 10%. From that point onwards, firing at this rate meant firing good employees. This fostered office politics and encouraged unethical methods of competition, which ultimately brought the system's efficiency down. This was the opposite of what was actually intended by using this rule. In Risk, what matters is to win, keeping up the efficiency of the system as a whole is not applicable. So go ahead: Remove the inefficient, compete with the efficient, and find your way up.

3.3.6 *Optimism*

Optimists will usually go the extra mile to get what they want, thinking that they can learn from issues. On the other hand, pessimists think negatively about things even though they can usually be right about them.

When an optimist and a pessimist deal with positive past events, an optimist describes them as *universal and permanent*. A pessimist describes them as *specific and temporary*. When analysing negative past events, the reverse is true. An optimist describes them as *specific and temporary* while the pessimist describes them as *universal and permanent*. As a result, the interpretation of an event comes down to which point of view one uses.

Thus, how would you deal with each type in Risk? Get rid of an optimist first because he will keep coming back at you stronger every time. With the pessimist, start a psychological war and push him even deeper towards his pessimistic point of view. He will automatically quit, make a wrong move, or just sit idle because he would (correctly from his point of view) estimate that his situation is hopeless!

Is it better to be an optimist or a pessimist? Generally, aim to be an optimistic yourself. Being optimistic means you are open to more ideas and you will tend to learn from your past mistakes. The game puts a lot of pressure on every player anyway and no matter how experienced you are, there is always a feeling that you might just be kicked out of the game in the next round. Attempt to be an *attentive optimist* instead. This way, you balance your views between taking too much or too little responsibility. Being a pure optimist can be dangerous as one can become arrogant and take credit for anything positive that happens and associate it with his own brilliance. When such a person falls, he falls a long way. An attentive optimist on the other hand focuses on the balance. For example, after a positive event such as winning the game, an attentive optimist takes credit for his own efforts, while he simultaneously understands that without luck and a bit of help from others at a critical time, he would not have been able to make it all the way.

So far, you have seen how to profile Risk players and anticipate the dynamics of their relationship. It is all too often that players possess great analytical and diplomatical qualities, but when a situation becomes emotional, they lose it completely and dig their own grave by behaving emotionally. Keeping yourself under control is vital for any successful world conquest.

3.4 *Being in Control*

> *"A government should not mobilise an army out of anger, military leaders should not provoke war out of wrath."*
>
> *Sun Tzu*

The game has been going on for an hour. Players around the table are starting to feel that the trenches have been dug and the main battles are about to begin. The situation is becoming tense as everyone is focusing on their moves. If you make a wrong move at this point, you probably will not have time to recover.

Albert is in a good position. He has a continent and lots of armies. There is a debate going on between two aggressive players. One of them invaded the other's continent and the other is naturally unhappy. Meanwhile, you need to approach Albert and get him to agree to a treaty over your desired border. Albert is unusually quiet. You suspect that he is following the conversation between the two and wants to know where it will lead. If they both get to fight each other, it is to his benefit, as a war of attrition will weaken both of them. Naturally, no one likes to interfere to resolve their issue.

You decide to seize the time and approach Albert. You say, "Do you see what is happening. We ought to be careful on these fronts or we will both get invaded. I was wondering if we can make a deal here, so that we can free up our resources for other fronts. Shall we make a deal?" Albert looks into your eyes. His voice is distinct and clear, neither loud nor quiet, "We can certainly consider it." Then he pauses, expecting you to fill the void. He wants to know what you have got to offer. He acts as if he is giving something very valuable away and you just want to get it off him.

As you start talking to him about the offer, he looks up, then the other way and starts to carefully listen to the ongoing conversation between the other two guys. Do you continue, or do you stop? By looking away, Albert is implying that he has no worries if he does not listen to you. He is testing you to see if you are an equal, or an inferior. If you can match him for presence, you may have a chance. You have to show that you have as much willpower as he has.

You interrupt the other two players: "Guys, Guys, it's OK. It's getting very loud, let's keep it down." Suddenly you have startled everyone. The two players stop talking. They are momentarily puzzled. Instantly, you turn back to Albert and say, "So what do you think?"

Albert is no longer quite comfortable. Now Albert has no choice but to respond. He cannot look the other way as no one is talking. Besides, he cannot repeat his trick twice; it is too obvious. You have matched his presence.

Albert says, "So, have you got something to give me?" He delivers this with a sarcastic tone. As if no rational being would suggest anything like that. He thinks that he is still superior.

You get annoyed, but you control yourself. You are in no mood to be defeated verbally, "This deal will help you as well as me. We will both win. As you can see, if you take this offer, it will benefit you greatly. We will both emerge as winners. We will honour this deal until only the two of us are left in the game." You now have delivered the specifics of the deal. Now he knows what you want.

There is one more thing you need to do. Show him, just as he showed you, that you do not really care if the deal does not go ahead. Demonstrate that you are actually doing him a favour! "Albert, this deal will help you greatly. I am only doing this for you because you are so trustworthy. I know I can count on you. If it was anyone else I wouldn't have bothered. There are many other ways I can win. But if you want to benefit from this, you have to accept it now. This deal will be meaningless in a couple of turns."

You have shown your presence and have given him a deadline. He is forced to make a decision immediately. As for you, all you care is that he accepts the deal on *your terms*.

Albert accepts the deal and you go on to win.

This story, illustrates why *Presence* is such an important quality to own and use at the right time. However, you need to have just the right amount of presence. The following shows the levels of presence you may have and how people may look at you accordingly:

- Little presence. You are not listened to. You are treated as a junior. Your input is neglected.

- With presence. You are a calm, calculating player. People have respect for you and your opinion. You are considered wise and a person who knows what he is talking about.

- Too much presence. You seem to be arrogant. You are treated as an aggressive person. You could be irritating and too loud. People may think you do not listen to them.

In the above story, Albert originally had the right amount of presence. Through your efforts, you managed to turn his presence into arrogance since he was not listening to you, and you exploited his weakness. You subsequently increased your own presence just to the right amount so that you could get what you want.

There are a number of key points you need to consider when you want to increase your presence:

- *Think equal.* Always consider your opponent as an equal. You need to believe that there is nothing he has that you do not. This boosts your confidence and makes it easier for you to control your body language. If you are going to win, you need to feel at least as strong as your strongest competitor.

- *Do not show your vulnerability.* Never show your weakness. As soon as your opponent discovers your weakness, he will be hard at work exploiting it. Be aware of your weakness, but do not let it consume you. If there is something you want, but that you realise you cannot have, the worst action you can take is to draw attention to it by complaining about it. An infinitely more powerful tactic is to act as if it never really interested you in the first place.

- *Be passionate.* In order to show people that you are the boss, you need to talk and fill the bandwidth. The best way to convince others that you are *the one* is to show how passionate you are about the subject. People have the tendency not to interfere with you, once they know a subject is very close to your heart. You can exploit this and influence others by your knowledge.

- *Do not let people interrupt you.* A person who is interruptible does not have much of a presence. If you manage to interrupt people, or people pause because you talked, then everyone assumes you have a higher presence. If you are attacked by inferior people, deflect the attack by making it clear that you have not even registered the attack. Look away and show how little the attack concerns you.

- *Talk.* If you are in a group of people and want to increase your presence, you need to participate. Undivided attention to the speaker usually influences him to address you while he is talking. Increasingly, others will also address you when you talk. If you want to participate in the conversation, you can:

  o Summarise the current conversation based on views.

  o Introduce new information into the conversation that changes its nature.

  o Show your view based on others' views that have been discussed so far.

  o Talk about a related story or an experience to capture the imagination of the audience and guide them to your desired direction.

Risk is a great game to practice on your presence skills. Use the above technique and evaluate yourself at the end of each game on how you wanted to perform and what you actually got in the end.

You need to experiment with everything. Those who take risks are usually more successful. There are numerous examples of successful people who always suggest that their secret to fame is that they took a *calculated risk*. Meryl Streep, one of the most acknowledged actresses, recalled in an interview with *The Independent* newspaper about her latest movie release and why she has been so successful in her career. So, what was the secret? She responded:

> *"A willingness to take risks, go out on a limb and make a fool of yourself. It's about choosing good scripts."*

The Message: take risk, but think about it before you do. So, go on, make a fool of yourself. After all, Risk is only a game.

This chapter focused on you and your understanding of others. The following three chapters focus on the three layers of your parallel thinking process. You need to be strong in every one of them to win repeatedly. The next chapter discusses tactics. Initially, the focus is mainly on the Risk board game itself. As you move on to following chapters, the scope of topics become wider and you will gradually be exposed to more non-Risk domains and skills.

4 *Tactics & Logistics*

*"In order to win a battle, one needs to know what the
enemy would do for each move that one would take
and this should be anticipated in the overall plan."*

Napoleon Bonaparte

Tactics deal with the design and execution of manoeuvres in
order to win battles. A quick look at history provides many
examples of good tactics that have changed the course of a
particular battle despite flaws in the overall strategy. A good
tactic is only effective as a short-term solution. Logistics deals
with the management and distribution of your resources.
Knowing how to micromanage your resources is a key in getting
the most out of any conflict.

In order to be able to look at the bigger picture with a long-
term strategy, you need to have control over the smaller
issues. In the three-layer approach, the idea is to start from
the bottom layer (tactics & logistics) and build your way up.
You need to master the rules and mechanics of the game (the
environment) and move on to learn how to form a winning
solution which will be your long-term plan (strategy). Finally,
you will learn how to influence other players to make it easier
for yourself to get what you want (diplomacy).

In order to be tactically great, you need to be familiar with the environment you are in and the *rules of engagement*. In Risk, this means knowing the map, the game, and the rules.

Before diving into detail on what the best tactics are and when to use them, it might be beneficial to quickly cover the rules used in Risk, and in particular in this book.

4.1   Early Game Tactics

"The spot where we intend to fight must not be made known; for then the enemy will have to prepare against a possible attack at several different points; and his forces being thus distributed in many directions, the number we shall have to face at any given point will be proportionately few."

Sun Tzu

Every player has a large number of options at the beginning of the game. The trick is to filter out your options to find a few critically effective strategies where you can be sure you have a chance of winning the game. These filters are as follows.

4.1.1   Which Continents?

"Military conquest is a matter of coordination not of masses."

Du You

The choice of your initial continent is important. Without a good starting position, you may find it exceptionally difficult to compete with other players who have a better strategic position. The initial continent depends on many factors such as the number of players in the game and the playing order.

The best way to find which continents are better is to evaluate them in practice. A series of votes by Risk players from around the world was collected on the dedicated website for this book at *www.totaldiplomacy.com*. Figure 4-1 shows the summary of these votes for the preferred continent depending on the number of players in the game. Figure 4-2 to Figure 4-5 show specific vote results based on the number of players involved. You can vote on the website on your preferred choice.

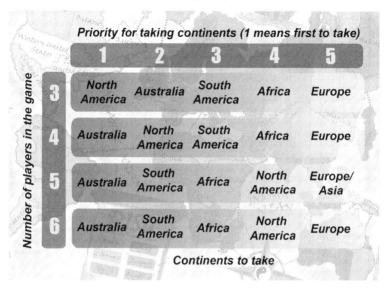

Figure 4-1. *The choice of initial continents depends on the number of players in the game.*

Notice that the preferred options are only suggestions; it is always possible to win the game no matter where you start from. With a sub-optimum start, you may have a rough time, but may just get there in the end!

Your initial position also depends on the overall strategy of other players. If the general wisdom of the group (or *house style*) is to disallow anyone to keep a continent, smaller continents are obviously more desirable.

Best Continent for Three-Player Game

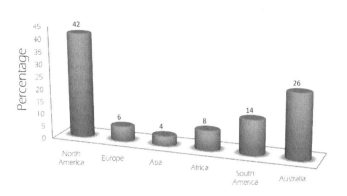

Figure 4-2. Preferred continent to take when playing against three players. Based on 1262 votes.

Best Continent for Four-Player Game

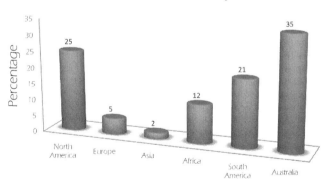

Figure 4-3. Preferred continent to take when playing against 4 players. Based on 766 votes.

Best Continent for Five-Player Game

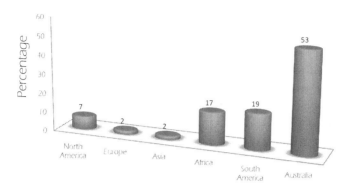

Figure 4-4. *Preferred continent to take when playing against 5 players. Based on 619 votes.*

Best Continent for Six-Player Game

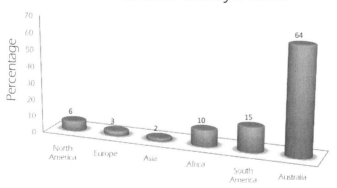

Figure 4-5. *Preferred continent to take when playing against 6 players. Based on 778 votes.*

4.1.2 Large or Small, Isolated, or in the Middle?

> *"The individualist without strategy who takes opponents lightly will inevitably become a captive."*
>
> *Sun Tzu*

Generally speaking, the smaller the continent, the better it is. Small continents are easier to capture and defend. However, not all of these continents are necessarily a good choice. Small continents can have limited access to the rest of the world and tend to be isolated. Indeed, some people prefer to stay isolated initially until they feel strong enough to suddenly emerge all-powerful and conquering. This dream, however, may die quickly as you will discover that an isolated power could be at the mercy of more resourceful and politically driven empires.

The best example for an isolated continent is Australia. It has only one border with the rest of the world (less than all the other continents) and is practically impossible to conquer in the early game once somebody has claimed it. It is usually highly desired. This is good news. However, there is also a trade-off. The problem with Australia is that there is no direction in which to expand. Usually the player in Australia lasts through the game to the end since Australia feels like a fortress to other players. Over time, however, the player falls behind as other players collect larger bonuses than him. Being isolated, he usually does not participate in world politics either. Before long, he is *eaten up* by the few remaining superpowers of the game! In short, Australia is a double-edged sword, be careful how you use it.

Machiavelli argued that in a strictly military sense, a fortress is invariably a mistake. It becomes the symbol of a power's isolation and everyone will know where to attack. The fortress may appear to be unconquerable, but it will be restrictive. Its isolation provides no protection and actually creates more problems than it solves. To make yourself powerful, you must place yourself at the centre of things. All activity should revolve around you and you should be aware of everything that goes on in the environment.

Remember that there is an alternative to the *continents-first strategy*. You can use *territories-first strategy* instead. In this method, your intention is not to go for a continent first. Instead you should get as many territories as possible, preferably connected. Notice that by taking six territories anywhere, you will get the same bonus as Australia or South America. The idea is that if you play for a continent, you will end up playing defensively as you want to protect *your* continent. In practice, if you can own eighteen connected territories anywhere on the world map, then you are better off than owing North America without a couple of territories left to conquer. Of course, later in the game you need to start focusing on continents as well as they cannot be ignored in the long term. It is your decision to select between these strategies, which depend greatly on your position on the map, your opponents, order of play and your style.

In any case, in the beginning of the game, you need to know *exactly* what your overall strategy is. This is critical. Establish which continents or territories you prefer to own and once you are in a particular continent or area, what type of players you are likely to encounter. Your move must always consider the psychological profile of each player. If you want to win, you have to use every trick of the trade at your disposal.

4.2   Cards or Continents?

> *"Get there firstest with the moistest."*
>
> **Nathan Bedford Forrest (an American Civil War General)**

One of the most controversial topics in tactical Risk is whether to go for cards, continents or both. This depends on a number of factors. Your strategy can be different in the beginning of the game from it is the end. It also depends on the rules of the game such as the growth sequence used for cashing cards.

You should always attempt to focus on the balance of power. At the beginning of the game, the following two trends define the number of armies each player owns: Armies *collected* for continents and Armies *lost* during battles.

As long as you can maximise your total number of armies while engaging in minimal number of battles, you will survive. Hence, you should focus on continents at the beginning of the game. Have patience and you will prevail. Cards do not provide a substantial amount of armies initially. However, it is relatively easy to collect them as one-army territories are abundant in the early game. Make sure you collect your cards.

Gradually as the game progresses, cashing cards becomes more lucrative and at some point this becomes more valuable than owning continents. Notice that as card values go up, it becomes more and more difficult to defend successfully on all borders. Someone can cash his cards and attack you pretty much anywhere he wishes. As a result, the dynamics of the game starts to change. At this point, it becomes more important to get your cards (and even others by eliminating them) than to defend your continents. In addition, it would be more desirable to use your cashed armies to inflict maximum damage on others: *Attack is the best form of defence*. In Risk, this is even more accurate as you shall see later.

The question still remains that at what point you would start caring more about the cards and less about the continents. This largely depends on the rules. Basically, over the years, players have been fine-tuning the rules to balance the game as strategies have evolved. The intention is to keep the game strategical and not random based on luck. At the same time, it is desirable to stop it from dragging on forever. After all, no one wants to engage in a long marathon game only to be kicked out by someone who got slightly luckier.

The variations of rules apply to two parameters: Cashed armies over time and continent bonuses. A number of different cash sequences are devised which influence the pace of the game. The most popular are as follows:

- 4,6,8,10,12,…: This sequence provides slow growth. It means that the first person who has a set will get four armies as bonus, the next player with a set will get six, then eight and so on. The game is longer and it is easy to calculate how many armies someone may cash.

- 4,6,8,10,15,20,…: The pace is slow at start, but increases as the game progresses. The game will reach a level where owning continents is no longer essential.

- 5,10,15,…: This is a very fast-paced game. Towards the end, the game is effectively decided by cards. Watch out for players who are waiting patiently ready to snap at you and take your cards. Your vulnerability is dramatically increased if you own four cards and haven't them cashed yet. Watch out!

- 4,6,8,10,12,15,18,21,24,27,30,34,38,42,46,50,55,…: This and the next sequence attempt to provide a gradual increase in the pace of the game in such a way that cards slowly become more important while the end game becomes less random. More complex sequences are suitable for online games, since they are easily tracked by the computer.

- 4,5,6,7,9,11,13,15,18, … and so forth until it is increased by five. Again, addressing the same growth issue, but in a different way.

In addition, continent bonuses can also be adjusted. For example, the bonuses for continents can be increased by 5% every round. Towards the end of the game, the bonuses of continents will make the continents almost as attractive as the cards. This is believed to provide a more strategic gameplay, as it stops players from abandoning continents. It discourages stockpiling armies without attacking each other, which is usually classified as a *marathon*.

In general, the cards are still the key to success. In the beginning of the game, the players get similar quantities of armies. Towards the end of the game, a player with cashed cards can control the flow of the game by threatening others. *You always need to collect your card in your turn, in particular when getting cards becomes more difficult.* Anyone who is left unable to collect one is automatically falling behind and will be subject to attacks and eventual elimination.

Similarly, *get continents in the early part of the game.* If you cannot get a continent, you may need to resort to other strategies such as '*Turtle*'. This strategy focuses on *passive growth* as opposed to continents. Following this strategy can be controversial. This is explained in detail later in the book.

4.3   Is Power All That Good?

"Appear to be lowly and weak, so as to make them arrogant, then they will not worry about you, and you can attack them as they relax."

Wag Xi

Being powerful is what everybody wants. However, *covert power* is much more effective that *overt power*. Someone who arrogantly makes trouble for others, just because he can, will inevitably attract adversaries. Be powerful, but hide your power, use it only when you have to.

It is usually a good strategy to cash cards as late as you can in the initial part of the game and as soon as you can towards the end of the game. Psychologically, it is preferable not to frighten other players with your vast amount of armies at the beginning of the game. It is a good motivation for them to attack you. Instead, hide your armies from other players by not cashing. Of course it is a different story if you are desperate! Towards the end, the number of armies on the map is larger. If one or two players attack you, you will soon become very weak. You should attempt to avoid any attacks and recover from your weak position as soon as possible. If you are in a good position, use your cards to weaken your key opponents before they become too powerful and out of control. If you can, make it more difficult for them to know how many cards you have. *The less they know the better*.

4.4   How Many Armies to Use

"Know when to fight; with how many armies to fight and be prepared to fight."

Sun Tzu

In many situations, you may find yourself with a choice of placing a number of armies before you start a blitz on an enemy. The question is, given the number of enemy armies and the number of countries you want to conquer, how many armies would you allocate for this purpose. Obviously, as a result of bad luck with the dice, some of your armies may get killed in the process. Of course, no one can formulate this quantity accurately as it depends on chance, but a rough guide is always beneficial when confronted with such a choice.

Suppose E is the total number of enemy armies and T is the total number of enemy territories of which you would like to conquer. The question is how many armies (F) would you place on your territory before the attack to make sure that you conquer the target enemy territories?

A number of formulas were explored and some were found to be the most effective. The most common formulas are as follows:

- F = 2E. Use the ratio of 2:1 against the enemy, which means that you need to place twice as much as the entire number of enemy armies you need to kill. You will place this amount in the territory you want to start the attack from.

- F = 1.5E + T. For example, if enemy has twenty armies in four territories that you want to conquer in this turn, then place F = 1.5 * 20 + 4 = 34 armies and start to attack. Hopefully, you will have enough to cover your losses and be able to put at least one army in each conquered territory.

- F = 2E + T

- F = 2.5E + T

- F = 3E

Figure 4-6 shows the preferred options based on votes collected on the book's website.

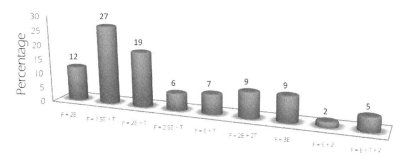

Figure 4-6. The popularity of each formula to place F armies before attacking T enemy territories which has E number of armies. Based on 827 votes.

4.5 Concentration of Armies

"Hence, when able to attack, we must seem unable; when using our forces, we must seem inactive; when we are near, we must make the enemy believe we are far away; when far away, we must make him believe we are near."

Sun Tzu

It is essential to concentrate your armies in the game. One-army countries can be conquered very easily. The best way to expand is to have strong borders where most of your forces should reside. The countries within your border should contain a minimal number of armies. This way your border armies are ready to be used as you need them rather than being stuck in the belly of your empire.

However, there are also exceptions to this rule. Sometimes, in a continent such as Europe, it may be beneficial to leave armies in non-border countries to reduce the chances of getting invaded.

Always attempt to minimise the existence of a *single point of failure*. Make sure you have a contingency plan so that if something goes wrong you can always be in control of the situation.

Spreading too fast and too soon will lead to disaster. Always place yourself in the same position as your enemies and strive to understand their choices against you. It has been observed that time and time again, a Risk player makes a smart move and wins his objective decisively only to ruin it all by going past the victory mark. He leaves thin borders behind and becomes weaker after a massive campaign. This means others will jump at the opportunity to bring him down there and then. In this regard Machiavelli states:

> *"Princes and republics should content themselves with victory, for when they aim at more, they generally lose. The use of insulting language towards an enemy arises from the insolence of victory, or from the false hope of victory, which latter misleads men as often in their actions as in their words; for when this false hope takes possession of the mind, it makes men go beyond the mark, and causes them to sacrifice a certain good for an uncertain better."*

Similarly, Jia Lin states that:

> *"Even if you prevail over others in battle, if you go on too long there will be no profit."*

Remember, that single-army countries are statistically easy to conquer and are therefore tempting. *Do not expand too rapidly beyond a sustainable level and do not leave any holes in your borders.* All it takes an enemy is a weak point in your defences. Before you know it, he will be inside your continent rubbing you off the continent bonus and making chaos. This is in particular more devastating at the beginning of the game since you rely more on continents' income than any other. Do not forget; a good opponent will never miss a chance to take advantage of your *weak borders* or your *weak status*.

Keep the number of your borders to a minimum at all times. Always plan this a few turns in advance so that you know how to expand. This is essential as you can concentrate your armies in each of your border countries, which deters potential attackers.

In a similar concept, leaving a *buffer country* between you and a large army can benefit you since the other player needs to use a fortification move before he can attack you. This is illustrated in Figure 4-7. In this figure each player is represented by a different colour pattern. Refer to key in *Page xiii* for reference.

Suppose you are playing as Black. If you leave North Africa as it is, Grey cannot use his fourteen armies in Egypt to start an invasion against you. He is forced to wait at least one turn to move his armies to North Africa before he can attack you. However, if you get North Africa, he can attack you straight away. Use this technique to buy time before someone attacks you.

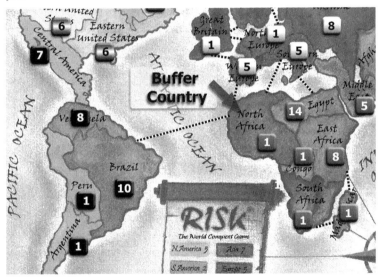

Figure 4-7. Buffer country between Black and Grey is left in Grey's possession so that Grey is forced to make a fortification move before he can attack Black.

4.6   *Let Them Leave*

"A surrounded army must be given a way out."

Sun Tzu

If you find a large army of an enemy in the belly of your empire, just let them leave. *Do not try to kill them all.* If you make it difficult for him, he will have no choice but to attack you. Once he realises there is no benefit for him being in your continent, all a player wants is to preserve his army. Once gone, his army becomes somebody else's problem. Good for you! Not only do you get rid of a large army, but you tie down someone else's armies too.

4.7   Exchange Country

"When a territory is of marginal benefit and is as easy to lose as is to win, then don't fight over it."

Cao Cao

Always aim to put yourself in a position that you can easily conquer at least one country every turn. This way you do not have to spend a large number of armies just to collect a single card. In the initial stages of the game, this is usually not an issue. However, towards the end, one-army countries become scarce. A common technique is to leave a one-army *exchange country* close to your borders and share it with other players. Each turn you can attack it with minimum effort and get a card. Other players will follow suit, as everyone is happy collecting a card every turn. This tactic is also known as '*card farming*'.

The exchange country also works as a *pressure valve*. If someone is unable to easily get a card, he is forced to start a massive attack on one of the fortified borders so he can get his card. Anyone can exploit this to his advantage. You or your enemy might conquer the exchange country and leave a large army behind. This will almost certainly annoy other participants of the *exchange country scheme*. The 'happy days' are effectively over! Make sure you know what you are doing.

This scheme is illustrated in Figure 4-8. Afghanistan is exchanged turn by turn and acts as a pressure valve since all borders between players are very strong. Without Afghanistan they are forced to spend a large number of armies to get a single card.

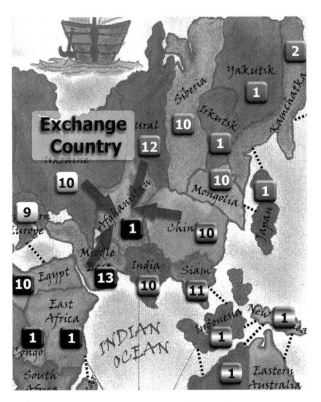

Figure 4-8. Afghanistan acts as the exchange country.

4.8   Intersection Ground

"'Intersecting ground' means the intersection of main arteries linking together numerous highway systems: first occupy this ground, and the people would have to go with you. So if you get it, you are secure. If you lose it, you are in peril."

Ho Yanxi

The owner of a territory that has access to numerous continents can exercise a great deal of power over others. Likewise, he will also be subject to attacks from others as they may need to get through him to get to their goal. Hence, attempt to be the first person to conquer such territories to maximise your political gain and lead the strategic attacks.

There are a number of choke points, or so called *intersection grounds* in the game that are absolutely critical to control. Owning them gives you more options when you want to attempt surprise attacks or respond quickly to enemy army rearrangements. A classic example is the Middle East. This territory has access to three continents and a large army in this strategic location can threaten players in Asia, Europe, Africa, and even Australia. There are of course other intersection grounds. The most common intersection grounds for the classic Risk map are presented in Figure 4-9. This is based on votes collected on the website.

You have now covered the tactical layer of the three-layer approach. The next chapter explores global strategic thinking and provides you with a number of lessons from history.

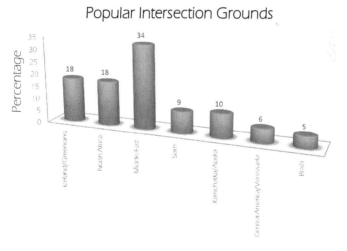

Figure 4-9. *The most popular intersection grounds. Based on 2205 votes.*

5 Strategy

"Military strategy is the employment of battles to gain the end of war."

Carl von Clausewitz, father of modern strategic study

In the past, military strategy was confined to the action of soldiers and solving military issues. However, in modern times, strategy is used to define the overall plan. As described in the previous chapter, using tactics is useful in resolving a local situation and any good general should know them well. However, it is the *overall strategic plan* and *diplomacy* that can make the difference between winning and losing!

Historically, over time the rise of technology resulted in ever more complex strategies which eventually led to an *operational strategy*. This involved planning for the efficiency of a nation at war as a whole and not just for the war activity itself. Georges Clemenceau famously said that: *"war is too important a business to be left to soldiers."* An important part of this grand strategy is diplomacy, which is the top layer in the three-layer approach. A nation may use diplomacy to avoid 'hot conflicts' altogether and strive to achieve its goal by anything other than brute force. This may involve alliances and negotiations with other nations to resolve conflicts without resorting to combat.

For example, consider chess. It can be argued that at any point in the game, a player searches to find the absolute best move.

If he takes this best move, he will end up in a better situation eventually. However, in Risk, diplomacy and politics add an endless number of possible paths to victory. The large number of options at your disposal is what makes Risk a truly wonderful game and a training tool. There is never a move, at any point in the game that can be classified as the perfect move. You always have many more solutions to think of. When playing Risk, you are constantly reminded of historical events as actions of players are analogous to actions of generals and leaders of nations. You can certainly learn from the evolution of their ideas and also understand the importance of decisions they have made. The huge human cost of wars is something that no one wants to bear. Rational reasoning and morality suggest that wars should be the last resort to resolving conflicts and avoiding the damage they inflict on humans. Of course as history shows, humans are not always rational!

It is beneficial to examine the evolution of different philosophies to further your understanding of conflicts. You can then use Risk as the platform on which to experiment with these ideas. Learn by doing:

"Experience is the best teacher"

5.1   Philosophy of War

"War is not merely a political act, but also a real political instrument, a continuation of policy carried out by other means."

Clausewitz

In general, there are three schools of thought in the *philosophy of war*:

- **Cataclysmic.** This school of thought looks at war as a cause for destruction and suffering of people whether the war is avoidable or inevitable. For example, Tolstoy presented war as a tool that does not provide any benefit, but only created suffering for the people. Gandhi's non-violent approach was inspired by Tolstoy's great masterpiece *War and Peace*.

- **Eschatological**. This view looks at war as a means to a final goal, perhaps a war that ends all wars and takes the society into a new state of equilibrium such as utopia or dystopia. The two main ideologies in this school of thought are *global* and *religious*. An example of the *global view* is the Marxism concept that states that a society leads to a communist world ruled by a proletariat after a global revolution that brings such a state. Examples of the *religious view* are the second coming of Christ in Christianity or the return of a saviour in Shi'a Islam, where a final war started by the saviour can bring a single faith and unify humanity.

- **Political**. Followers of this ideology think that war is the extension of politics and is a tool to use to enforce one's power over others.

The *political* view is perhaps the ideology that is most familiar and recognizable today, and it is the dominant view. A look into 20th century history shows that most of the major conflicts such as both world wars follow this ideology.

One of the most important proponents of this strategy was Clausewitz, who inspired subsequent generals after him. He was a Prussian with a background in philosophy. Clausewitz was not a military commander such as Napoleon, who was his contemporary. He was a military philosopher and was interested in the examination of war.

He undertook to write a careful philosophical and systematic examination of war in all aspects, as he saw it and taught it, and the result was his principal work, *On War*, the West's premier work on the Philosophy of War. His examination was so careful and considered that it was only partially completed before his death.

It is an arguable point that Clausewitz can be compared with the ancient Chinese philosopher, *Sun Tzu*, and *On War* can be compared to *The Art of War*. In short, Clausewitz's ideas have been widely influential in military theory. *On War* is still being taught in military academies.

The main philosophy portrayed in *On War* contains the following major lines:

- *Rational.* The decision to wage war ought to be rational, in the sense that it should be based on estimated costs and gains of war.

- *Instrumental.* War should be instrumental, in the sense that it should be waged in order to achieve some goal, never for its own sake; and also in the sense that strategy and tactics ought to be directed towards just one end, namely towards victory. War is therefore the continuation of politics through other means. War should never be seen as a purpose to itself, but as a means of physically forcing one's will on an opponent.

- *National.* War ought to be national, in the sense that its objective should be to advance the interests of a national state, and that the entire effort of the nation ought to be mobilized in the service of the military objective, i.e. *Total War.*

Clausewitz did not believe in the *strategy of attrition*. Here, the idea was to wear down the enemy using limited warfare. Clausewitz instead believed in occupying enemy territory rather than destroying his army. Along the same lines, Antoine-Henri Jomini (one of Napoleon's officers) believed in two basic principles of strategy:

- Concentrate against fractions of enemy force.

- Strike at the most decisive objective.

The strongest of Clausewitz's points is the concept of *Total War*. The idea is to use all of the resources of the nation to fight with the opponent. The use of this methodology is very pronounced in the 20th century world wars and it is even used today. However, this ideology has also been criticised for being responsible of much of the damage inflicted in both World Wars.

For example, B.H. Liddell Hart states that if the influence of Clausewitz's *On War* had been blended and balanced by Sun Tzu's *Art of War*, Civilization might have been spared much of the damage suffered in the world wars of the 20th century.

In the context of Risk, a balance between *Total War* and *The Art of War* seems to be the desired direction. This means an ability to achieve most by spending the least, while at the same time following the goal to the very end with all the means at your disposal. Perhaps we can call this *Total Diplomacy*.

5.1.1 Taoism

> *"To win without fighting is best."*
>
> **Sun Tzu**

A magical monkey establishes a monkey civilisation. The monkey declares himself king and becomes the leader of the established territories. The monkey king then goes on quests and eventually overcomes a 'devil'. He steals his sword and returns.

Upon returning to his land, the proud monkey shows off the devil's sword to his citizens. He then goes on and sets up a practice of swordsmanship. To do this, he issues his citizens toy swords and teaches them how to use them. The monkey civilisation therefore masters the art of making toy weapons.

However, the problem is that the monkey king is not yet *ruler of himself*. One day, the monkey king, in a backward logical reasoning, comes up with a revelation. He thinks that if the neighbouring countries realise that his civilisation was engaged in martial arts and making weapons (albeit toy weapons), they may assume that the monkeys were preparing for war. This meant that the neighbouring countries could take *pre-emptive* action against the monkeys, in which case, they are forced to fight a real war with toy weapons!

That was bad news. The monkey king (being so clever of course) decides on a pre-pre-emptive action and orders the stockpiling of *real weapons*. He therefore initiates an arms race.

This story is alarmingly similar to what happens today in international politics, and it is rather disconcerting. The monkey has exercised power without *wisdom*. By his backwards-logical thinking, he has gone so far that he has reached the limits of possibilities and is on the way to raising madness and ultimate destruction for everyone. The final solution imposed by the divine god was that the monkey king should put a ring of *compassion* on his head. If he misbehaves, the ring of compassion brings him pain, so that he can learn.

This story originates from *Journey to the West* (also known as His-yu chi or Xiyou ji), which is one of the *Four Classical Novels* of Chinese literature originally published anonymously in the 1590s during the Ming Dynasty. It draws on Taoism sources prior to this and explores what happens when one uses force without intelligence.

On similar ground, the ultimate strategy advocated by *The Art of War* is to use knowledge of yourself and your opponent in order to win without fighting, or if combat is ultimately necessary, *to accomplish the most by doing the least*.

This approach is characteristic of *Taoism*; the ancient tradition of knowledge that fostered both the healing arts and the martial arts in China.

In one of the classic works on Taoism, known as the *Tao-te-Ching* or *The Way and Its Power*, Lao-Tzu applies the same principle to human society that Sun Tzu applies to warfare. Lao-Tzu wrote:

"Knowing others is intelligence"

"Knowing yourself is true wisdom"

"Mastering others is strength"

"Mastering yourself is true power"

A master Risk player following these will have no problem winning against all others.

5.1.2 Principle of Least Effort

> *"Satisfaction lies in the effort, not in the attainment."*
>
> *Gandhi*

You decide to go shopping. You enter a shop, have a look around and suddenly stumble upon the trousers you were looking for. You have a thorough look at them. You like them very much, but do not want to buy it in case there is something better out there. You have only just started your shopping. Therefore, you come out of the shop and for the next hour explore all the major places in the shopping centre. Meanwhile, you have seen half a dozen more pairs of trousers and have been making a trade-off in your head. In the end you decide that the first ones were in fact the best ones after all and you decide to go back and buy them. Later you half-jokingly tell your friend how strange it is when you end up buying the first item you see.

Well, as always there is a reason behind this kind of behaviour. It is best described by the 'principle of least effort'.

The principle of least effort is a theory of user behaviour held among researchers in the field of library and information science. Within the context of information seeking, the principle of least effort was first noted by librarian and author Thomas Mann in his influential 1987 book, *A Guide to Library Research Methods*. Mann lists the principle of least effort as one of several principles guiding information-seeking behaviour.

The principle states that an information-seeking client will tend to use the most convenient search method, in the least exacting mode available. Information-seeking behaviour stops as soon as minimally acceptable results are found. This theory holds true regardless of the user's proficiency as a searcher, or their level of subject expertise. The principle of least effort applies not only in the library context, but also to any information-seeking activity or general search activity.

For example, one might consult a generalist co-worker in the same office building rather than a specialist in another branch of the company, as long as the generalist's answers are within the threshold of acceptability.

Going back to the shopping example, once you have seen the first trousers, all other trousers are compared against that. Somehow the first trousers have become the norm and all others are either rejected or provisionally considered. In short, the search process has been short-circuited.

Similarly in the context of Risk, players are performing a large number of searches. They like to know where everyone is heading, which borders are the weakest, which players are most vulnerable and so on. Following this principle, one can deduct that most players do not perform a comprehensive search. The chances are that someone will miss an optimal strategy because he was content with the one he just found as adequate.

You can exploit this in two ways. First, if you put more effort into your search, you will have an advantage over others. Second, always believe that other players may make a mistake (however good they are) and be prepared to take advantage of the opportunity when it arises. This could be your only chance against good players.

Another fascinating concept is that many variables do not follow a normal distribution curve. It is famously recognised that 20% of a project takes 80% of the resources. This relationship has been observed in many diverse systems. Twenty percent of the staff creates 80% of the problems. Equally, 20% of the staff creates 80% of the revenues (different set probably). Twenty percent of the components on an electronics circuit board are responsible for 80% of the failures.

This is universally known as the 'Pareto principle'. In 1906, Italian economist Vilfredo Pareto created a mathematical formula to describe the unequal distribution of wealth in his country, observing that 20% of the people owned 80% of the wealth. Pareto's Principle can be a very effective tool to help you manage your tasks effectively.

In Risk, one can use this principle to focus on what matters most. Twenty percent of players are those who cause most of the problems. In a five or six-player game, this turns out to be a single person. All you have to do is look out for the one person who causes you trouble. There is *probably* one person who is stronger and more experienced than you. There is one who is weak. There is one who may stab you in the back, and so on. All you need to do is to spot the individual and act appropriately. All you need to know, based on Pareto Principle, is that you may not need to spend your entire effort on everything. You only need to focus on a few issues to get the most results: *Work smart, not hard.*

Having covered the philosophy and principles behind strategical warfare, it is time to focus on Risk and see what the best overall strategies that will lead you to victory are.

5.2   Blocked Player

> *"Overcome your opponent by calculation."*
>
> *Li Quan*

First and foremost, always know your opponents. If you know how strong they are and where they are heading, you will have much more chance of dealing with them. You should always count the total number of armies of all players in each turn. It tells you precisely who is the most powerful and who is the weakest. In general, the idea is *to wipe out the weak and fight with the strong*. This is not always easy and thus you need a strategic plan.

When attacking, make sure that you have enough armies to complete your move. These manoeuvres can sometimes be very dangerous. If you go all the way and manage to get all of his countries but one, you have spent all those precious armies to the advantage of your competitors. Someone else will get that last country and collect the *bounty* (i.e. cards). Hence, you have to make a decision: *to go for it, or not to go for it*.

Pay attention that other players cannot take advantage of the weakness of a player too easily. One way to prevent them from taking your bounty is by isolating one of the countries of the weak player inside your empire. Make sure only you can attack it. Thus, even if someone conquers all other countries of the weak player, you will be the only player who is capable of conquering his last remaining country. This tactic is illustrated in Figure 5-1. In this example, the last remaining Black armies are in Irkutsk. The Black armies are surrounded by Grey. Black is not easily accessible by other players. They may experience a heavy loss going through Grey's border before they can take Black. Grey is taking no chances by making sure that Black cannot do much damage inside his own empire by surrounding him with strong forces.

Figure 5-1. Surround a weak player, so that no one else can take it. Irkutsk is blocked for access.

5.3 What to Do?

"If someone else can do it for you, then don't do it yourself."

Popular Proverb

Master Sun beautifully describes where you need to focus your attention when deciding where to attack:

> *"So when the front is prepared, the rear is lacking, when the rear is prepared the front is lacking. Preparedness on the left mean lack on the right, preparedness on the right means lack on the left. Preparedness everywhere means lack everywhere."*

When you are about to get a new continent, only attempt to conquer the continent if you can get all of the countries in that continent, and you are sure that you can hold it in the next turn. Anyone who completes conquering a continent can be subject to attack by just about everyone.

Always attempt to keep up with the strongest player and do not let him advance further ahead of everyone else. Of course, this does not mean that you need to fight with him yourself! Rather, get someone else to do the job. Motivate other players to do it for you.

5.4 What Not to Do?

"Patience is a virtue"

Popular Proverb

The Shah of Persia had sentenced two men to death. One of the men, knowing how much the Shah liked his stallion, offered to teach the horse to fly within a year if the Shah would spare him his life. The Shah, fancying himself as the rider of the only flying horse in the world, agreed.

The other prisoner looked at his friend in disbelief. "You're mad," said the other prisoner. "You know that horses can't fly. What made you come up with a crazy idea like that? You're only putting off the inevitable."

"Not so," said the first prisoner. "I have actually given myself four chances for freedom. First, the Shah might die. Second, I might die. Third, the horse might die. And fourth … I might teach the horse how to fly!"

Never underestimate the power of possibilities. The future may be brighter than you think.

For example, if you have just conquered a continent and got attacked, make an effort to remain patient. If you are in a situation to contain the attack, do not attempt to get that one remaining country in your continent every turn. In a few turns, your enemy might be under heavy attack himself and may not have the option to deal with you. Do not give others excuses to attack you every turn. Wait a few turns to recover and then claim your lost country in a way they can never get it back.

5.5   When to Nail?

> *"Do not confront force with force; instead use your opponent's strength and turn it against him."*

A fundamental philosophy in the ancient sport of Judo

Nailing is defined as placing a large force in a player's continent to disrupt his plan to get that continent. The best analogy for this is as if you have a military base in someone's land. You may benefit from this, though at the same time, your opponent may become aggressive towards you. There is a trade-off when you want to *nail* someone.

- *When is it good?* Nailing is generally used to slow a player. You want to rub him off his continental bonus and are willing to allocate certain number of armies for this purpose. Sometimes, especially if you have a smaller continent, it will be beneficial to nail your neighbour's bigger continent, so that he will not become too strong too soon. If you have long-term plans for that continent, your nailed armies will ultimately be useful as you can spend them while conquering the continent. Hence, nailing can be a wise tactical move.

- *When is it bad?* A nailed player may easily interpret your army placement as an aggressive move towards him. It will be in his best interest to remove your armies form his continent. It makes him hostile towards you for no reason. This is not desirable since you have made an enemy for yourself without achieving much.

The short-term benefit may be to your advantage, though the long-term benefit is debatable.

The best move, if you can time it well, is to nail a neighbour so that he becomes weak and the subject of attack by others. Since he is weak and cannot retaliate against you. He will be struggling to get his continent. A weak neighbour is extremely useful as it lets you expand easily.

Notice that nailing can be a useful tactic in Risk games where rules are modified or the goal of the game is not global conquest. If you know someone needs to get a particular continent to win, nailing that continent is a logical move.

In an special case, suppose you find yourself in South America and are confronted with two experienced players in North America and Africa. If they prove to be hard to deal with, you may find yourself squeezed between them. They practically tell you that they will invade you whenever they please. How would you resolve this situation?

Again, nailing can be a useful tactic here. Early in the game, you can nail one of your neighbours to prevent him from getting his respective continent. He will not expand as fast as others (including you) since he does not receive continual bonuses. This way you have broken the symmetry and hopefully will not be squeezed too much.

5.6   *Total Elimination*

"To have ultimate victory, you must be ruthless."

Napoleon Bonaparte

In 1934, Mao and some 75,000 poorly equipped soldiers fled to the desolate mountains of western China to escape Chiang Kai-shek's much larger army in what has since been called the Long March. China was determined to eliminate every last communist, and by a few years later, Mao had less than 10,000 soldiers left. In 1937 Japan invaded China and Chiang made a calculated decision that the communist were no longer a threat, and he preferred to concentrate his armies on the Japanese. Only ten years later, communists returned all-powerful and encompassing.

Chiang had made a fundamental mistake. He should have *totally* eliminated his enemy . An enemy that has become weak will always seek to get ignored so that he can survive. He may then recover and can always come back for revenge. Crush him when you can, in body and in spirit.

In Risk, if you have a chance to eliminate a player, conquer him and get his cards. You may become weak temporarily, but it is much better to get rid of your sworn enemy rather than leave him out. Otherwise he will cash his cards and will come knocking on your door all full of hate and revenge!

5.7   How to Recover if all Failed

"In battle, there are not more than two methods of attack: the direct and the indirect; yet these two in combination give rise to an endless series of manoeuvres."

Sun Tzu

One day Voltaire, the famous French philosopher, was walking in London and suddenly found himself surrounded by an angry crowd who were shouting at him, "Hang him. Hang the Frenchman." Voltaire calmly and cunningly addressed the mob, "Men of England! You wish to kill me because I am a Frenchman. Am I not punished enough in not being born an Englishman?" The crowd cheered his thoughtful words, and escorted him back to his home. This amusing story from *The Little Brown Book of Anecdotes* captures an extremely important concept that no matter how hopeless a situation may seem, there can always be a smart way out. All you have to do is to believe that such a way exists and explore every imaginable option.

For example, in Risk, if for any reason you find yourself in a weak position, you can switch to a strategy which is known as the 'Turtle Strategy'. Suppose you suddenly find yourself under attack turn after turn. You are left with only a few countries and not many armies. The best strategy you can follow now is to make sure that the next player does not wipe you out of the game. *Never lose hope, however small you think your chances are*. You can always win the game and conquer the whole world even if you have only one country.

The solution is to use *passive resistance*. Find a location on the planet that you think is close, reachable and is completely out of the way of other players. Yakutsk and Japan are good examples, since players usually have no incentive to attack them. Thus, move to this isolated country and attempt to bring all of your remaining armies there. This is now your new home. Do not worry about losing your one-army countries in the process. You are not in a situation to care about such issues!

Once you have successfully emigrated, aim to concentrate a reasonable amount of armies in this newly found country so that no one can get rid of you without seriously weakening himself against other players. At this point in time, killing you will not have any direct benefit for other players. You do not even have a continent to lose. Removing you would only cost them. Hence, you are exploiting the selfishness of other players by preventing them from attacking you.

There is, however, an exception. If you have a high number of cards, such as four or five, you will automatically be considered a great target, especially in the later stages of the game. If you have cards, cash them in and put them on the map. You will simultaneously decrease their incentive to get the bounty, and make it more costly to attack you. As a minimum, if you can, hide your cards so other players cannot easily see how many you have.

Performing this manoeuvre is an art and needs *active diplomacy* during the process. If you got this far, you only need to build up for a few more turns while others carry on fighting with each other. All you need to do is to be ignored. Eventually, if you are ignored for long enough, you can return as a powerful nation ready to compete with others.

Make sure that you will always get your all-important card in your turn so that you are not falling behind. Since they use their armies and you do not, you will eventually become as powerful as they are.

Beware that 'Turtling' (The act of using the Turtle Strategy) is considered controversial. If everyone employs this strategy, the game basically comes to a halt as no one will be fighting anyone else. This is undesirable for everyone. This topic is thoroughly examined later in Section 8.7.

5.8 Learn from History

> *"Fool me once shame on you, fool me twice, shame on me."*
>
> *Chinese Proverb*

History is a great teacher. It shows us that events seem to repeat themselves over and over again. The civilisations constantly find themselves in the same set of conflicts experienced hundreds or even thousands of years ago. The underlying mechanism to advance the civilisation through conflict resolution seems to remain the same. One can learn a great deal from history and avoid repeating the same mistakes. This section provides a number of historical crises and attempts to examine them in the context of Risk.

5.8.1 Schlieffen Plan

In World War I, Alfred Graf von Schlieffen, the German field marshal and strategist, envisioned a new plan for containing a two-front war where Germany may end up in the middle while the French could attack from the west and the Russians from east. The Schlieffen Plan hence provided a strategy with an objective to defend in the east and then concentrate the main army in the west for a decisive victory. For the plan to work, the German armies had to go through the two countries of Luxemburg and Belgium, who were neutral. This meant that the army went to the west through the north (See Figure 5-2). The intention was to destroy the French army itself as opposed to the war industry or capturing cities. The distribution of the army was set to be 90% for the west and 10% for the east.

The critical part of this strategy was to finish the western front quickly so that the army having finished the job in the west could return to the eastern front and take an offensive position.

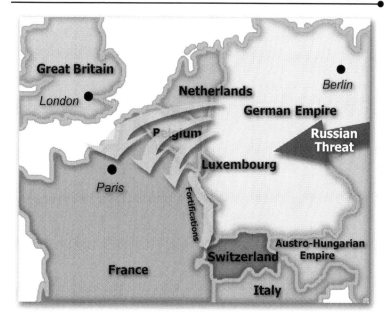

Figure 5-2. The Schlieffen plan. Germans allocated 90% of their army to go through north via Belgium and Luxembourg towards the west and planned to return to the east to cover the eastern front against the Russians.

Schlieffen's idea, as you may know, did not go according to plan. Germans underestimated just about everyone: Belgians, French, Russians, and British.

The Schlieffen Plan is a much-studied strategic manoeuvre in history with numerous suggestions on why it was genius, even though it did not work, and what could have been done instead to ensure victory.

Some argue that one of the critical parts of this plan was *timing*. It was essential to make sure that the western front could finish the job quickly and be ready for the eastern front when the Russians arrived. Kaiser Wilhlem II is famously quoted as saying, "*Paris for lunch, dinner at St. Petersburg.*"

What happened was that the Belgian Resistance caused more trouble than anticipated and the British entered the war when they were not expected to do so. The French could mobilise faster thanks to their railway system, which meant they could put up a tougher fight than expected against the Germans. This all meant that the Germans were delayed in completing their western front campaign. In addition, the Russians managed to mobilise faster and hence advanced more in the eastern front. This forced the Germans to make a decision. They had to take some of the armies from the western side and use them for the east to adapt to the new circumstances. This temporarily helped the situation in the east, though it resulted in weakening the western side. The end result was the two-front war that the plan had tried to avoid!

At the outset, the plan sounds rational. If you find yourself in such a situation, with armies on two fronts both outnumbering you, it may be worth considering. However, much emphasis should be made on the timing of the execution of this move. Once the plan is underway, *it is all or nothing*. In this situation, you should pay a lot of attention to the capability of the other players at that moment in time. You should add in contingency measures to make sure that even if something unanticipated occurs, you can still survive the dilemma. As always, identify those parts of the plan that have the highest risk and devise a number of alternatives if something unexpected happens. In history and economics, the research shows that time and time again most people underestimate the true nature of *risk* and consistently make decisions without considering its impact.

5.8.2   Carpe Diem

"Seize the Day"

The Suez Crisis is one of the most captivating international crises of recent history, which led to a large change in the balance of political power in the world.

In 1954 a new type of political leader, Gamal Abdel Nasser, a strong Arab nationalist, emerged as the leader of Egypt. Nasser announced that he was nationalising the Suez Canal Company (partly, he said, to pay for the Aswan dam, which the West refused to finance).

Britain and France were alarmed. France, who engineered the canal and had interests in it, was hostile to Nasser. Egypt was also helping the Algerian rebels. Britain could not accept Egypt running the Suez Canal, even though they had previously agreed to remove British troops from Canal Zone. The canal had now acquired a new importance: a passageway for oil to get to Europe.

Anthony Eden, prime minister of Britain at the time, refused to accept that the world had changed. He told his government colleagues that he would not allow Nasser to "have his thumb on our windpipe".

As a result, Britain and France made a secret tripartite plot with Israel. Israel was longing to have a go at Nasser anyway because of Palestinian Fedayeen attacks and historical reasons. The plot was that Israel would invade Egypt across the Sinai Peninsula. Britain and France would then give an ultimatum to the parties to stop fighting or they would intervene to *protect* the canal.

And so it played out. The Israelis even had to *moderate* their attack in case they won before the *intervention* forces could arrive. As planned, the British and French went in to *save* the canal.

There was only one thing wrong. Britain had not told the Americans. President Eisenhower, concerned about wider relations with the Arab world and horrified at such an adventure, was not amused. The president was an advocate of decolonisation because he believed it would liberate colonies, thereby strengthening U.S. interests, and presumably make other Arab and African leaders more sympathetic to the United States. Meanwhile, Eden had ignored Britain's financial dependence on the U.S. in the wake of World War II. There was a run on sterling. Eden was forced to bow to American pressure to withdraw. The Chancellor of the Exchequer told the cabinet that the only way to save the situation was an IMF loan backed by the United States. The Americans, however, refused to back it. Britain was told by them to go no further and to evacuate promptly.

The fallout was huge. The Suez Crisis is widely taken as marking the end of Britain, along with France, as world powers. British and French troops left Egypt by December 1956.

In the meantime, the Soviets eagerly rushed in to aid Egypt, which was considered a friend of the Soviets, and a nation not overly friendly to the West. As a result, Egypt now firmly aligned herself with the Soviet Union, which armed the country and other Arab nations for the continuing struggle against Israel.

This all meant that Britain and France could no longer act alone on the world stage. They did, however, draw different conclusions.

Since then, Britain has been reluctant to oppose any U.S. policy. France on the other hand went its own way, led in due course by de Gaulle. She left the military command structure of Nato and turned to leading Europe alongside a newly prosperous Germany. Just as Britain always thereafter tended to side with the U.S., so France tended to oppose it.

The result was that the U.S. and the Soviet Union emerged as new political superpowers leading their corresponding allies around two opposite poles in the power spectrum.

In the end, there is no doubt that Suez represented the end of a long phase of British imperial history. Margaret Thatcher in her book, *The Path to Power*, on reflection on the crisis famously states that: "As I came to know more about it, I drew four lessons from this sad episode." Her conclusions were:

1. We should not get into a military operation unless we are determined and able to finish it.

2. We should never again find ourselves on the opposite side to the United States in a major international crisis affecting Britain's interests.

3. We should ensure that our actions are in accord with international law.

4. He who hesitates is lost.

Interestingly enough, a look at today's developments suggest that British international politics is still very much in line with the above guidelines, in particular the strategy of siding with U.S. on all major international crises affecting Britain!

There are a large number of lessons one can learn from this story. Power balance on the world map changes during successive crises. A Risk player could take advantage of a crisis (in this case Soviet Union) and carry on with his own agenda, while the rest of the world (i.e. other players) focus on something else.

As you might have noticed, change of power on the board is just as swift as it is seen in the real world. The following major instructions can be drawn from this historical event:

- Make the crisis look as if it has been initiated by the 'bad guys' and then aim to take advantage of it by playing the innocent (even though it was you who started it with a plot).

- Watch out as it can go horribly wrong if you ignore the strong player. You may need to keep him in the loop.

- Get someone to attack someone else while you and your allies appear to be only protecting your own resources.

- If you have become a strong player lately, like the U.S. in this event, and are waiting for an opportunity to exercise your power, wait for a crisis. When a crisis unfolds, *carpe diem*: seize the day. This will be your chance to influence the strongest players and bring them down without directly fighting them.

- It is not always clear which strategy is best to follow, even if it sounds clever to you. In this crisis, France and Britain chose to go through different paths. In Risk, one player (like France) may decide not to cooperate with 'the emerging strong player' because he destroyed their plot. While, another player (like Britain) can always decide to support the position of the strongest players in future crises because ignoring that may be futile for him. Which strategy is better depends greatly on other players in the game and how you will align yourself with them.

Just make sure you do not hesitate, whatever you do!

6 Diplomacy

"Weapons are instruments of misfortune to be used only when unavoidable."

Sun Tzu

Diplomacy is the art and practice of conducting negotiations between nations. It concerns getting other nations to listen to you and negotiate over crises and resolve issues through peaceful means. In an ideal world, all issues should be resolved through diplomacy and no nation should end up in a war. This is why war is always seen as the result of *failed diplomacy*. This inevitably means that the politicians involved in the diplomatical affair have not been able to do a good job or they would not have failed.

The following lesson from history will shed light on the extent of a diplomatical act and how powerful it can be.

6.1 How to Take a Country Without a Single Shot?

"You can fool all the people some of the time, and some of the people all the time, but you can't fool all the people all the time."

Abraham Lincoln

Hitler had grabbed control of the German Army. It was 1938. He was preparing for his next move. His aim was to expand, rapidly and decisively. Hitler set out to engage in his gangster diplomacy.

His very first victim was Dr. Kurt von Schuschnigg, Chancellor of Austria, a country being torn apart from within by Nazi agitators and also feeling threatened from the outside by Germany's newfound military strength. Hoping for some sort of peaceful settlement with Hitler, Schuschnigg agreed to a face-to-face meeting at Berchtesgaden.

On the chilly winter morning of February 12, 1938, Schuschnigg, having been picked up by Papen, the German Ambassador to Austria, arrived at the steps of Hitler's villa and was greeted by the Führer himself. Standing behind Hitler were three generals who were going to be present in the discussions. Schuschnigg was somewhat taken aback by this.

Hitler led Schuschnigg into his villa and up to the great hall on the second floor, a big room featuring a huge plate glass window with sweeping views of the Alps, and in the far distance, Austria itself. Schuschnigg, in his character, began the conversation with a graceful titbit about the magnificent view, the fine weather that day and a flattering remark about the room they were in. Adolf Hitler cut him right short, "We did not gather here to speak of the fine view or of the weather!" Thus began two hours of hell in which the quiet-spoken Austrian Chancellor was lambasted without mercy by the Führer.

"You have done everything to avoid a friendly policy!" Hitler yelled. "The whole history of Austria is just one uninterrupted act of high treason...And I can tell you right now, Herr Schuschnigg, that I am absolutely determined to make an end of this. The German Reich is one of the great powers, and nobody will raise his voice if it settles its border problems."

After regaining his composure, Schuschnigg tried to settle down and said, "We will do everything to remove obstacles to a better understanding, as far as it is possible."

However, Hitler did not let go, "That is what you say! ... But I am telling you that I am going to solve the so-called Austrian problem one way or another ... I have a historic mission, and this mission I will fulfil because providence has destined me to do so...who is not with me will be crushed..."

Hitler then said, "Listen, you don't really think you can move a single stone in Austria without my hearing about it the next day, do you? I have only to give an order and all your ridiculous defence mechanisms will be blown to bits. You don't seriously believe you can stop me or even delay me for half an hour, do you?"

Hitler pointed out that Austria was isolated diplomatically and could not halt a Nazi invasion. "Don't think for one moment that anybody on earth is going to thwart my decisions. Italy? I see eye to eye with Mussolini...England? England will not move one finger for Austria...And France?"

An exasperated Schuschnigg finally asked, "What exactly are your terms?"

To which Hitler replied, "We can discuss that this afternoon."

Schuschnigg was a chain smoker and was not allowed to smoke in front of the Führer. During the lunch break, he could finally relieve himself of the urge.

By the afternoon, the forty-one-year-old Schuschnigg had aged about ten years. He was then introduced to Germany's new Foreign Minister, an amoral character named Joachim Ribbentrop, who presented him with a two-page document containing Hitler's demands. All Nazis presently jailed in Austria were to be freed. The ban against the Austrian Nazi Party was to be lifted. Austrian lawyer, Dr. Arthur Seyss-Inquart, a staunch Nazi supporter was to become the new Minister of the Interior with full control of the police. In addition, Nazis were to be appointed as Minister of War and Minister of Finance with preparations made for the assimilation of Austria's entire economy into the German Reich. This was, Schuschnigg was told, the Führer's final demands and there could be no discussion. Ribbentrop told Schuschnigg to accept the demands at once.

This is when one should pause and consider what options the Austrian Chancellor had. The questions were: Should he sign them? Was surrender necessary? Was there an alternative? To get support of other world powers such as Britain and France may not be easy. As it turned out, Britain and France may not have been able (or had enough incentive) to do anything if Austria was invaded. Would that mean Schuschnigg should lose hope entirely?

Schuschnigg was to give up his country at the point of a gun. This, by all standards, was a stressful situation to be in. Under such pressure, the Austrian Chancellor wobbled and said he would consider signing, but first sought assurances that there would be no further interference in Austria's internal affairs by Hitler. Ribbentrop gave friendly assurances that Hitler would indeed respect Austria's sovereignty if all of his demands were met.

Schuschnigg had one last chance to make a stand. He was summoned again to the Führer. He just had to make the best of this. He found Führer pacing excitedly up and down.

Hitler said, "Herr Schuschnigg ... here is the draft document. There is nothing to be discussed. I will not change one single iota. You will either sign it as it is and fulfil my demands within three days, or I will order the march into Austria."

Schuschnigg, somewhat weak, said he was willing to sign, but informed Hitler that under Austrian law only the country's president could ratify such a document and carry out the terms. He added that there was no guarantee the agreement would be accepted by Austria's president.

"You have to guarantee it!" Hitler exploded. However, Schuschnigg said he simply could not. Hitler then rushed to the doorway, opened it and shouted, "General Keitel!" Then he turned to Schuschnigg and abruptly dismissed him. Schuschnigg was taken to a waiting room and left to ponder what Hitler was saying to Keitel.

Schuschnigg did not know he had just been the victim of an outright bluff. There were many generals that day surrounding the Führer and the scene was set. When Keitel arrived to ask for orders, a grinning Hitler told him, "There are no orders. I just wanted to have you here."

Thirty minutes later, Schuschnigg was again ushered into the presence of Hitler.

Hitler said, "I have decided to change my mind, for the first time in my life. But I warn you, this is your very last chance. I have given you three additional days to carry out the agreement." That was the extent of the dictator's concessions. The document was Austria's death warrant.

Schuschnigg departed Berchtesgaden, accompanied during the ride back to the border by a somewhat embarrassed Papen. Papen could not refrain from trying to cheer his Austrian friends up. "You have seen what the Führer can be like at times!" Papen consoled him. "But the next time, I am sure it will be different. You know, the Führer can be absolutely charming."

Of course, the rest was history. Hitler had taken Austria without firing a single shot. He now had his eyes on Czechoslovakia. Next-door Czechoslovakia now trembled at the thought that it was surrounded on three sides by the German Army. Hermann Göring assured the nervous Czech government, "I give you my word of honour that Czechoslovakia has nothing to fear from the Reich." And so the story continued...

One can learn a great deal from history. Hitler obviously pushed his opponent with no limits on moral. He was set on his goal and did not care less if his means were not considered fair. Equally, Schuschnigg was too weak and too far behind to figure out what was happening to him. He thought that there was no choice but to give up his country, while the reality was that his choices were blurred systematically. He was convinced by the Germans that his best option was to surrender. The Germans used every psychological trick in the book, and as history showed, they were pretty successful in this particular case. Ultimately though, this was the beginning of the end for them.

Diplomacy is one of the most rewarding experiences in Risk. It is equally an important skill in real life too. Dealing with your friends, your partner, your associates, your colleagues and even the butcher down the road, all involve certain levels of diplomatic skill. Practicing diplomacy never hurts anyone and is certainly not a waste of time or resources. It has been seen numerous times that cunning diplomacy can save the day and save you many hours of painstaking work. Master diplomacy and learn how to deal with people effectively and with minimal effort.

Diplomacy is the key in any strategic situation. Why do you need diplomacy in Risk? Because y*ou can never go against the whole world just with war*! In the previous chapters, you were exposed to different tactics and strategies. In this chapter you will learn how to get the most by putting in the least.

6.2 Alliances & Treaties

> *"Those who come seeking peace without a treaty are plotting."*
>
> *Sun Tzu*

Making alliances is usually perceived as one of the most important acts in diplomacy. This section expands on the concept of alliances in Risk and provides you with a number of examples.

Why should a player need to make a treaty? Since you cannot fight with everyone simultaneously, you need to engage with others one at a time. No matter how powerful you are, you need to resist the temptation to attack a lot of players at once. You need to be able to influence the flow of the game with something other than direct force.

Niccolo Machiavelli states in his famous book, *The Prince*, that it is always wiser to choose a side rather than be neutral. Machiavelli provides the following reasons to support his argument:

- If your allies win, you benefit whether or not you have more power than they have.

- If you are more powerful, your allies are under your command; if your allies are stronger, they will always feel a certain obligation to you for your help.

- If your side loses, you still have an ally in the loser.

Machiavelli also notes that it is wise for a prince not to ally with a stronger force unless compelled to do so.

Alliances can be broadly divided into two types:

- *Total Alliance*. This alliance is established when two players consider each other as friends. They agree not to attack each other. If one of them is attacked by an enemy, his ally will automatically come to his rescue. An enemy of one is also an enemy of the other. Since only one person can win in Risk, alliances are usually terminated when only the two allies are left in the game.

- *Treaty*. This type is used when a specific issue is negotiated by a number of players. Treaties usually have a deadline or can be set to expire when only the two participants are left in the game. For example, two players can make a treaty between two countries or over a border. They should state that they will adhere by the terms of the treaty.

In Risk, treaties are much more common. A total alliance can be considered as a hostile act by other players. For example, suppose you approach another player by saying, "Let's have a deal. We will never fight each other." This suggests an alliance for the rest of the game with no specific limits (i.e. no terms and conditions). There are two reasons why making a total alliance can be a problem:

- By making a total alliance, other players will certainly be tempted to follow suit. Overall you may not achieve any advantage.

- A total alliance makes your game extremely inflexible since towards the end of the game you may find yourself continuously *squeezed* by your allied partner. You may simply lose the game as a result of lack of options. The alliance will be under pressure, which increases the incentive of each party to break the deal.

As opposed to a total alliance, any player with a treaty or a *border alliance* has a great advantage over those who do not have one. A treaty releases your precious armies from one of your fronts. Not only do you not have to worry about that front anymore (within reason), you can now strengthen your other front by the amount of army you just saved. This can easily lead to more decisive battles and pave the way for more successful campaigns. Sun Tzu wisely states that:

> *"If you do not compete for alliances anywhere, do not foster authority anywhere, but just extend your personal influence, threatening opponents, this makes town and country vulnerable. No alliances lead to isolation."*

You have two options when making alliances and treaties: Either you find the need and approach other players, or they approach you. You have to treat each case separately and consider your position.

6.2.1   You Approach Others

> *"When you have the means but are not getting anywhere, seek appropriate associates, and you will be lucky."*
>
> *Sun Tzu*

As stated above, having a treaty is always better than none. You should always strive to find a player with which to make a treaty. Initially you should approach your immediate neighbour to make a treaty. You can then secure one front and then focus on others.

If you are under treat and in a serious situation, a *border alliance* is a must. Under such circumstances you need *anyone's* help. You want to stop others from attacking you and making you even weaker. Eventually, you can return as a world-class power when you are fit enough.

Do not give up on a player who is not so keen to have an alliance or a treaty with you. The power balance in the world changes rapidly. By the time a turn has passed, he may have second thoughts and you may get what you want, if only you ask him again. *Do not take 'no' for an answer.* Aim to have one or two border alliances with those that you do not want to fight with.

Remember, in any alliance you need to get something in return for anything you give. *Political haggling is the key to success.*

Always put yourself in your opponent's position and understand his needs. The art of negotiation and techniques on how to get what you want are discussed later in Chapter 7.

If you want something from an ally, appeal to self-interest. When you turn to an ally for help, do not bother to remind him of your great history and good deeds. He will find a way to ignore them. Instead tell him what he will gain and he will listen to you. People's resistance will fall dramatically if they see how it is going to benefit them. Find their interests. Master the art and there is no limit to your achievements.

Once you have made an alliance, *generally*, you should not break it. In doing so, other player will always remember you as a player who cannot be trusted. You will not be very popular in the next game! However, there are exceptions to this rule, as you shall see soon.

Similarly, you should not make an alliance with someone who has broken them in the past. If they have done it once, they may very well do it again. If someone broke a deal, attacked you on an unfair basis, or just fought with you from the beginning of the game for no particular reason, aim to fight only with him. Make a clear statement for everyone that if someone treats you this way, your only aim in continuing the game is to get rid of the annoying player. Do your best to make sure that the player is weakened as much as possible before you are kicked out. If you are losing badly, there is not much you can do anyway, but at least you have made a statement and might have made it easier for yourself in the next game.

Indeed, you should have a strategy when breaking or honouring deals, especially when it is repeated over time. This fascinating topic is discussed later in Section 8.4.

6.2.2 Others Approach You

> *"When they are fulfilled, be prepared against them; when they are strong, avoid them."*
>
> *Sun Tzu*

If someone else approaches you and offers you a deal, you should not necessarily jump at the idea. You need to go through the following checklist:

- The most important consideration is to see whether you need another deal at all. If you already have a treaty or treaties with other players, having another one may not be such a clever idea as it may block your expansion and limit your options.

- Make sure it is wise to have a treaty with this player. If he has a history of breaking deals, reject his offer at once.

- If you have just invaded this player and he is offering you a deal to make peace, with no offer of a treaty, then you cannot trust him as he could be plotting.

- Consider the impact of accepting such a deal, or the impact of your actions on other players. If others have a tendency to become hostile to anyone who makes a deal, you should be careful with your decision.

Once the player has passed the above checks, only then would you move to full negotiation mode and start discussing the specifics of his offer. You need to consider what he is offering and what he wants in return from you, and if this is worth the effort.

A few examples are provided below to show you how alliances work in practice.

6.2.3   *Treaty Example 1: Playing as Africa*

In this example you are playing as *Stripe* starting from Africa. This is shown in Figure 6-1. Upon evaluation of your position, you realise that you have two main options:

1. *Move toward east and north and expand to Europe or Asia*. You can make a deal with the player in South America. Once you can secure your border with a treaty, you can then focus on other fronts.

2. *Invade South America*. South America is a small continent and is therefore desirable. As a bonus, you

do not even end up increasing the number of your borders once you have conquered South America. In this case you will be expanding westwards and securing east (North Africa, Egypt and East Africa) through treaties will be extremely helpful.

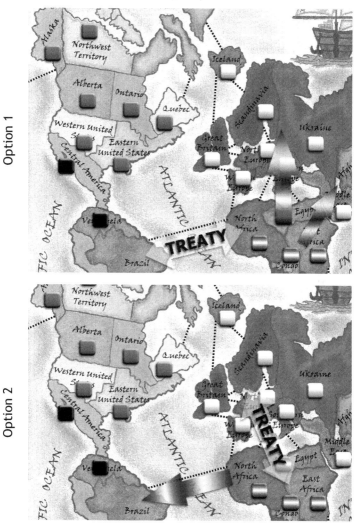

Figure 6-1. Treaty Example 1: You have two options for making treaties when playing as Stripe.

In this scenario, making treaties with either side is certainly an advantage. You need to trust the player you want to make the treaty with. The last thing you want is to make a treaty, move your armies elsewhere and then get invaded by a large force from your weakest border.

6.2.4   *Treaty Example 2: Playing as Europe*

Suppose you are playing as *White* and reside in Europe. Europe is strategically interesting since it is in the middle of the world and has access to everywhere. This means you can attack anyone as you wish. It provides a fair number of bonus armies, though you can use it only *if you can keep the continent*. Being in the middle of the world has its drawbacks: almost everyone has access to Europe and can be a direct threat.

The trick with Europe is that if you can get a couple of treaties with other players, it is almost guaranteed that you will win the game. You have the following options (the options are illustrated in Figure 6-2 and Figure 6-3):

1. *Treaty with Africa.* This will secure your southern border. Once the south is secure, you are left with expanding into North America or Asia. The player in Africa will be happy to have a treaty with the player in Europe since, as explained in the previous scenario, he can concentrate on South America.

2. *Treaty with Asia.* Expanding to Asia is not usually wise early in the game since it is a difficult-to-get continent. No one is usually very strong in Asia and there is no point making a treaty on this border.

3. *Treaty with North America.* You can make a treaty with North America and expand to Africa or Asia.

Your choice largely depends on the type of players and the distribution of armies on the map. As you can see, in *Option 1*, only one treaty with Africa can make Europe as fortress-like as Australia, but with two and a half times more extra armies. The pass to victory is already set!

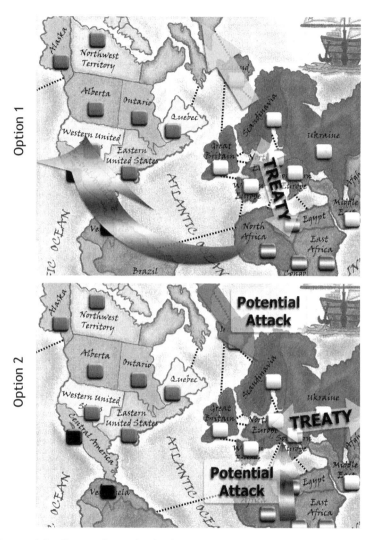

Figure 6-2. Treaty Example 2 (Options 1 and 2): You have three options when playing as White.

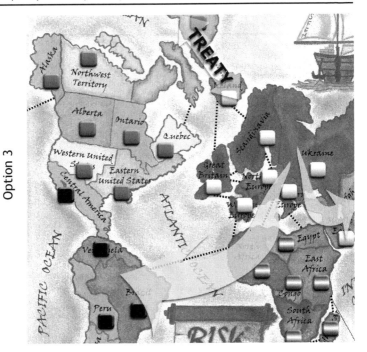

Figure 6-3. *Treaty Example 2 (Option 3): You have three options when playing as White.*

6.2.5   Treaty Example 3: Playing as North America

If you find yourself in North America playing as *Grey*, you need to think carefully to make sure that you can take advantage of your situation without others getting too concerned about your higher continent bonus. There are basically three borders to protect and expand from. The Asian side is not critical in the early game as usually there are no strong threats in Asia. This leaves North America with two options. Your choice between these options depends greatly on the current situation and the type of players you are playing against.

1. *Dealing with South America.* If the player in South America has already made a treaty with Africa over the Brazil-North Africa border, he has only one direction in

which to expand: *North America*. This example is shown in Figure 6-4. Hence, he is not going to be interested in treaties over this border, otherwise he will not be able to expand to anywhere else. You in North America are only left with one choice: *make a treaty with Europe*. This simply shows how important it is to be the first to make alliances and treaties. As more and more treaties are made, your options are reduced and so is the willingness of players to make yet another treaty.

Figure 6-4. Treaty Example 3: Dealing with South America and making a treaty with Europe while playing as Grey.

Invading South America is not a bad choice after all. In fact it is quite ideal since one continent can be conquered without increasing your number of borders, which is always an extremely important point to consider when expanding.

2. *Dealing with Europe.* Suppose Europe has already made a treaty with Africa on its southern border. This is shown in Figure 6-5. As a result of the treaty, Europe will be interested in expanding to North America. You now have no choice but to make an alliance with South America or you will end up with two fronts. The problem is that your options are limited. This is bad news indeed! South America may easily realise that you are in a weak position and will probably exploit this. He will not be interested in cooperating with you. This unfortunate event happened because you were late in making up your mind in selecting who you could make a treaty with! By the time you decided on your overall strategy, Europe had already made a treaty with Africa. The moral of the story: *Do not hesitate!*

As you have seen in this section, deciding on alliances mainly depends on your ability to perform a trade-off on your potential options and to being able to take decisive action. However, trade-offs can be manipulated by your opponents. You should be aware that your opponent can play many psychological tricks on you and you should deflect them as much as you can. The following section explores common manipulation techniques working on your most vulnerable emotions.

Figure 6-5. Treaty Example 3: You, playing as Grey, are forced to deal with Europe and have ended up at the mercy of South America.

6.3 Psychological Warfare

> *"If opponents are numerous, they can be made not to fight."*
>
> **Sun Tzu**

The U.S. Department of Defence defines psychological warfare as:

> *"The planned use of propaganda and other psychological actions having the primary purpose of*

influencing the opinions, emotions, attitudes, and behaviour of hostile foreign groups in such a way as to support the achievement of national objectives."

Most of the events throughout history involving psychological warfare utilised tactics that instilled fear or a sense of awe towards the enemy. Making the enemy afraid of you can make it a lot easier for you to get what you want. It is critical to know how not to become afraid of an adversary, while at the same time making them afraid of you. The following sections focus on different aspects of psychological warfare.

6.3.1   Rule by Fear

"Benefits must be conferred gradually so they are appreciated more thoroughly and harm should be inflicted all at once. Both harm and benefits should not serve as quick solutions to problems."

Niccolo Machiavelli

The Mongol empire, founded by Genghis Khan, was the largest contagious land empire in world history. The Mongols achieved this incredible expansion by having three main advantages: *rapid movement of the army, self-contained logistics* and *fear*.

As for rapidity, Genghis' army and his strategy were based on his tribal levies of mounted archers and just as important the vast horse-herds of Mongolia. The Mongolian army had an average of five horses per man! Hence the entire army could move with incredible speed. As for logistics, since horse milk and horse blood were the staples of the Mongolian diet, Genghis' horse-herds functioned not just as his means of movement, but also as his logistical tail. All other necessities could be foraged and plundered. In comparison, the rival armies such as Persians, Chinese, Arabs, and Europeans were comparatively immobile and heavy. The Mongolians had little problem overcoming them.

As for fear, Genghis' achievements and those of his successors were based upon manoeuvre and terror. The point of Genghis' strategic assault was to control the psychology of the opposing population. If they were confronted with fortified cities, they used any means they could to break them. They even went as far as using limited biological warfare. Their reputation of being excessively aggressive worked in their favour greatly. Killing all the citizens of a city, just to set an example, was not something they would lose sleep over. It is estimated that under the rule of the Mongol Empire, thirty million people were killed and the population of China fell by half in fifty years of Mongol rule. Mongols used every fear tactic they could conceive by using terror, mass extermination, and wiping out urban populations that had refused to surrender. This lead to the destruction of almost all major cities! Simply put, they *ruled by fear*.

By a steady and meticulous implementation of this strategy, Genghis and his descendants were able to conquer most of Eurasia. Thus, the Mongolian horde achieved for two centuries an unparalleled dominance.

We can see that using the so-called *triple-tactic* (rapidity-logistics-fear) in Risk can be quite effective in fast expansions. However, do not be surprised if you lose all your friends! Rapid manoeuvres and maintenance of supply lines are tactical issues and are already covered in previous chapters. It is the fear factor that is more complex to initiate or handle. Not being afraid of fear tactics is also just as important. The last thing you want is to be afraid of your opponent and give up the initiative. Once you become afraid and start believing that there is no hope, you have lost your greatest asset: The ability to think your way out of the crisis and overcome your fears. You can either get sucked deeper into the mud (by becoming more and more afraid) or rescue yourself by any clever means you know.

Sun Tzu was asked, "When a large well-organised opponent is about to come to you, how do you deal with it?"

He replied, "The answer is that you first take away what they like, and then they will listen to you." There is always a way, however hopeless a situation may appear to be.

Fear tactic is usually initiated through propaganda. This is discussed in the following sections.

6.3.2 Propaganda

"The broad mass of the nation ... will more easily fall victim to a big lie than to a small one."

Adolf Hitler, in his 1925 book Mein Kampf

Propaganda is a term used to describe the distribution of information, usually in a way to benefit the initiator. In English, the term has a negative bias. However, *distributed information* does not have to be untrue to count as propaganda. In reality, it may omit many truthful statements that turn out to be highly misleading.

Propaganda is basically the manufacture and distribution of Factoids. Factoids refer to unverified, incorrect, or invented *facts* intended to create or prolong public exposure, or to manipulate public opinion.

The generation of factoids to support one's intention, especially in times of crisis, is something that has been occurring in history for a long time. Its modern version was greatly enhanced by the work of Joseph Goebbels, the Propaganda Minister of Nazi Germany, where he was responsible for feeding the people with whatever information he could *manufacture* to convince them of their cause.

The Goebbels technique, known as *argumentum ad nauseam*, is a policy of repeating a point until it is taken to be the truth. He also pioneered the concept of broadcasting (by using single frequency radios), so that he could deliver his message, again repeatedly, to his audience. As it turned out, this method was quite successful in convincing the German population that it was in fact the rest of the world that was being aggressive towards them!

Another similar concept is *conventional wisdom*, a term coined by the economist John Kenneth Galbraith in *The Affluent Society*. It describes certain ideas that are generally accepted as true by the public, though in reality may be false. Many urban legends, for example, are accepted on the basis of being conventional wisdom. Interestingly, conventional wisdom is often seen as an obstacle to introducing new theories and explanations.

In politics, the idea can be turned on its head to take advantage of people's belief in conventional wisdom. Political parties usually use 'talking points' to convince their audience that what they say has always been true. Talking points are statements that are repeated over and over to eventually become conventional wisdom, regardless of whether they are true or not.

Political strategists issue talking points, which are small pre-prepared arguments or phrases, to supporters of a party to be used repeatedly in debates, speeches and talk shows. The strategy is to create a meme and make the idea a common assumption by sheer means of repetition. Talking points are often used as labels such as 'XYZ member', 'fanatic', 'extremist', 'loss maker', 'anti-revolutionary' and so on. The major difference between a talking point and a slogan is that they are sneaked into speeches where they should naturally feel they belong, thus suggesting that the concept is simple and is common knowledge. Slogans on the other hand are advertised freely as a new message.

Labelling is widely used and people have the tendency to generalise and stereotype others into a rigid number of categories. Of course, nothing in real life is black and white, though in practice people might prefer to look at it that way.

In Risk, labelling can be used to represent another player as a particular type and expect others to deal with him as such. For example, if you continuously say 'good player' when you are talking about someone, everyone might start to think that he is a very good player. In reality, he may or may not be a good player. That is not the point. Your aim is to get the attention of the people to the fact that 'the player' is very good, and of course if he is not dealt with early on, everyone is going to be in trouble. Hence, collectively, other players may start to think that they need to deal with him as soon as possible. The key in using talking points is repetition. Make sure you repeat them enough.

Propaganda can be used in different ways and may incorporate deceptive tactics. There are three types of propaganda:

- *White Propaganda*. The source of the propaganda is known. For example a radio station in Britain spreading lies about the Germans is involved in white propaganda. It is basically an overt psychological operation.

- *Black Propaganda*. The source pretends to be from the other side. An example is a British radio station (such as Soldatensender Calais) located in Germany that broadcasted in German. It pretended to be Nazi extremists accusing Hitler and his henchmen of going soft while also focusing on alleged corruption of Nazi Party members.

- *Grey Propaganda*. The source of the propaganda is not known. For example, a website can provide delicately written political articles that support the cause of the owner. The articles appear to be written by someone who seems to be neutral, such as an attractive super model! Though in reality, the site is owned and maintained by a far more sophisticated political party targeting a particular audience. In this case that audience is probably fifteen to twenty-five-year-old males!

In any case, the combination of white, black, and grey propaganda can indeed produce a complex situation where you cannot rely on what you hear. As always, you need to check the source of any information you get and compare it with other trustable sources. If in doubt, use common sense.

In a report on Hitler's psychological profile prepared during the war by the United States Office of Strategic Services, Hitler's primary rules were categorised as follows:

- Never allow the public to cool off.

- Never admit a fault or wrong.

- Never concede that there may be some good in your enemy.

- Never leave room for alternatives.

- Never accept blame.

- Concentrate on one enemy at a time and blame him for everything that goes wrong.

- People will believe a big lie more than a little one.

- If you repeat a lie frequently enough, people will eventually believe it.

As history showed, these, as immoral as they might seem, were effective in controlling the masses and the enemies, at least for a while.

Just as in real life, Propaganda is also an important part of playing Risk. Propaganda works so well sometimes that it makes you wonder if the game is only controlled by this.

In the context of Risk, propaganda is an ability to give a mix of true and false statements so that you can effectively mislead others and hide the true purpose of your activities within the game. The idea is then to influence other players' opinions and aim to modify their understanding of the game so that their actions will benefit you. In short:

> *"It is the art of convincing others of something, whether it is true or not. What matters is not the truth, it is the achievement in convincing others."*

At any stage of the game, if there are any issues that need to be resolved, you have to act rapidly in spreading your propaganda to change popular opinion in your favour. Let's consider an example. Suppose your enemy wants to invade another player that you have a treaty with, and that you do not want this to happen. Spread your propaganda by stating that: "The enemy is the strongest player in the game since he can afford to invade. Who knows who is next on his list? He should be contained," and so on. By this, the world opinion may start to shift against him, and as it has been iterated several times, you cannot fight the whole world. The response to propaganda is anti-propaganda. In this case, your enemy will seek to convince others that you are lying, trying to avoid attention yourself, and that you are trying to confuse others. To be effective in a propaganda war, you need to have the ability to convince people. This is a talent that can be improved with practice. A comprehensive analysis of the *Art of Debate* is given in Section 7.

What makes propaganda different from other methods is that the propagandist is willing to change people's understanding through deception and confusion rather than persuasion and understanding.

An interesting feature of propaganda is *reinforcement*. The idea is that if people believe in something that is actually false, they will be continuously in doubt if the concept is true. They would like to resolve the concept and get to the bottom of it. As a result, they are very receptive to reassurances that may reinforce the concept and assure them that all is right. This method takes advantage of the human behaviour where one prefers to accept data from those sources that provide an 'agreeable' piece of information.

In practice this means that if you see a player who is already contemplating a certain idea (perhaps even initiated by you), you may keep reinforcing it until all doubts are removed.

For example, if a player is suspicious that his neighbour is about to concentrate his armies on his border, you can use propaganda to reinforce this. This is achieved by providing information to support his suspicion (irrespective of whether the information is true or false). This can suit your needs, since the player would then focus on that particular border instead. He may move his armies away from your border, which can make life easier for you. You can use your armies elsewhere.

6.3.3   *Propaganda Techniques*

"History is the version of past events that people have decided to agree upon."

Napoleon Bonaparte

There are a number of techniques used for propaganda which are based on social psychological research and *logical fallacies*. Propagandists use arguments that, while sometimes convincing, are not necessarily valid. The following shows a number of such techniques:

- *Repetition* (Argumentum ad nauseam). Repeat an idea an endless number of times. An idea that has been repeated many times tends to have a higher probability to be accepted as fact.

- *Appeal to Fear*. Make people afraid so that they follow your recommendation.

- *Black or White*. Provide only two choices. The better idea can then be easily enforced as no one wants to take the bad choice.

- *Follow the Crowd*: If a number of people are already participating on an idea, get others to join the crowd, or they will be left behind. No one likes to be isolated.

- *Intentional Vagueness*: By being intentionally vague, the audience needs to derive its own conclusion. Rather than providing the explicit idea, the audience is manipulated into ignoring the validity of the ideas given and instead fill in the gaps themselves. This way they will be more likely to accept the argument as they have participated in its construction.

- *Red Herring*: This is to provide irrelevant data and then draw conclusions from it. This needs to be used with care as it may backfire.

- *Labelling*: This is to put a label on someone or some entity to describe them in an abstract way. This is a very powerful technique to categorise someone as a person that the target audience fears, hates or dislikes. It usually puts the person into a defensive mode. Even if it is resolved, the effect may always remain in the mind of the audience and can always come back to the surface.

- *History*. Use *historical facts* to influence people's decision-making process. If people accept that something has been taking place for a long time, they may take it for granted. Remember, that historical facts can be altered or fabricated to support your own cause. An interesting quote from George Orwell in his book *1984* makes this more clear:

> *"If, for example, Eurasia or Eastasia (whichever it may be) is the enemy today, then that country must always have been the enemy. And if the facts say otherwise then the facts must be altered. Thus history is continuously rewritten. This day-to-day falsification of the past, carried out by the Ministry of Truth, is as necessary to the stability of the regime as the work of repression and espionage carried out by the Ministry of Love."*

- *Indirect Assumptions.* When it is difficult to explicitly and directly provide a concept, it can be repeatedly implied or assumed. For example, if you say, "Player A wants to attack me irrationally," it can provoke other players to either object to this or to simply dismiss it. In reality, Player A does not even want to attack you. However, you can imply it by saying, "As everyone knows, I will be attacked by Player A (which I can't do anything about) I am afraid I need to invade your continent so I can survive." This creates sympathy and takes the focus away from the *factoid* that 'Player A wants to attack me irrationally' to 'I have been forced to invade (against my intention)'.

6.3.4 Yes, But No

> **"Doublethink means the power of holding two contradictory beliefs in one's mind simultaneously, and accepting both of them. To tell deliberate lies while genuinely believing in them, to forget any fact that has become inconvenient, and then when it becomes necessary again, to draw it back from oblivion for just so long as it is needed."**

> **George Orwell, 1984**

Doublespeak is a language that is deliberately constructed to disguise or distort its actual meaning, often resulting in a communication bypass. Doublespeak originates from similar phrases George Orwell coined in his novel, *1984*, such as doublethink, newspeak, etc. Doublespeak is mostly used by a government agency or organisations to cover up something unpleasant. The idea is that an organisation may find the need to talk about something that has negative connotations to large portions of the public, and avoids backlash by replacing the term with a new one that most people will not recognize as the same thing.

A few examples of doublespeak are as follows:

- *Defence*: War.

- *Classified*: Secret.

- *Move on*: Any incarnation of "now is not the time to play the blame game, there will be plenty of time later, let's move on".

- *Failed state*: A weak enemy.

- *Liberate*: First invade, then destroy, and then steal!

- *Nation building*: Imposing or influencing a new domestic policy.

- *Playing politics*: Generally, any side may accuse the other of playing politics with an issue when it is losing the debate.

- *Spin*: This implies an effort to portray events in a light favourable to the one creating the spin.

- *Neutralise*: To kill, damage reputation, distract or to politically render the entity ineffective.

- *Surgical strike*: To perform a military attack. This phrase evokes a medical metaphor to suggest that warfare is a form of healing, as if a regime was a 'cancer' or 'tumour', while the *warrior-leaders* are trustworthy surgeons.

In Risk, doublespeak should be used to manipulate other players' opinions. Use it when you are about to take an action that you know others dislike or that would make them hostile towards you. Attempt to disguise your action behind a similar sounding phrase with potential positive meaning.

The following are a few examples of such doublespeak phrases in Risk:

- *Player X is too strong*: We need to attack him.

- *I never make deals*: If I do make deals, I may break them.

- *That's an unfair suicide attack*: That was a surprise attack I was not prepared for.

- *Player X is a newbie*: Player X just attacked me. He should have attacked someone else.

- *I need to make a tactical move here*: I need to invade you so I can gain a strategic position, though I don't want you to get worried.

- *We should get together to balance the world power*: If we don't take action now, we are both doomed.

- *Do you even know how to play the game?* Your attack has ruined me and I am extremely annoyed.

- *Good effort*: Well, that didn't really go according to plan, but I am glad that at least you did something.

Equally well, you need to watch out for other players' interpretation of events and think beyond what they say. Always focus on what they do and not on what you hear.

We can learn a great deal from George Orwell's book, *1984*, as he shows us a world that we do not want to end up with. However, the similarity between the events portrayed in the book and today's events make you think that society can always be on the verge of disaster, and we should never lose sight of the essential qualities of life and the reason for being.

The book addresses many issues from totalitarian governments to dynamics of warfare and propaganda, government control over the population, and in particular how to successfully deceive people into believing what you want them to believe.

For example, an interesting analogy can be made between the world portrayed in the book and a special case in Risk. As you may know, the Risk game can be played from three players up to six players. The game is designed in such a way so that a player should eventually win. However, certain styles of gameplay (in combination with specific rules) can bring the game to a halt. The game may get stuck in a specific mode when a number of players are involved in a *perpetual war* with no one being able to win. The situation mostly occurs when there are three players in the game, either right from the start or when other players have been eliminated and only three players are left.

The world gets equally divided between three *super-states* where any two are always fighting the strongest. As the fight goes on, one of the two players becomes stronger over time and eventually ends up as the most powerful. At this point, his ally switches strategies and starts fighting him instead. This cycle repeats as long as players adhere to the same strategy of survival. No one can win against the other two, so everyone is fighting just to survive.

This phenomenon, amazingly enough, is identical to the political geography portrayed in *1984*. There, three super-states of Oceania, Eurasia, and Eastasia are involved in a never-ending war.

In one of the episodes in the story, a book is given to the main character that describes the world as is. The book, written by Goldstein (who in the plot is considered as the chief enemy of the state), explains that: "Each super-state is so strong it cannot be defeated even when faced with the combined forces of the other two powers. The allied states occasionally split with each other and new alliances are formed. Each time this happens, history is rewritten to convince the people that the new alliances were always there, using the principles of doublethink. The war itself never takes place in the territories of the three powers; the actual fighting is conducted in the disputed zone."

Goldstein later even suggests that the three superpowers may not actually be at war, particularly as Oceania's media provides completely unbelievable news reports on impossibly long military campaigns and victories. However, as with many facets of the novel, the disputed existence of a war is neither confirmed nor denied, and the reader cannot be sure whether a war actually is in progress or not. In fact, it is entirely possible that the other two powers themselves are fabrications, and the entire world is controlled by a single entity!

When you end up in a three-player game and you all know what to do to survive, then you might as well call it a day and restart another game. Let's just hope this does not happen in the real world.

6.3.5   *How not to be Intimidated*

"All Your Base Belong to Us"

Intimidation is the threat of using power to get others to do what you want them to do. It is an attempt to frighten or overawe someone by speaking or acting in a dominating manner intending the person to do what you want.

The following makes this clearer. Intimidation means:

- Making others feel like you are more powerful or forceful than what you really are.

- Using verbal and nonverbal cues to let others know you are not going to reward any unfaithfulness to what you desire them to do for you.

- Using status and strength to get others to respect and obey you.

- Using quick temper, anger or rage to get people to do what you want.

- Convincing others that you are the *only one* with enough experience, wisdom, intellect, and insight to give direction or to have the *correct* answers to life's problems.

Intimidation is usually considered as a negative quality, something to be avoided. If you adopt an intimidating role, you will:

- Find that the costs of *getting your way* all of the time are greater than you expected when you find yourself lonely and disconnected from others.

- Believe that the only goal in life is succeeding in getting your way at any cost and become totally consumed in the pursuit of acquiring power, control, position, and status.

- Run the risk of becoming a lonely, isolated person with few close relationships and many enemies out there to get you.

- Not be accepted, approved of, or sought after by others, who will never get a chance to see the *real you* whom you have locked behind your intimidating mask.

As in any environment, you may find yourself with an intimidating player in Risk. To know how to deal with an intimidating person is critical. To start with, you first need to realise that you are the subject of an intimidation act. That is not necessarily trivial as the intimidation process can be padded with goodies to deceive you into thinking that the requests are all normal.

What you need to do is to look at patterns of behaviour and notice if this is applied to everyone else as well. An intimidator usually intimidates everyone. It is much easier to become aware of this process when it is applied to someone else.

One of the best ways to avoid being intimidated is to *counter-intimidate* the very same person. This usually makes the person *back off* and may lead him to think that it is not worth bothering you. At the same time, you should change how you feel. You can replace your fear with another milder emotion such as laughter. Make the intimidator a very comical character in your head and keep repeating it until you no longer feel afraid when confronted by this person.

As with all behavioural traits, intimidation exists in greater or lesser manifestation in each individual person over time, though for some it can be a more significant compensatory behaviour as opposed to others.

Here is an interesting example of intimidation. Consider an online Risk game. In these games, players can usually communicate only via text chatting during the game, and even that is done minimally and is heavily abbreviated. As a result the level of misunderstanding can be extremely high. There comes a point where a player (say Player A) decides to attack a particular individual (say Player B), who obviously would not be pleased! However, it is a game after all, sooner or later someone has to be attacked. Player B may therefore decide to *intimidate* Player A. One of the common techniques is that Player B says: "Player A is a ####. Ah ####, yet another newbie!!!" (Insert your own swear words in place of ####). He attempts to tell everyone that there is a newbie in the game and that he is ruining it for them. He practically tries to get everyone to gang up against Player A to get rid of him so that they can have a *better game*. Basically, Player B is intimidating Player A with his 'superior' knowledge of the game and showing that he is an insider while Player A is just a newbie and should not really be there at all. Eventually, Player A gets kicked out of the game having no support from anyone.

As you may imagine, this can have a very negative effect on you if you are Player A. However, attempt to look at it from a strategic point of view. Player B is just applying his *novel strategy* to get rid of you, whether moral or immoral. Once you realise that this is not personal and it is just another strategy, it will be much easier for you to work out a counter strategy. All you have to do is to let him and others know that he is acting irrationally and that he is intimidating you. You might be new to the game and it is *only fair* to be given a chance. Get others to sympathise with you and *talk him out of it*. Remember, the best way to shut someone up is by flooding the communication medium yourself, i.e. *talk a lot*.

In any case, Risk is a convenient environment to deal with intimidation. You can practice intimidation and how not to be intimidated yourself. Remember, the more you know how a particular behaviour works, the more you can handle it. Use the Risk game as an aid tool with which to practice.

6.4   Politics

"Discovery consists of seeing what everybody has seen and thinking what nobody has thought."

Albert Szent Gyorgyi

A wasp called Pin Tail was on a quest to find a way that would forever make him famous. One day he thought of a great idea. He set out for the king's palace. He entered the palace and stung the little prince, who was in bed. The prince woke up and started to cry loudly. The king and his courtiers rushed in to see what had happened. The wasp stung the prince again and again and the prince was now yelling. The courtiers tried to catch the wasp. The result was that they got stung one by one. The whole royal household rushed in, the news soon spread and people flocked to the palace. The city was in an uproar. All business came to a halt!

A name without fame is like fire without flame. There is nothing like attracting notice at any cost.

Politics in general is a process of conflict resolution by which groups make decisions. Although politics is generally applied to governments, it is observed in all humans. Everyone needs to know how to deal with other people through politics. Good politics is usually responsible for the success of a particular individual.

Politics in Risk, which is a game of strategy, is even more influential. A player who is capable of getting more than his share from every negotiation and who in general is politically more active than others has a higher chance of winning. As always there are various techniques that can be used. The following summarises some of the more relevant topics.

6.4.1   How to become a King?

A man said to a Dervish: "Why do I not see you more often?' The Dervish replied, "Because the words 'Why have you not been to see me?' are sweeter to my ear than the words 'Why have you come again?'"

Mulla Jami, quoted in Idries Shah's Caravan of Dreams

For many centuries the Assyrians ruled upper Asia with an iron fist. In the 8th century B.C., however, the people of Medea (now north-western Iran) revolted against them and finally broke free. Now the Medes had to establish a new government. Determined to avoid any form of despotism, they refused to give ultimate power to any one man, or to establish a monarchy. Without a leader, however, the country soon fell into chaos, and fractured into small kingdoms, with village fighting against village.

In one such village lived a man named Deioces, who began to make a name for himself for fair dealing and the ability to settle disputes.

He did this so successfully that soon any legal conflict in the area was brought to him, and his power increased. Throughout the land, the law had fallen to disrepute; the judges were corrupt, and no one entrusted their causes to the court anymore, resorting to violence instead. When news spread of Deioces' wisdom, incorruptibility, and unshakable impartiality, Medean villages far and wide turned to him to settle all manners of cases. Soon he became the sole arbiter of justice in the land.

At the height of his power, Deioces suddenly decided that he had had enough. He would no longer sit in the chair of judgment, would hear no more suits and would no longer settle any disputes. He complained that he had been spending so much time settling disputes that he had been ignoring his own affairs. He retired. The country once again descended into chaos. Violence was on the rise again. The Medes held a meeting of all the villages to decide how to get out of their predicament. "We cannot continue to live in this country under these conditions," said one tribal leader. "Let us appoint one of our number to rule so that we can live under orderly government rather than losing our homes altogether in the present chaos."

So, despite all that the Medes had suffered under the Assyrian despotism, they decided to set up a monarchy and name a king. The man they most wanted to rule, of course, was the wise Deioces. He was hard to convince. The Medes begged and pleaded. Without him the country had descended into a state of lawlessness.

Deioces finally agreed and became the King of Medes. However, he imposed a number of conditions. An enormous palace was to be constructed for him, he was to be provided with bodyguards and a capital city was to be built from which he could rule. The capital city was named Ecbatana, which is modern day Hamadan. The palace was made at the centre of the capital with seven walls, each with a different colour and was made inaccessible to the ordinary people. Deioces established the terms of his rule: No man should be admitted to the king's presence. Everyone should consult him by means of messengers. No one in the royal court could see the king more than once a week, and then only by permission. It was indecent for anyone to laugh or spit before him. Deioces thought that if people saw him habitually, it might lead to jealousy and resentment and plots would follow. He hoped that a legend would grow that he was a being of a different order from mere men.

Deioces ruled for fifty-three years, extending the Medean Empire. He established the foundation of what would later be the Persian Empire founded by Cyrus the great, his great great grandson. Cyrus, as the leader of the Persian people in Anshan, conquered the Medes and unified the two separate kingdoms into the Persian Empire, which eventually became the largest empire the world had ever seen.

This story shows that Deioces realised the power of politics and absence pretty well. He served too many people, which in turn meant that people started to take his services for granted. He realized that unless he showed them how it would be without him, he would no longer be able to exercise power. Hence he set out to show them just that, and in the process got himself to become the indisputable power, the king.

If you want to be noticed, you need to show them your true value and establish your brand. Once people get the taste of what you offer, they will start to come to you in the hundreds. Although you should always beware not to fade into the background by becoming part of the furniture. Make sure you stand out, evolve, change yourself, deny your services to others and make them beg for you and your wisdom. If you want to become the best, you should be the first person to believe in it.

6.4.2   Brinkmanship

> *"Brinkmanship is the ability to get to the verge without getting into the war."*

John Foster Dulles, United States Secretary of State

In international politics and foreign policy, brinkmanship refers to the practice of pushing a dangerous situation to the brink of disaster in order to achieve the most advantageous outcome. This is achieved by forcing the opposition to make concessions. The idea is to perform diplomatic manoeuvres by creating the impression that one is willing to use any method at one's disposal rather than concede.

For example, the threat of nuclear force in the Cold War was often used as the force to push the opponent to make a concession, which in this case worked as a deterrent. The British intellectual Bertrand Russell famously compared nuclear brinkmanship to *a game of chicken*. The principle between the two is the same, to create immense pressure in a situation until one person or party backs down.

The game of chicken is a game in which two players engage in an activity that will result in serious harm unless one of them backs down. It is commonly applied to the use of motor vehicles whereby each drives a vehicle of some sort towards the other, and the first to swerve loses and is humiliated as the 'chicken'. Yes, it is rather odd!

The idea is to push your opponent into making a decision (swerve), or otherwise be doomed. One person has to give up for both of them to survive, otherwise they will both collide and perish.

In Risk, this is similar to a situation where both parties are engaged in an arms race over a particular border, or in general are competing to remove their opponent from the game in a single attack. Both know that they cannot attack the other player and get their continent or remove them and survive themselves, while at the same time they need to keep the threat up to force the other party to concede (give up the costly arms race).

The use of brinkmanship as a political or diplomatic tool can lead to what is commonly known as 'slippery slope'. A threat is not worth anything unless it is credible. At some point, the aggressive party may have to back up their claim to prove their commitment to action. As a result, in order for brinkmanship to be effective, the threats used are continuously elevated (such as the arms race and the accompanying political threats in a Risk example). However, the deeper one goes, the greater the chance of arguments *sliding* out of control.

One tactic to use in the game is for one party to signal their intentions convincingly before the game begins. For example, if one party disables their steering wheel just before the match and shows it off to everyone, the other party would be compelled to swerve. He has no choice but to respond to the new circumstances. This shows that sometimes reducing one's own options can be a good strategy. Another clear example is a protester who handcuffs himself to an object so that no threat can be made which would compel him to move (since he cannot move).

In Risk, the classic option is to make an alliance with a neighbour. If you have only two directions to expand and have now made an alliance with someone, there is only one direction left for you to go. If this happens to be the border where the arms race is taking place, it is simply *tough* for the other guy. He should back off or else, as you have no choice but to invade.

6.4.3 Slippery Slope

"For want of a nail the shoe is lost, for want of a shoe the horse is lost, for want of a horse the rider is lost, for want of a rider the battle is lost, for want of a battle the kingdom is lost."

George Herbert

One day an Arab and his camel were travelling across the desert. Night came and the temperature became colder. The Arab put up his tent, tied the camel to it, and then went to sleep. The temperature became slightly colder. The camel asked the Arab if he could just put his nose in the tent to warm up. The Arab agreed that the camel could just put his nose in because the tent was small and there was no room for both of them. The camel's nose became warm. A bit later, the camel asked the Arab again if he could just put his fore legs in because it was very cold. The Arab reluctantly agreed that the camel could only put his fore legs in and no more. Again, after a while the camel asked the Arab if he could put in his hind legs or else he won't be able to make the journey the next morning with frozen legs. So the Arab agreed and the camel moved his hind legs in.

The Arab went back to sleep again, with difficulty in the crowded tent. When he woke up the next time, he was outside in the cold and the camel had the tent to himself! This is known as *the camel's nose* or the *slippery slope*.

The slippery slope is an argument for the likelihood of one event given another. Similarly, the problem with brinkmanship is that the sequence of threats can get out of hand. Invoking the slippery slope means arguing that one action will initiate a chain of events that will lead to a generally undesirable event later.

The slippery-slope arguments are usually constructed based on induction made from a possibility that a particular predicate becomes true. The argument is usually as follows:

If A occurs, then the chances increase that B will occur.

Where A and B are events, situations, actions, etc.

For example: "There is 95% chance that if a tree falls, it will hit another tree. We conclude that many trees will fall."

On the face of it, this sounds rational. However, we just know from common sense that this does not happen in reality. The conclusion is of course wrong. If calculated, there is in fact 92.3% chance that only fifty or fewer additional trees will fall. The momentum is reduced every time a tree is dropped and eventually this momentum dies and no more trees will fall.

What is interesting is that the argument usually *sounds right*. In this particular case, we just knew from experience that it cannot be true. However, on matters where you have very limited or no knowledge, a slippery slope argument can easily catch you off guard. You need to consider each argument on its own and perform a reality check on it.

Another more real-life example illustrates this point better. Consider the following argument:

> *"If we grant a building permit to build a tower block in a community, then there will be no bound on the number of building permits we will have to grant for tower blocks and the nature of this city will change!"*

This argument instantiates the slippery slope scheme as follows: First suppose k building permits are issued. One then argues that the situation of k permits is not significantly different from the one with $k + 1$ permits. In addition, issuing permits to build a hundred tower blocks in a city of 300,000 will clearly change the nature of the city.

In most real-world applications such as the one above, the naive inductive analogy is flawed because mathematical induction cannot be applied to imprecisely defined predicates. To put it another way, every time a building permit is issued, the environment is changed and the argument should be adjusted to reflect this.

In Risk, this can be used to construct arguments for potential invasion. For example:

> "If you don't make a deal with me, then I have no choice but to invade you. If you are attacked, then you will become weaker and may lose your continent. When you become weak, another player may attack you, and soon everyone will invade you from every direction and you will be out of the game in no time!"

You are trying to convince the player that if he is attacked once, then there is no end to being attacked, and of course anyone who is attacked many times will eventually lose. Your argument *sounds* logical, though in reality there is no reason to believe that a single attack will be followed by subsequent attacks with a similar probability. The chances are that the nature of the game will change, or you simply might get attacked by someone else, which may also transform the situation. What matters is your ability in convincingly delivering a slippery slope argument, even though it is entirely flawed.

Various arguments similar to the above example can be constructed. In particular, you can use such arguments when people are busy debating with each other. Distracted players are more likely to miss the flaws in the logical structure of the argument.

6.4.4 Conflict Escalation

> *"Strength does not come from physical capacity. It comes from indomitable will."*
>
> *Gandhi*

Conflict escalation is the escalation of a situation to make it more destructive, more confrontational and more painful. In effect it is about making the situation *less comfortable* for the other party.

Gandhi was one the most successful users of this methodology. His main aim was to reduce the conflicts altogether and end up with a peaceful society without the use of violence. However, to get there it was necessary to escalate conflicts by using protests, strikes and similar acts until a response could be garnered from the opponent. Each response resulted in a change in the society which meant the situation was ripe again for yet another escalation that could lead to another change. Gandhi was indeed very clever in using this approach as not only did he achieve his objectives (freeing India from the imperial colonising force), but he also managed to do it gradually and peacefully.

Calmly getting somewhere is of course easier said than done. In Risk, conflict escalation is best described as when a player pauses the game and initiates a long debate on the future of the game, perhaps working out alliances and the like. Since it could be his turn, he has control over the game and other players are therefore forced to deal with him. The more he pauses the game, the more agitated others may get (as they want to get on with the game). The player can then take advantage of this and force a deal upon someone. If the opposite happens, you can always state your *irrational* demands loudly and expect this player to agree with them. If not, "Then tough!" The player's ability to convince you is not your problem after all.

Another form of conflict escalation is through the use of force. By stockpiling armies near someone's borders, you raise the possibility that an attack is imminent. You can then break into a negotiation stance where you provoke the other party into disagreeing with you, or even better to attack you, so you have all the excuses to attack him in return. Of course, you will be telling everyone that it is only fair to give a response.

What would you do if you find yourself on the other side of conflict escalation? This is perhaps best described by the *Broken Window Theory*, conceived by the criminologists James Q. Wilson and George Kelling. It argues that minor nuisances, if left unchecked, turn into major nuisances. If someone breaks a window and sees it is not fixed immediately, he gets the signal that it is all right to break the rest of the windows and maybe set the building afire too! What this means is that if a problem is not addressed promptly, it could become a lot harder later on as the conflict is escalated. In Risk, if someone invades you and gets no major reaction, he may think that it will not cost him politically to attack you repeatedly as there is nothing to lose. Of course, your response should be proportional. The challenge is to give a response but not to escalate it into a conflict. Make sure that it does not appear that nothing has been done about it, while at the same time, not give in to the hands of the conflict escalator by continuously responding to his artificial conflicts.

The opposite of conflict escalation is *conflict resolution*. This is the process of resolving disagreements between a number of parties. This is usually achieved by listening to and providing opportunities to address each side's needs so that all needs are satisfied. Conflict resolution usually involves another group or individual who is considered to be neutral on the subject in their opinion. The conflicts can be negotiated between the two members via the mediator. A mediator is an outside party who separately evaluates the position of each side in an attempt to resolve their differences and *mediate* the process.

In Risk, suppose you end up with a dispute over certain aspects of your empire. You need to negotiate your way out. You need to know that just because you may disagree with the other party, it does not mean that there is nothing that can be done. A mediator can sometimes help the process of getting both sides to reach a reasonable outcome. The only difference is that, in Risk, the mediator may not necessarily be *neutral* since he is most likely a player himself. This is even better since you can convince the mediator to be on your side (even by giving him incentives). You can end up as two against one. If you want to win at all costs, convincing the mediator should be the least of your worries.

Suppose you want to escalate a situation in Risk to a crisis. This is not necessarily difficult. All you need to do is to make sure that after the escalation you look innocent.

To escalate a situation you can say the following:

- *Generalising*
  - You are always attacking me.
  - That is just typical of you.
  - You are so unfair.
  - You are such as an aggressive player.
  - You are a newbie.
  - You have a reputation for breaking deals.

- *Blaming*
  - If it wasn't for of your attacks, I wouldn't be in this position.
  - You stabbed me in the back. You deserve everything you get.

- *Rules*
  - It is against the code of conduct to attack me at this stage of the game.
  - It is illegal to gang up against a single player. It is not fair.

- *Intimidating*
  - You always target me in the game. I should report you to the moderator.

- o Is this the first time you are playing this game? You are such a loser.

- *Exaggerating*

    - o This is an outrageous manoeuvre.

    - o Your move has slowed the game down to a halt. Now we are going into a long marathon all because of you.

If you find yourself in a position where you want to prevent a serious conflict from occurring, there are a number of methods you can follow to prevent it. These are as follows:

- *Generalising.* If someone is generalising, make it specific and temporary. Attempt to focus the conversation on the issue at hand and what is taking place now. Say that labelling does not help anyone, but it is mere stereotyping.

- *Blaming.* Aim to focus the blame on something else. You can say, "Look, I had no choice but to take this option. It's just bad luck. The nature of the players in the game dictates that the game should progress this way. If I wasn't attacked myself, I wouldn't have to make such decision at all."

- Rules. If someone states rules to you, mention that rules are agreed based on a democratic system. You can put any rule under question and expect a new vote on it. Campaign for it to bring others to your side. However, be careful with a hostile crowd. Getting a vote might be exactly what they are looking for.

- *Intimidating.* An intimidator is always looking for easy prey. If you make it difficult for them, they will focus on someone else. Intimidate the intimidator!

- *Exaggerating.* Stick to facts. Let your opponent know that he should scale down his claim to concepts he can only back up with evidence.

To be in control of a conflict, you need to keep calm and not get carried away with emotions. The side that can stay focused in the logical land always has the upper hand.

6.4.5   *Mutual Assured Destruction*

"If I go down, I will take you with me!"

Conflict escalation may lead to a situation where you may benefit from raising the conflict, but simultaneously do not want it to get out of hand. To protect yourself, you may need to make sure that the other party gets destroyed, if anything happens to you. Mutual assured destruction (MAD) is a doctrine of military strategy where a full-scale use of nuclear weapons by one of two opposing sides would effectively result in the destruction of both the attacker and the defender. It is based on the theory of *deterrence* according to which the deployment of strong weapons is essential to threaten the enemy in order to prevent the use of the very same weapons. The strategy is effectively a form of *Nash Equilibrium*, in which both sides are attempting to avoid their worst possible outcome. This is further explained in Chapter 8.

In MAD, a *first strike* (for any reason) will be retaliated against with similar or stronger force, possibly destroying both parities (*second-strike capability*). The idea is that since no one wants to be destroyed completely, no one would *dare* attack the other.

In Risk this concept is also referred to as *committing suicide*. A player may decide (rationally or irrationally) that he has no choice but to attack another player *all the way*. This usually leads to both parties engaging in a long destructive battle where both end up extremely weak and subject to further attacks by other players until annihilation. The player which is subjected to this suicide act is never amused and understandably thinks the other player has been unfair. The fact that a *suicide* can take place is sometimes used as an intimidating factor, forcing the other player to bow to the intimidator's demands.

The practice of actually carrying out the suicide is usually frowned upon (as it would be if any nation launched nuclear weapons!) and should be left as a last resort, if at all.

Similarly, Mutual Assured Destruction is also used to balance the increase of armies on a border between two players. An attack by one may lead to such a huge loss that both players may have difficulty surviving. Therefore, the armies on both sides get inflated over time without being actually used. This cold war style escalation will continue unless a new situation arises that may unbalance this strategy. These could be:

- Another player with similar force enters the scene. At this point any two can gang up against one, effectively eliminating the weaker player's capability to destroy them.

- A new alternative option emerges. For example, it becomes possible to fight through a different border, which as a result the attacked player would suffer greatly. For example, he may lose an important continent and may not be able to respond effectively to destroy the attacker. In other words, it is no longer *assured destruction*.

- Both sides are vulnerable to a surprise attack by the other due to new cards being introduced into the game (*First-strike capability*). This can unbalance the power to the point that the attacked player is no longer able to show that he can destroy the attacker once he has been attacked. Again the destruction capability is no longer assured.

- A third player attacks one of the two players engaged in MAD. This weakens one of the MAD players to an extent that the MAD player is no longer able to convince the other of his own *destructive* capability.

Basically, it all comes down to having second-strike capability. If you are dead before you can retaliate, then, well, you are dead! As you might have imagined, this strategy can sometimes be *mad*!

6.5 Economics

"Having money brings about its own problems. Do you want to have the problems of the Rich or the problems of the Poor?"

Rich Dad (by Robert Kiyosaki)

You may wonder what economics has to do with Risk. It has been stated that economics is a science primarily concerned with incentives. Incentives drive individuals actions and the science of economics attempts to understand, analyse, and predict the individuals' actions in different situations. In Risk, everyone has a different set of incentives, with only one common goal: Winning the Game. As a result, economics should become a handy tool.

Economics is primarily concerned with trending and predicting the future. Fortunately, it comes with a large set of statistical tools to measure how people respond to those incentives. All you need in any given situation is some data. You can then use the tools and start predicting, or at least understanding.

Individuals have a large set of incentives which change over time. The most important emotional factors that influence incentives are perhaps *greed* and *fear*. One needs to control these emotions to succeed. The problem is that in the heat of the action, this can be difficult.

You can take advantage of other people's greed. Someone who is dying to get a continent might be willing to trade a lot for the privilege. This is a great opportunity to start negotiation. He could be blinded by his greed and you can cash in on that. After all, if he really wants it that bad, why should he not pay for it?

Fear of an imminent attack, especially at the wrong time, is another emotion you may feel in the course of the game. In Risk, you may never become too afraid since, after all, the worst that can happen is losing a game. In real life though, fear can have a deeper effect on you.

The general understanding of fear and greed is that people either go too far because of greed or get out of something too quickly because of fear. In economics, this is usually known as 'following the crowd mentality'. If you are not a leader of the crowd, the chances are that you will not benefit from what you are perusing. You need to be on the *edge*. In Risk, it means to be politically active and to think one step ahead of others. You need to be able to predict the flow of the game and where it is heading, know who is going to fight whom, who is after what, and so on. Once you know what others want, you can start to influence their opinion (and their *incentive matrix*) to guide them towards a direction that would benefit you the most.

If something goes wrong, never fear. Stick to your position, cut losses, move on and never lose hope. People tend to put too much emphasis on the most recent activities. As a result, their actions are usually exaggerated. There always comes a time when they exaggerate in the opposite direction, which could be to your advantage.

The next section expands on incentive analysis.

6.5.1   Incentive Analysis

"Power is just an idea. If you don't think you have it, then you probably don't. Just believe in it and it will come to you. Use the great power of the mind to your advantage."

Ehsan Honary

Information is power. If you know the history of players in the previous games, or if you know them personally, then you can take advantage of it by attempting to predict their gameplay. Doing this systematically is quite beneficial.

Economics, as explained earlier, deals largely with incentive analysis. An understanding of incentives can be valuable in any situation where people (or entities for that matter) compete for resources. Generally, incentives can be divided into the following main categories:

Economic Incentives

A person expects a form of material reward in exchange for acting in a particular way. In Risk, this is usually represented by a desire to have more armies.

For example, in a six-player game, conquering North America can be difficult in the crowded game. Suppose you find yourself and another player in North America based on the random placement of armies at the beginning of the game. You now have to decide who is going to go for the continent. Since getting the continent can be difficult, you may decide that you want to leave for South America instead. However, you do not just leave. You start by giving an economic incentive to the other player so that he thinks he ends up in a better place if he stays in North America. You can tell him, "If you want North America, and I think it's a good choice because it has a larger bonus, I can leave the continent for you and go for South America. Just open up the way so I can get out." The other player is now tempted to stay in North America. He was already worried that he may have to fight with you over it. Now he no longer has to spend his precious armies to get rid of you and he can get the continent for himself. Of course, you may end up with South America far sooner than him and with your strong armies (as a result of continent bonuses) come back to conquer North America while he is struggling to secure it.

Moral Incentives

A person acts in a way that is widely regarded as the right thing to do. Similarly, a person will not act in a way that is considered indecent. In Risk, players have the tendency to play a fair game and not gang up against a single player in an irrational way.

For example, to control players you can use a moral incentive to stop someone from attacking you by indicating that such an attack is 'immoral'. You may be new to the game and you can tell other players to give you a chance. What is the point of playing with them, if they do not let you survive in the game, at least initially? To put it another way, the Risk game has to be enjoyed for its own sake and you would not enjoy it if you really did not have a chance.

Social Incentives

This is an incentive where a person's failure to act in a particular way may result in *pain* being used against them (or their loved ones) by some members of the community. In Risk, you are restricted by similar social restriction as you have in any other environment. For example, swearing, bullying, shouting, abusive behaviour and the like are extremely discouraged, and there is an incentive not to behave in this way.

Online Risk games provide an interesting example for social incentives. As with any online activity these days, players need to adhere to a *code of conduct*. This is usually put in place by the website. Players must follow the code or otherwise they will be disqualified. As a result, players tend to follow suit and behave in a reasonable way. If you see someone swearing at you in a chatbox, you can always give him an incentive to stop his abusive chat. All you have to say is that his conduct is not fully compatible with the terms and conditions, and if he continues to use foul language, he will be reported to the moderator. This is usually quite effective in silencing the offending player, and in the process saves you the hassle of dealing with a rude player.

Personal Incentives

An individual person may act to satisfy his desire, pride, personal drives, life ambitions, etc. Your personal incentive in Risk can be your competitive desire to win against your friend, or at least to stay in the game before he is kicked out.

Personal incentives are well known and are sometimes frowned upon in the Risk community. Some players have an exaggerated sense of pride and think they can do what they like without being affected by the consequences of their actions. They feel so confident that they start invading everyone. Of course, a sense of pride can be exploited by other players. A player may end up making a wrong move and you may benefit as a result. A number of friends, especially if they have played against each other in the past, may have a strong personal incentive to *compete*. It is absolutely critical for you to spot this as soon as possible and adjust your moves accordingly. For example, if you find yourself stuck between two *competing players* who are determined to take revenge on each other, just get out of the battlefield and flee to the other side of the planet. Watch them as they kill each other and then make your move to take the prize.

Manipulating incentives can be tricky and unpredictable. An interesting piece of research provided by Steven D. Levitt in his popular book *Freakonomics* will shed light on the complexity and delicacy of incentive manipulation. Levitt provides the following story: "Imagine for a moment that you are the manager of a day-care centre. You have a clearly stated policy that children are supposed to be picked up by 4 p.m. But very often parents are late. The result is that at day's end, you have some anxious children and at least one teacher who must wait around for the parents to arrive. What would you do?" The day-centre consulted a pair of economists and they came up with this: "Fine the tardy parents!"

Consequently, the day-centre started to charge three dollars for each late pick-up. Before introducing the fee, the economists collected data on late arrivals so they could compare it with the situation when they introduced the fee.

Once the fine was introduced, the number of late pick-ups promptly went...up. Before long there were twenty late pick-ups per week, more than double the original average. The incentive had plainly backfired.

What happened was that the day-centre substituted a moral incentive with an economic incentive. Parents could simply buy-off the moral incentive. They no longer had to stop what they were doing and rush to the day-centre to pick up their children. In addition, the fine was small and this signalled to parents that the actual cost of being late was not really that much. Indeed, when the fee was lifted, the number of late pick-ups stayed the same. Now they could arrive late, pay no fine, and feel no guilt. A moral incentive was successfully replaced by an economic incentive which then led to getting both eliminated. The situation actually got worse.

This is a good example of *unintentional consequences* of introducing abrupt rules/guides/directions to fix a problem, only to cause another somewhere else. There are numerous examples of such schemes made by governments in a rush to resolve an outstanding issue (such as reducing high petrol costs by subsidising it) only to realise later that the proposal has flopped (increased inflation and lots of traffic). Thorough analysis is essential to avoid surprises later on.

Similarly, in Risk, be thoughtful about the consequences of your incentive manipulations. However, you should always be careful not to get obsessed with finding patterns and should always stick to scientific methods. The next section described this further.

6.5.2   216

> *"When you earnestly believe you can compensate for a lack of skill by doubling your efforts, there is no end to what you can't do."*
>
> *despair.com*

Pi, directed by Darren Aronofsky, is a fascinating dark psychological thriller that explores obsession in finding patterns in the real world. It is certainly worth watching, especially for anyone who is interested in mathematics. The main character of the film, Max, is in search of patterns. He wants to predict the stock market. In the process of his research, he manages to blow up his computer, which before doing so spits out a number which is 216 digits long. Max is fascinated by this number and sets about finding out if it is a *special number* which can be used to predict the future. After getting seriously excited to the point of madness, he pays a visit to his mentor, a wise old man called Sol, who used to be a mathematician himself. It turns out that Sol also ended up with a 216 digit number as a result of a bug he had in his program a long time ago. They start to have a conversation over a Go game which is quite fascinating:

> *Sol*: "The Go board itself represents an extremely chaotic universe. And that is the truth of our world Max, it can't be easily summed up with math. There is no simple pattern."
>
> *Max*: "But as Go game progresses, the possibilities become smaller and smaller, the board does take order. So all the moves are predictable"
>
> *Sol*: " So, So, ..."
>
> *Max*: "So maybe, even though we are not sophisticated enough to be aware of it, there is a pattern. An order underlying every Go game, maybe that pattern is like the pattern in the stock market, the Torah, this 216 number."
>
> *Sol*: "This is insanity, Max."

Max: "No, maybe this is genius, I have to get that number!"

Sol: "Hold on. You have to slow down. You're losing it. You have to take a breath. Listen to yourself. You're connecting a computer bug I had with a computer bug you might have had and some religious hogwash. You want to find the number 216 in the world; you will be able to find it everywhere. 216 steps from a mere street corner to your front door. 216 seconds you spend riding on the elevator. When your mind becomes obsessed with anything, you will filter everything else out and find that thing everywhere. 320, 450, 22, whatever. You have chosen 216 and you will find it everywhere. But, Max, as soon as you discard scientific rigour you are no longer a mathematician, you are a numerologist."

The moral of this story is not to become obsessed with what you already know about something. By being obsessed, most of the time if not all the time, you will find what you are looking for, though that may not mean you have solved the problem. Instead, look at it from an objective point of view and consider *all* possibilities. In Risk, you need to be unbiased when you are looking for other players' incentives. If you already assume what someone is planning to do, your mind will work hard to find enough evidence to support your predefined theory, even though it may be false. People usually have the tendency to think this way and only those who are disciplined can succeed.

A classic technique in propaganda is to take advantage of this phenomenon by providing a manufactured piece of information through different sources to the masses. People are more likely to accept news if they hear it from different sources, especially if the sources appear to be independent. In fact, once they start to suspect that something is true, they actively seek to confirm their findings in everything they see. Needless to say, this can lead to disaster exactly when they least expect it.

6.5.3 Cheating

"For every clever person who goes to the trouble of creating an incentive scheme, there is an army of people, clever and otherwise, who will inevitably spend even more time trying to beat it."

Steven D. Levitt, Freakonomics

Steven D. Levitt provides another interesting story in *Freakonomics* on the habits of cheating.

Feldman's research institute fell under new management in 1984. As a result, Mr. Feldman had a look at his career and grimaced. He decided to quit his job and sell bagels.

Originally, the bagels had begun as a casual gesture when he as a boss would treat his employees whenever they won a research contract. Then he made it a habit. Every Friday, he would bring in some bagels, a serrated knife and cream cheese. Eventually he was bringing in fifteen dozen bagels a week. In order to recoup his costs, he set out a cash basket and a sign with the suggested price. His collection rate was about 95%. He attributed the lost 5% to oversight but not fraud.

After quitting his job, he focused on bagels instead. Every morning, he would deliver some bagels and a cash basket to a company's snack room; he would return before lunch to pick up the money and the leftovers. It was an honour-system commerce scheme, and it worked. Within a few years, Feldman was delivering 8,400 bagels a week to a hundred and forty companies and earning as much as he had ever made as a research analyst. He was a happy man.

Feldman kept rigorous data on his business, so he could measure his collected money against the bagels taken. Did they steal from him? If so, what were the characteristics of a company that stole versus a company that did not? Under what circumstances did people tend to steal more, or less?

When he started his business, he expected a 95% payment rate, based on the experience at his own office. So, what was his result? Each year he dropped off about seven thousand boxes (small plywood boxes with a slot cut into the top) and lost, on average, just one box to theft. How about the money taken inside the boxes? He found that he only got 87% of his stated price for all the bagels sold. Feldman concluded that his presence must have deterred theft in his own office. The data also showed that smaller offices were more honest than big ones. An office with a few dozen employees generally overpaid by 3 to 5% an office with a few hundred employees.

Weather had an impact too. Nice weather inspired people to pay more and cold, rainy or windy weather made people cheat freely. For years Feldman delivered to a company that was spread out over three floors which had an executive floor on top and two lower floors with sales, service, and administrative employees. Feldman found that employees further up the corporate ladder cheat more than those down below. He wondered if perhaps the executives cheated out of an overdeveloped sense of entitlement. What he did not consider is that perhaps cheating was how they got to be executives in the first place!

In a six-player game of Risk, 87% means one person on average cheats in every game (if cheating is at all possible). In a casual game (especially with a board game as opposed to a computer game) this is more likely. Time and time again, it has been observed that towards the end of the game (when pressures are high), players have a higher tendency to cheat. A common cheat is to exchange bigger armies on the board when they are placing their tokens. After all, it only takes a casual mistake to put an 'X' (large army) in place of an 'I' (small army). If caught, they can always claim that they simply made a mistake. If not caught, they get extra armies for free at a critical time (i.e. when attacking), which by the time the other players realise this, it could be too late. Some of them might even be out of the game by then.

In any case, always watch out for a cheater. Remember, you do not have to get every cheater red-handed. Only catch those that are cheating against you. Someone who cheats on the number of his armies while fighting your strongest enemy is actually helping you and it may not be to your advantage to stop him. Of course, you should keep an eye on the cheater in case he starts to use his skills on you.

6.6 Big It Up

"No single raindrop believes it is to blame for the flood."

despair.com

People usually have an affinity to exaggerate. Stock exchanges are the prime example. News on a company may make the stock price increase very rapidly, only to see a while later the opposite take place. Similarly, humans put a lot of emphasis on recent news. This effect can also be observed when someone is telling a story in a social situation. Usually, to get other people interested, the storyteller would twist the statistics or exaggerate the story to a level that people would find interesting to listen to. This is very common in many cultures and there are many aphorisms reflecting the concept. Equally, if there is a problem, it is made to look more important than what it is and sometimes it is so exaggerated that it may make you feel that the end of the world is coming.

However, as bad as this may sound, it is sometimes important to do so as you can get the attention of people who may otherwise not be interested or not have time for *such things*. For example, it is perfectly reasonable to exaggerate on *global warming* since it is an important issue that needs to be addressed, and there is a lot of reluctance and laziness in doing anything about it. In short, you need to *big it up*.

In Risk, you can also pick up an issue and *big it up*. Make an issue of the biggest problem there is and players will start listening to you and come to your rescue. All you have to do is to slightly exaggerate the problem's effects on the game and expand it. You can use *slippery slope* arguments (Section 6.4.3) to deceive players into thinking that a cascade of events is indeed inevitable. The end of the world (or in this case, the end of the game) is coming and that if they want to be around when this happens, they need to do something about it now: and *your solution* is the only way to address it. Make sure you make it clear how *your plan* may benefit them in the long run. As stated earlier, if you want others to listen to you, make it personal for them and show them how your scheme may benefit their lives.

In this chapter you have seen how effective diplomacy can be in resolving issues without the direct use of force. Good diplomacy is always used in parallel with a good strategy and a clever execution of tactics and logistics to support it all. Diplomacy, however, is the key to success. Like everything else, diplomacy is a skill that can be improved with practice. At the heart of diplomacy lies the art of debate and the know-how to control and influence people. This topic deserves expansion and is the subject of the next chapter.

7 The Art of Debate

"All the world is a stage, and all the men and women merely players."

William Shakespeare

One of the great things about Risk is that it has a considerable amount of depth. There is always more than one way to achieve a particular goal. This keeps it interesting no matter how many times you play it. The game encourages you to negotiate over conflicts, which forces players to make deals and debate with each other.

Negotiation is a key skill in diplomacy and in day-to-day real life. It is essential to master it. In this chapter, tactics and techniques on different aspects of debating are presented.

7.1 How to Influence Others?

"It's lonely at the top, but it's comforting to look down upon everyone at the bottom."

despair.com

Every action human beings take is motivated either out of a need to avoid pain or a desire to gain pleasure, or a combination of the two. What you link pleasure and pain to determines how a person will respond. If you want to influence a person's behaviour, you need to attach pain to the direction you do not want him to move in, and pleasure to the direction you want him to move toward.

Being able to influence other people is a skill you cannot live without. Those who are masters of influencing tend to become very successful in life. They have the ability to use other people more to get where they want to be, and do not need to work too hard to get there. Influencing depends on many parameters such as charm, charisma, personality, quick thinking on the spot, and so on. No one is born with these qualities (and let us ignore the super attractive Hollywood movie stars for now). At some point you need to develop these skills and learn how to use them. Most people who influence others successfully in a *natural* way have learnt and practiced the skill in their childhood, perhaps as a result of the environment they have been brought up in. For the rest of us, we need to practice the skill until we can master it. The best way to practice is of course to do this in a systematic way. As usual, Risk can come to the rescue. There are plenty of opportunities in Risk where you may need to influence others so you can get what you want. As mentioned earlier, since Risk is only a game, you can be more experimental and not so concerned with your approach. This lets you practice various techniques more freely and efficiently.

When you attempt to influence others, make sure that you consider their needs too. It is all too easy to make decisions that will only benefit you. Make sure that you also consider where they would end up when you have performed your act. In short, *think about other's needs all the time.*

The following nine tactics will help you to influence others, in Risk or in life.

7.1.1   Logic

"The reasons behind this are..."

Concept:

Making a factual reasoning to convince someone of your cause such as the logical reasoning of a step-by-step invasion to conquer an enemy.

Example:

"There are two reasons why getting rid of the player in Africa is a priority ... First, it becomes much easier to stage the set for the invasion of South America and second, it gives you a backdoor access to Europe..."

When to use:

Use it when you want to influence people's decisions by logic.

Backfire:

Weak reasoning without the *correct* facts can backfire. It is much harder to influence people if you do not have evidence for your argument.

7.1.2   Inspiration

"Imagine when it is only me and you in the game..."

Concept:

Suggesting what *may* happen as opposed to fact-based reasoning. This appeals to emotions more than logic.

Example:

Making an alliance usually involves some inspirations. You can picture a post-alliance world and show how wonderful the world would be.

"Guys, we need to do something about Player A (which is the most experienced and powerful player). If he is left on his own, he will come to kill us all. Imagine a world without him. We need to get together and attack him one by one until he is weak. Let the ball roll..."

When to use:

Use it when it is difficult to present the argument with facts and evidence. It is also useful when getting players emotionally involved in the subject.

Backfire:

The actual *delivery* of inspirational speeches is critical. You need to be passionate and attempt to raise the emotions.

7.1.3 *Participation*

"Don't you want to take over the world?"

Concept:

Asking a number of questions where the answers will lead the other person to draw his own conclusions.

Example:

Use a series of questions that will lead to what you want. The other person needs to get to your conclusion by himself:

> You: "Do you want to take Europe?"
>
> Him: "Yes."
>
> You: "Do you want to have another player on your side, so your back is covered?"
>
> Him: "Well, that would certainly be useful."
>
> You: "Would a treaty here free your armies, so you can use them against Europe?"
>
> Him: "Yes, that helps."
>
> You: "Would you like to make a treaty with me over here?"

When to use:

This is very effective since the other person feels responsible and actually part of the reasoning process. In particular, this is used against someone who is more powerful than you. After all, powerful people do not like to be told what to do. You can guide them to your desired conclusion, but they get there by themselves.

Backfire:

This tactic is particularly hard to use since it is difficult to know the answers in advance. You need to be careful that the questions are not too broad (as to become irrelevant) and not too narrow (so that the other person can see where you are going). You need to practice this tactic to master it.

7.1.4   Uplift

"You are a good player."

Concept:

Making someone feel good about themselves and start listening to you.

Example:

"You played very well in the previous game. I can trust you 100%. I think it will be great if we get together again, make a treaty and beat them all."

When to use:

Used when you want to influence people with similar or less power.

Backfire:

If used in an obvious way, it has a reverse effect. They can see that you are just saying this to make them do something for you. If this tactic is used against someone more powerful than you, then it looks like you are sucking up to him. Use wisely.

7.1.5   Deal

"Let's have a deal."

Concept:

Offering something to someone in return for something.

Examples:

- "I will not attack your continent if you don't attack mine. Should we make a deal?"

- "If you move your armies away from this border, I will move mine away too."

- "If you move your armies out of my continent, I will move mine out of yours too."

When to use:

This tactic is used when you want something that someone else has and you do not mind giving something in return. It is also beneficial in a sense that when two people make a deal together, they both feel better about each other, which can defuse future problems. You can also separate the *give part* and the *take part* temporally. For example, you can suggest that you will not attack his border, which happens to be vulnerable at this point. A few turns later, you can then suggest that he move his armies away from a certain territory so that you can pass through easily without wasting your armies in the process.

Backfire:

It is important to make a fair deal, or at least make it appear to be. Be careful with how much you offer. If you offer too much, you may look like a naïve player. If the other person is hesitating, make sure that you provide the details of the deal precisely and professionally (even as much as writing it down on a paper!). Make it look serious.

7.1.6 Favour

"Can you help me please?"

Concept:

Asking for something you want.

Example:

"We are both in a good situation, you in North America and I am in the south, it would be wonderful if you expand north either through Europe or Asia. Not through South America, please."

When to use:

This is powerful only if the other person cares about you. In Risk, this is best used with a player that already has some relationship (treaty, alliance, agreement, etc...) with you and you know if asked nicely, they may try to help you. You can also use this against someone who you know may not refuse your offer, your girlfriend, your mother, and the like.

Backfire:

Since Risk is only a game, such favours may not be honoured. They may also feel that you owe them one, which means that you would need to return the favour. If you do not return the favour, they could become more resistant to you in the future.

7.1.7 Collective

"Everyone always does it this way..."

Concept:

Using view of other people to influence someone.

Example:

Assume you are in Europe and are trying to influence someone in Africa: "Everyone always goes for South America. It is a known fact that having the continent gives you a much better chance of winning."

When to use:

This is especially effective if what you state is in line with the view of the person you are influencing. If he sees that someone like him has gone through this before, he will be more inclined to go through it too. This tactic is strongly related to *peer pressure*. A relatively new player may also attempt to copy the strategy of more experienced players. If the more experienced players make alliances with each other, the chances are that the new player will be interested too since everyone is doing it. At the same time, if the experienced players start backstabbing each other, he may think that such behaviour is normal and will join the crowd of backstabbers!

Backfire:

Some people prefer to go against the crowd and want to be different. Your argument might have the reverse effect in this case.

7.1.8 Policy

"It is my code of conduct that..."

Concept:

Showing your power based on a certain principle or rule.

Example:

You have made a treaty with someone. He is about to break it. "Let me be clear about this. It is my policy that if anyone backstabs me, he will be marked. I will never ever trust him again in this or future games."

When to use:

Authority is effective as a quick response to a problem. It is very blunt and sometimes provocative. It is better to use *Policy* as a last resort.

Backfire:

If this tactic does not succeed, you have almost no choice other than force. The other problem is that it can have a negative effect on your relationship. Equally well, this can lead to a reverse outcome when used on certain people. They may choose to do exactly the opposite of what you want them to do, precisely because you tried to exercise authority over them.

7.1.9   Force

"Do it or face the consequences..."

Concept:

Exercising power.

Example:

"If you invade me, despite the agreements we have, I will use anything I have at my disposal, including my allies, to remove you from the game. I will fight to the bitter end."

When to use:

Use only in emergencies.

Backfire:

Since this is a powerful influencing tactic and is effective in bringing short-term results, it can be very tempting to use, especially when combined with *Policy*. As with *Policy* this can also have a negative effect on your relationship, even when the event has passed. Let's say you do not want to lose your friend over a game. Using this tactic can give you a great sense of power , but it can all go wrong and stay wrong. Use only as a last resort.

7.1.10 Example A

Use the above influencing tactics roughly in the order presented here. You can devise a sequence to influence a target player. The sequence depends on your strategy and the situation. *Questions* are better used before others. *Favour* and *Deal* are more effective after other tactics have been employed. *Policy* and *Force* are best left for emergency only. The following is an example of a series of tactics to use. Once each tactic fails, you can execute the next tactic.

Situation: Can be attacked by two powers simultaneously (Player B and C). Need to cover my back with Player A.

Objective: To make an alliance with Player A.

Your argument is as follows:

- *Logic:* "These two players are getting together against us. We need to get together to be able to withstand their attack since we cannot stop them on our own individually."

- *Collective:* "It is well known that players who make alliances are more likely to win than those who do not. Because they tend to fight less than those who stay without friends and spend their precious armies while fighting all the time."

- *Deal.* "If you don't attack me over this territory, I will not attack you either."

- *Policy.* "If you don't make an alliance with me, I am forced to respond to their moves and my response may not be beneficial to you."

- *Force.* "If you are not with me, then you are against me. I need to get your continent so I can have enough extra armies to withstand their attack and try to survive. You have left me no choice, but I give you one more chance."

The trick is not to go straight from *Questions* or *Deal* to *Policy* or *Force*. Once you use the extreme measures, it is hard to use any other. You cannot suddenly become nice when you have been so blunt. Instead, seek to persuade the player with other tactics until you have exhausted all options before resorting to more forceful tactics.

7.1.11 Example B

Situation: Player A keeps idling in a single country on the map collecting armies and does not attack anyone. He is growing more powerful every turn, and he is becoming a stronger threat. Something needs to be done about him.

Objective: Remove him from the game.

- *Questions:* "Don't you think the game has become slow?" Response: "Yehh"

- *Questions*: "Where do you think we would be once he has twice the armies he has now?" Response "In big trouble."

- *Inspire:* "Imagine the world with only four of us. The game would then gather pace and we would all have a chance of winning."

- *Logic:* "We need to participate with each other so we can remove him successfully in a fair way."

- *Deal:* "Let's make a deal. Everyone should attack him a bit until he is out of the game."

- *Policy:* "Anyone who doesn't attack him when it is his turn would be subject to attacks himself."

As stated, using the milder influencing tactics is always better than the more forceful ones.

7.2 How to Negotiate?

"A good negotiator won't take NO for an answer."

Negotiation usually reminds people of dealing with a car salesman or negotiating in a job interview. In Risk, negotiation is a great way to settle issues before they get out of hand. Whatever the context, the principles stay the same. Negotiation concerns the fulfilment of your own needs, nothing more, nothing less. If the other person chooses to react adversely, so be it. It is no big deal.

At the heart of negotiation is access to information. The one who knows more on what they want and what the other party wants will have a far greater chance of getting the most out of the negotiation.

People usually have two *fears* when they negotiate: One is that they will lose and look like an idiot, the other is that they will win a deal that is great for them but unfair to the other person. They feel worse about the latter. Hence, controlling fear is the key to success.

Every negotiation is a trade. You give something to get something in return. The trick is to simply ask. Just go ahead and pop the question. If you get a 'no' or a 'maybe', then you can either negotiate from there or forget it if the matter is very small. However, you will be surprised how often the answer is 'yes'. Asking is a lot like fishing. As long as you have got your line in the water, anything is possible. But if you do not have your line in the water, you will almost certainly get nothing.

However, where would you use negotiation in Risk? There are many examples. If you see that you are involved in an erosive war, aim to negotiate for a truce or make an alliance with a player to get rid of your enemy. Act quickly or nobody will bother to get allied with you. They will just wait to see when you two become weak enough so that they can take you both.

A secret negotiation is probably the best type of diplomacy in Risk, though it is almost impossible (unless you play online and the software has the capability). If you are playing Risk with your friends sitting around a board game, the situation can be slightly different. If you attempt to have a secret negotiation with somebody, other players will assume that the two of you have come to an agreement, even if you have not! This might be enough for them to line up against you just because you talked in secret and probably behind their backs. This makes the rest of the world your enemy: bad news!

Sometimes you can initiate negotiations before even the attacking stage of the game starts. At the beginning of the game, you may still be wondering which continents to choose, and another player might also be asking the same question. Start a *passive negotiation* by telling him how nice it would be if you had a deal so you did not have to worry about each other. Right from the start you have an advantage over others since you no longer have to worry about your neighbour, and you can focus on others. This way no armies will be misplaced or wasted on unnecessary attacks.

What is the most effective way to end up with a deal? First, you need to know what you want, what the other party wants and how strongly you or he thinks about it.

7.2.1   *LAS and MSP*

"Know your limits."

There are two types of negotiations:

- *Positive*. This is a negotiation where both parties are interested in engaging in a deal, perhaps to exchange a commodity of some sort. You want to make the deal to your advantage or at least a win-win situation.

- *Negative*. In this type of negotiation, one party is by no means interested in having any negotiation at all. You usually need to use some sort of a threat to bring the other party to the negotiation table and place your demands directly.

You may need to approach the other person differently depending on the type of negotiation. Once you know what you want, you need to find your *Settlement Range*. The Settlement Range is the range of all possible settlements you would be willing to make in any given negotiation, from the very best to the very worst. The bottom end of the Settlement Range is called the *Least Acceptable Settlement* (LAS). This is the minimum point at which, when you make a deal, you still think that the negotiation has been to your advantage. The top end of the Settlement Range is called the *Maximum Supportable Position* (MSP). This is your opening position in the negotiation which the other person may probably not accept, but it is a position you think you can *support* and settle on.

A non-Risk example will clarify this. Suppose you want to sell a car. You comprehensively research and evaluate the car's worth. Remember, this is not how much you would like it to be. This is a purely mechanical way of calculating what the value of the car is when converted to currency. Suppose you think it is worth £4000. This will be your LAS. You would certainly not sell below this value. There is a distinction between your LAS and your wishes. You can also use the concept of *Sure Offer* (a guaranteed offer from someone) to set your LAS. However, you still need to calculate your LAS from scratch to know if the Sure Offer is actually worth it.

Your MSP, as the name suggests, is a value that you can *support* in a negotiation. This is the value you wish to get. For example, you may wish to get £6000 since the absolute top-notch car similar to yours is advertised as such and you do not think yours should be any less.

Remember, confusing what you want with your LAS can be fatal to the health of your negotiation. Keep your hopes and expectations out of the picture entirely when calculating your LAS. Your starting position is always with your MSP. In any negotiation, you get only one opportunity to state your opening position. After that there is no way to change it.

Now imagine that both parties have two pairs of numbers: a MSP and a LAS. A number of possibilities exist. A common possibility is shown in Figure 7-1.

In *Case A*, the seller has selected his pair better than the buyer. He has managed to set his pair higher than the buyer and has a higher chance of settling on a value that will benefit him. For example, the seller wants to sell his car at £6000

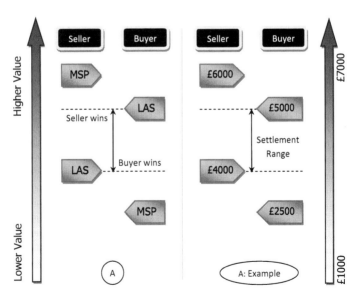

Figure 7-1. A typical scenario for buyer and seller (left). An example is shown on right that illustrates the concept.

while the buyer does not want to pay anything more than £5000 for the car. The seller thinks it not worth selling the car for less than £4000, while the buyer hopes he can convince the seller that the car is not worth more than a mere £2500.

A number of other possibilities are shown in Figure 7-2. In *Case B*, no settlement may be reached as the two ranges have no intersection. In *Case C*, the buyer has misplaced his MSP. He has basically overestimated the minimum value of the car. He can easily be pushed to pay more money for the car. In *Case D*, the reverse is true. The seller has misplaced his MSP and so the buyer is well placed to push the price down. In *Case E*, the buyer has misplaced both the MSP and the LAS. He basically thinks the car is worth more. Obviously the seller will be very happy!

In short, if you bid behind the other person, you would only get as much as you asked and would never be able to ask for more to match the other person's LAS. All you need to do is to keep you LAS secret and aim to correctly guess the other persons LAS.

How high should you go? The answer is that you should go as far as you can and still be able to justify your demand.

You should overcome your reluctance to make demands, not just little ones, but big ones. Because the simple fact in life is that if you do not ask, you will not get, and if you ask for a little, that is exactly what you will get: a little.

Extensive research has been carried out for a long time on the psychology of negotiation. All research points to one indisputable fact: People with high aspiration levels reach better settlements much more often than people with low aspiration levels. In other words, if you aim high, you will do much better than if you aim low.

In any negotiation you may feel a certain amount of tension. There are two reasons behind this: One is that you may wonder if you can actually make a deal with the person; i.e. does your settlement ranges overlap? The other is that once you have moved the other person to somewhere in your range, you may wonder how good a deal you can get out of it? Greed after all is a strong emotion.

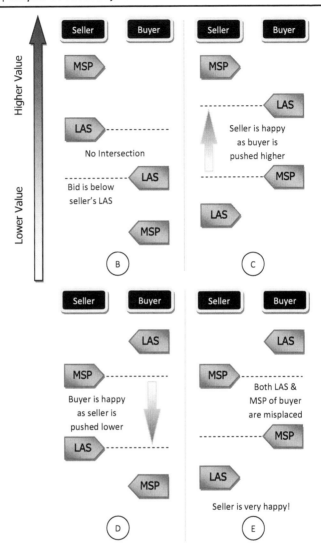

Figure 7-2. Other negotiation possibilities based on LAS and MSP set by the seller and buyer.

Hence, before any negotiation you need to ask yourself two fundamental questions: "How is he likely to respond when I propose to negotiate?" and, "If I get what I want out of this deal, what kind of position will he be left in?"

In any case, do not *assume* anything about yourself. It is quite possible the value you put on what you have is less that the value someone else puts on it, especially if they know more about it than you do. Time and time again, people who end up regretting the experience they had in a negotiation realise that they have made a single fundamental mistake. They *assumed* what they had (or the other party had) was worth X amount and based their entire negotiation around it. Once you realise that what you assumed was wrong, it will only lead to despair. Be open to new information. In particular if you are in the middle of a negotiation and you realise that you can get more than what you hoped for, update your position as you move on. Just keep calm, and adjust quickly to the new circumstances. Keep a poker face and play the game with new values. Remember, at the end of the day, it is only a game.

7.2.2 Negotiation Strategy

"Everything happens just the once. You can't relive it.
If you spend all your time trying to relive it, you'll
miss whatever happens next."

Graham Masterton, from 'The chosen child'

Theodore Roosevelt in his 1912 presidential campaign was planning a final whistle-stop journey called 'Confessions of Faith' which bore a *presidential* picture of himself. Three million copies were printed when it was discovered that the picture was copyrighted by Moffett Studios in Chicago. The penalty for copyright infringement was one dollar per copy. Roosevelt's options were few. There was not enough time left to print a different set of pamphlets using a non-copyrighted picture. Not distributing the pamphlet would hurt the former president's chances for re-election in an extremely tight race. Simply going ahead and distributing the picture without the consent of the copyright owner would expose the campaign to a staggering liability. A final option was to negotiate with Moffett studios for the right to use the picture. Not surprisingly, Roosevelt chose the last option. He asked George Perkins, his campaign manager, to carry out the negotiations on his behalf.

Well, there was a lot of money at stake for Roosevelt. He certainly did not want to pay $3 million dollars just for copyright! That was a lot of money in those days. He also did not want to get into big legal trouble just after he had been elected and to risk his entire election over such a simple oversight. This is when you should put down the book and start thinking about the problem. What would you do if you were in Roosevelt's position? What are your least and best expectations. Work out your MSP and LAS and compare them with what actually happened.

George Perkins went at it right away. He immediately sent the following cable to Chicago (in those times communication systems were not as sophisticated as they are today):

> *"We are planning to distribute many pamphlets with Roosevelt's picture on the cover. It will be great publicity for the studio whose photograph we use. How much will you pay us to use yours? Respond immediately."*

The same day, Moffett Studios wires back its reply: "We've never done this before, but under the circumstances, we'd be pleased to offer you $250."

It is fascinating how you can turn the tables around with only four sentences! This story makes an important point. In setting our aspiration level, we tend to focus on our own situation. We would have been happy to settle for half a million or something similar. Moffett Studios, of course, made the same mistake. However, George Perkins did not: he set his target by looking at the problem from the other side's perspective. The danger of falling into this trap is real. We understand our own position, but know little about the other side's position, and set our target based on what *we* know. We work out what we want to get from the deal and fix the expected benefit we are hoping to get. To avoid the trap, you have to look outward: what is the other player's perception of the problem and what options does he have?

One of the systematic ways to do this is to look at your opponent's BATNA or *Best Alternative To a Negotiated Agreement*. This is the course of action that will be taken by a party if the current negotiation fails and an agreement cannot be reached. Hence, if the current negotiation is converging on something which is less valuable than your BATNA, there is no point carrying on with it. Remember, always think about the other player's BATNA to see if you are pushing too far or too little. Once you know you have got them in a tight corner, you can squeeze. Sometimes, however, comparisons between different possibilities (or BATNAs) are not that easy since they are not always quantifiable or comparable.

Negotiating is just like any other skill. You just have to practice it until you get better. Here are a number of guidelines on strategies you can use.

Raise doubts about getting a better settlement:

- *Build the credibility of your MSP.* Seek to sell your position at MSP and make it as supportable as possible. You need to tell the other player that your opening position is *really* close to your LAS and he should not bother trying to push it down. This also helps to cover your true LAS, which is of course your top secret.

- *Conceal your need for the deal.* A person who needs something badly does not have much ground to stand on. You are most likely not going to get what you want if you are unable to keep secrets. Nor would you have any chance if you show your fears and weaknesses, your need for the deal, your doubts, and worst of all the location of your LAS. The other player knows right away that you need what they have, and they can make you pay for it. For example, if you badly need to protect your border, do not let your opponent know that you are so vulnerable (keep his attention away from it systematically). Negotiation is about keeping secrets. Remember, a slight hesitation, or slight eagerness to settle on your part can be a big giveaway.

Increasing the need to settle:

- *Goodies.* Add something to the deal at the right time to tilt the equation to your side. This is something that does not have to cost you much, but looks very attractive for the other party. For example, you can shift some of your armies away from a particular territory. It might help him a lot and might not be that important for you. If it helps you to get the deal, always consider it.

- *Threats.* A threat is usually used in those negotiations where the party wants to avoid you. Threats can be used to effectively change the balance of the negotiation by adding something negative to the other party's equation. Use threats selectively and only as a last resort. The tougher you negotiate, the tougher the resistance will be.

Change circumstances:

- When new factors are added to the scene, negotiation can tilt towards you. Again you can initiate this change yourself. For example, if you approached another player and he refused to deal with you, be patient. Wait a few turns and build up some armies next to him or show him the benefit of cooperation with you. Then approach him again with a new offer and a new settlement range.

The key is that you are exerting pressure on the other party to settle where you want him to. The pressure, ultimately, is what is going to enable you to get what you want out of your negotiation.

Aim to increase the number of options you have. The more options you have, the more leverage you can use in the negotiations. The next best is to make the other person *think* you have options, even if you do not. Do your best to conceal your degree of need for the deal. Give him the impression that you have no great stake in settling with him at all. Let him believe that you have other alternatives if he stops listening to you. Equally well, always think what his options are and determine if he is bluffing.

Sometimes when the negotiation does not go as planned, you can seek to involve other players. A bit of help from others can be quite effective. Timing is everything in negotiations. Needs, fears, environment, and in short anything that might have an impact on negotiations are subject to change at any moment. Do not negotiate as if you live in a fixed world. In a six-player Risk, each turn is like an eternity. By the time it is your turn again, the world might have significantly changed. You can always initiate another negotiation when your turn comes. You never know what you may get this time.

7.2.3 *Planning*

> *"Sweet dreams are made of these! Who am I to disagree? Travel the world and the seven seas! Everybody's looking for something. Some of them want to use you! Some of them want to be used by you! Some of them want to abuse you! Some of them want to be abused."*
>
> *Lyrics from Eurythmics*

In 415 B.C., the ancient Athenians attacked Sicily. They believed that the attack would put an end to the sixteen-year-old war and that it would bring fortunes beyond their imagination and would make them more powerful. The invasion went disastrously wrong. They did not anticipate the problems and dangers of fighting far away from home. The enemy, fighting in their own home, were naturally more resistant. They put everything they could into stopping the Athenians. When the war broke out, all the Athenian enemies banded together against the Athenians. The result was that they ended up with multiple fronts with fiercely fighting enemies. This led to the destruction of the Athenians, one of the greatest civilizations of ancient times. They got carried away by the potential glory and failed to carefully calculate their moves and anticipate their enemies' reactions.

Planning is extremely important. One should always consider the consequences of his moves; especially those that are considered most brilliant. Your plan in a negotiation should be thoughtfully designed. The less thinking you have to do on your feet while you are in the negotiation phase, the better. A bit of planning will go a long way. Use the following as a guide:

- *Gather information.* What is the status of the game? What is the status of the player? What position is he in? Is he confident, vulnerable, desperate, etc?

- *Research the player.* You need to know what his mentality is. Profile the player.

- *Anticipate the reaction of the player to your deal.* What shape will he be in after the deal? Is he going to like your offer and gain from it, or does he want to get away from you? Just knowing what you may expect will increase your confidence and reduce the tension.

- *Anticipate the future of the negotiation.* If you have to deal with the player in the future, your negotiation style will be different than if you do not.

  a. If you do not have to play again in the future, you have many more options. You can be ruthless.

  b. If you have to deal with him again, you need to establish yourself as a credible negotiator. Be very professional. First impressions die-hard. Aim to build mutual trust and respect.

- *Line up your assets.* Show the player that you mean it.

  a. In negative negotiations, if you are planning to threaten the other party, make sure to line up your threat so that your threat looks more convincing. For example, suppose you want to force someone to negotiate with you. Move your armies towards a weak point of your opponent (establish a threat) and then initiate the negotiation. The player can easily see the imminent danger and may back off.

  b. In *positive negotiations*, it is better to show off everything you have. For example line up the allies who will back you up on your demands.

- *Hide your weakness.* If you are vulnerable, then you do not want the other player to know how bad your situation is. If you are holding four cards and have no card combinations, pretend as if you do have a combination. Do not let the other player take advantage of your vulnerability.

7.2.4 Negotiation Example: How to Turn the Table?

"When the great lord passes, the wise peasant bows deeply and silently farts."

Ethiopian proverb

Ryanair is one of Europe's largest low-fare airline. It has steadily expanded in the past twenty years and now carries in excess of thirty-five million passengers per year. The philosophy behind the operation of the airline is to produce a no-frills ticket and use a single type of plane to cut costs (among other things). One type of plane reduced operational costs as the airline could use the plane on any route and manage the training of employees more efficiently. The formula proved to be successful and the airline expanded rapidly.

It was the beginning of 2005. Due to its expansion, Ryanair needed to buy new planes. The situation was as follows:

- *Ryanair:* Used Boeing 737-800. Three years ago, they had already ordered a hundred planes from Boeing and some had yet to be delivered. Rapid expansion meant that they needed to order more planes for new destinations. Ryanair wanted to place a large order and approached the airline industry.

- *Airline industry:* Consists of two main players: Airbus based in Europe and Boeing based in U.S. Both corporations needed the order badly as they had to meet end-of-year targets. Boeing and Airbus are fierce competitors.

- *Airbus:* Wants to win the new Ryanair order for the A320. It wants Ryanair, which is a European company, to order these and subsequent planes from them. Effectively this will rub Boeing from their current advantage.

- *Boeing.* Expects a lucrative order from Ryanair and thinks it is in a position to charge higher than normal as it thinks Ryanair is in a tight corner. Boeing is counting on the order and the subsequent service charges.

Approach

Ryanair's philosophy is to have only one type of plane (they already have mostly 737-800). It was not in its interest to break that philosophy and buy a different kind of plane. Overall, Airbus was not an attractive option at all. However, Boeing could command a high price as they could also see Ryanair's position and wanted to take advantage of it. Ryanair was effectively forced to buy from Boeing, which meant that they could be pushed hard in negotiations. Ryanair wanted a hundred and forty new planes. The catalogue list price for 737-800 was around $60 million. This was indeed a large order and there was a lot at stake. The question was how could Ryanair protect itself from being pushed into an undesirable deal?

Solution

Ryanair approached Airbus and opened direct negotiations over the A320 planes. It appeared that Ryanair was *seriously* considering switching to Airbus. They did thorough research over long technical negotiations with Airbus to see what kind of a deal they could get with Airbus. Ryanair leaked the negotiation news to the media and turned it into a major issue. Boeing was extremely afraid. They had already lost some orders on other planes to Airbus and were certainly not interested in a repeat scenario. They simply did not want to lose a large order such as this to their prime competitor.

Ryanair was now ready to face Boeing. With the offer from Airbus in their hand, they approached Boeing. They had done their homework and had set the scene for a negotiation that they hoped would be beneficial to them. Ryanair had effectively turned the tables. Not only they were going to resist Boeing's high pricing, but they could also bargain hard for a discount. That is exactly what they achieved in the negotiations.

In February 2005, Ryanair ordered their planes priced at $51 million. In addition they got a significant amount of concessions such as support services, credit allowances and free winglets that improve fuel efficiency and reduce operational costs. If the concessions were factored in, the price per plane was as low as $29 million; less than half of the list price!

This amusing story shows the importance of preparation before a negotiation. It also shows how Ryanair took advantage of a classic situation to set one negotiating party against the other. By exploiting the weaknesses of the two Airline manufacturers and their great appetite for new large orders, Ryanair managed to command the negotiations and settle on its preferred deal.

The extremely successful negotiation by Ryanair has saved them an incredible amount of money, measured in billions of dollars. How much effort should Ryanair go through to get a similar saving by only improving the flight costs? The simple answer is: a lot.

A good negotiation can save you a lot of hassle, eliminate the use of your valuable resources and pave the way for future success and better competition with your rivals. You do not have to use direct force when you can achieve the same by clever diplomacy and crafty negotiations.

7.2.5 Negotiation Tactics

"You are only as strong as your alternatives, and the more attractive your alternatives, the more power you have."

David J. Lieberman, Never Be Lied to Again

The following tactics can be useful when you are in the heat of negotiations. As always, they should be mastered by practice.

The Player Who Cares Less, Wins

You must be able to walk away. If your opponent senses any desperation in you, you are doomed.

When you are desperate, your vision can become blurred. You may see facts exaggerated. In such situations, *you should never make a decision out of fear*. In desperation, your thinking becomes more emotional than logical. If you think you have no choice, you are doomed to select whatever option is in front of you. It blocks your mind and prevents you from exploring other options.

To overcome this problem, increase your alternatives, and at the same time narrow the other player's choices. This way you tilt the equation significantly to your side. The equation that determines the balance is simple: It comes down to *who needs who more*.

All you need to do is to demonstrate to your opponent that what he has offered can easily be obtained through other means, such as from other players. This decreases his power significantly and hence his leverage. Remember to always think about your alternative choices and other player's choices when you are dealing with them. It is the best way to discover their weaknesses.

Turn Weakness into Strength

When you have got nothing, you have nothing to lose. If you find yourself in a tight situation, you may be able to use this to your advantage. Suppose you have been attacked and you have lost a big chunk of your empire. Since you are already running out of options, you can use this to limit the options of others. You can say that you have no choice but to attack one person with all your armies unless they let you pass through. The other player will think twice before making his decision. You have taken advantage of your weakness to force the other party to negotiate with you on *your terms*.

Timing

In negotiations, timing is everything. Sometimes a bit of delay can be to your advantage as circumstances will change. As you know, in Risk, the balance of power changes very rapidly. If you do not have enough bargaining power, wait a few turns and you may end up in a much better position. For example, an opponent that you wanted to negotiate with might be greatly under pressure from another invading force, and when you come to the negotiation table, he may need you more than when you needed him a few turns before.

Similarly, setting up artificial deadlines can also force the other party to act fast and hence put pressure on him. This forces one to speed up the process of negotiation and perhaps accept the deal on someone else's terms. Example: "If we make a deal as we discussed, we will both end up in a better position. But we need to do this now. I need to know how to distribute my armies. I can't wait any longer. You need to make a decision, so we can benefit from the deal before we are invaded by others."

Top-Up Your Requests

You can add extra requests to your deal, even though you do not care about them as much. You can then attempt to bargain for them hard, and just before the end of the negotiation you may drop your requests in an attempt to show that you are willing to come down from your initial position. Of course, since you do not care much about those items that you will no longer get, you have not lost much in the deal.

For example, suppose you are discussing a treaty over a border between your continents. Unfortunately, your opponent also has a number of armies in a continent that you are about to secure. You want to get rid of the army and get a deal. However, the deal is what you are really after. Therefore, you can start the negotiation by stating that you want the armies to be removed as well as having a treaty over the border. Your opponent may disagree. You carry on bargaining and towards the end, if he is still resisting, you drop your demand to remove his armies from your continent. He may suddenly think that what you are asking is a fairer deal. From your point of view, you have managed to get your border secured and you can get rid of his armies by killing them anyway, which does not cost you much (and in any case your relative power will not change against him if you kill his armies).

Packaging

Similar to Top-Up, you can also raise other important issues at the beginning of the negotiation and link them to your main objective. However, this time you actually want these bundled issues to be noticed and taken care of.

For example, suppose you have South America and Australia. The other player has Africa and a rather large army in Siam, which threatens your Australian continent (See Figure 7-3). You want to make a treaty over Brazil/North Africa. This is your main objective. However, you can also attempt to raise the issue of the existence of that large army in Siam. After all, it is to your advantage to get rid of it so you can expand from there. The African player might be very keen to get this deal to succeed and wants to secure his border.

If you raise this issue before dealing with the main objective, he would be forced to deal with it. He may then accept to move his armies away to a neighbouring country. If you have raised this issue towards the end of the deal, he may not have been keen to deal with it, as he would have thought that he had already secured the deal. Like any good player, he will enjoy the ability to put pressure on you with a large army in a different part of the planet.

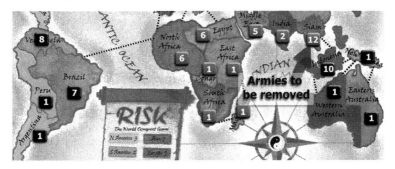

Figure 7-3. *Example of packaging tactic.*

You need to make sure that you bring these issues before the main objective is dealt with. Once the negotiation is settled, the other player may not have enough incentive to deal with you anymore and may easily sweep it to one side as a separate problem to be dealt with in a different negotiation.

Beware that concessions are like candies. Do not assume that because you just took a good chunk of your deal off (or added something in), the other player will worship you and definitely make a deal with you. Instead, he will probably think that the candy was tasty and will come back for more. Do not come down from your MSP in large steps. Give away in small steps, but make them *look big*.

Good Guy/Bad Guy:

This tactic involves using two people. One plays the *bad guy* and the other plays the *good guy*. When you negotiate with the bad guy, you get forced into thinking that you do not have much chance of tilting the deal to your side. The good guy then steps in to resolve the crisis, which makes you trust him further. You prefer to deal with the good guy as opposed to the bad guy and the offer made by the good guy is more likely to be accepted.

An example in Risk is as follows: Two players are allies (or have a treaty of some sort). They have a mutual interest to reduce the power of the player in Europe. One of them starts negotiating with Europe in an intimidating way, almost pushing it to an outright war. The other ally then steps in and attempts to defuse the situation by giving an offer, "If Europe takes X amount of armies away from territory Y, I will move Z armies from here. Then there won't be any hostilities at all. My ally (*the bad guy*) promises that he won't attack Europe."

The European player prefers to deal with the good guy than with the hard-bargaining bad player who intimidates him. The European may think that since the bad guy does not want to upset his own ally (i.e. the good guy), the bad guy will probably not object to the superior offer provided by the good guy. Hence, the European player will be much more enthusiastic to accept the deal.

Silence

Silence can be an effective negotiation tactic. It acts like a black hole, just waiting there for someone to fall into. If the person you are negotiating with is silent, will you rush in to fill the gap? Even perhaps making concessions just to make sure that there is some noise in the room.

The action and reaction for the silence tactic is as follows:

- *Making silence.* Leave bits and pieces of silence lying around throughout the negotiation and watch to see whether people jump into them. This forces them to talk and perhaps gives you more information about the circumstances surrounding the negotiation.

- *Confronted with silence.* Once you recognize that the other side has started a silence contest, go into denial. Say something like, "Now that I've had a chance to think about that," or "Well, that's an interesting idea and here is what I propose," or something similar. It sends the message that we just had a thoughtful moment rather than a silence contest.

Random Strategy

Sometimes you need to change your strategy altogether. If you happen to negotiate with regular players, they may discover a pattern in your negotiation tactics and play into that. Imagine if they have worked out your pattern. Suppose you always start high and as soon as you have achieved a reduction on their side, you give in. They could use this pattern against you. Hence, every now and then, play the *tough guy* or be slightly unreasonable just to disrupt their understanding of your negotiation pattern.

Policy

Make something your policy and state that this *policy* must be followed at all costs. This sets an artificial limit on your LAS and takes away any negotiation on this point. The other negotiators are forced to abandon their requests since it is against your policy.

The reverse tactic is: "Nothing is set in stone." You should challenge anyone's policies. If you can change the circumstances, they will be forced to rethink their position. Suppose you approach a player (Player A) to make a deal. He flatly tells you that, "I never make deals. I don't believe in them. It is my policy." What would you do? Of course, your aim is to get him to the negotiation table so you can get what you want without direct force. Instead of directly getting into a potentially costly argument over whether it is wise or unwise to have deals, you can use a more indirect approach to address the issue. You can change the circumstances. You can approach another player (Player B) and make a deal so that Player B's armies are released to be used against player A and not you. You can move your armies close to Player A's border and have another attempt at making a deal. This time, however, he is confronted with Player B's armies on one front and your armies on the other. It would be in his interest not to engage on both fronts simultaneously. He may start to listen to you, despite his policy!

Be on the lookout for opportunities where you can seal off the bottom part of your *Settlement Range* and place a limit on what the other person can negotiate out of you. Deadlines, policies, personal ethics, rules (even those that are artificially made up on the spot) can all work towards this end. We all played with a cousin, a friend or a colleague who tried to beat us in a game by re-interpreting the rules and giving us a distorted biased version of it, did we not?

The visibility of this tactic gives it high credibility since you can say something like, "I can't help you and here's why." However, beware that setting up policies introduces a high risk of a deadlock, in particular if the options you have left for the other person are not within his *Settlement Range*.

Make Him Regret

When you are in the middle of a deal and realise that the other player is not responding well to your arguments, you can appeal to guilt. You can take away what you just put on the bargaining table and state that you have changed your mind since it is too good! You can say, "Well, I thought about it and I am not sure now. Maybe we shouldn't make this deal. It's no longer the same as it was in the last turn. This may not work very well for me." Emphasise that you think this is too good an offer for the other player and you are actually considering pulling out of it. The other player then gets concerned that he might be losing something great. He may hesitate and start to have doubts. At this point, you can get him back to the negotiation table.

Quid Pro Quo

In a negotiation, always keep an eye on the progress of the dealings. If you think your original offer is not getting anywhere, aim to work out the problem to find a suitable solution. Quite often, if you find yourself in a deadlock and cooperatively attempt to get around the issues, you both stand to win.

When in a deadlock, *quid pro quo* (I give, so that you give) can be a useful technique to get the negotiation going. It is basically the exchange of something of value for something of similar value with your opponent. Since you can play it out step by step, it will make it easier to see what you are offering and what you are getting back in return.

Hopeless

Sometimes, a player may say right up front that he will not budge. He may say, "I'm sorry, this is pretty much the best I can do," or, "I'm afraid there's not a whole lot of room for negotiation here." He will formulate his words to comfort you, so that you will not bother to ask. His intention is not to shield himself, but to deceive you. If a player used such a phrase, it means that he knows he can be converted. He wants to tell you up front so that you will not ask. He knows if you ask, he will cave in. Sometimes, players who strongly assert an opinion or view, do not even hold it themselves, but nevertheless want you to believe in them. This is why they will not feel a need to compensate for their belief.

Credibility

Your display of information also creates uncertainty for the other player as to how good a deal he can get from you. People tend to lose much of their resolve when they are face-to-face with a well-informed opponent. They become quiet, not wanting to run the risk of saying something that sounds foolish or is wrong.

Starting to play online Risk can sometimes be stressful since you may think that you are new and others are far more experienced and knowledgeable than you are. Do not be intimidated. Instead, turn this on its head by boasting on your own experience elsewhere which they most likely do not have. Behave in a mysterious way. One of the best ways to show your credibility is to use technical terms common in that particular domain or community. Once you start to use their language, they start to think that you belong to their community and will trust you more. If you appear to know a lot of terminology, others will think that you must be an expert and effectively go into listening mode when dealing with you. Your presence will be significantly increased.

Boldness

It is important for you to be bold in whatever you do. People admire the bold and despise the timid. It seems that people have a sixth sense when it comes to detecting weakness in others. If in your initial encounter with others you show willingness to compromise or back down, you will encourage those who are not even bloodthirsty to come and tear you apart. A bold move will make you look larger than you are and will automatically put people on the defensive when considering your subsequent moves.

7.2.6 Tips

> *"Your goal is to get what you want, not to deny the other party what he wants."*

How to negotiate with multiple-goals

Multiple-goal negotiations are a special and often confusing case. The basic steps you take to plan them are the same ones you take in simpler negotiations. All you need to do is to break down the problem into smaller parts and solve them one by one. You need to research each goal separately and discover what the other person can do to help you for that goal. Once you know what you want, and what you can get, decide on your settlement range for each goal. In the end, think about how you can bundle all of them together as a package and which goals are your priorities. You would then be in a good position to trade goals with each other if necessary.

How far to go

There is no right answer to the question of how much you should risk in a negotiation. The longer you hold out for a better deal, the better you will do. However, the probability of a deadlock also increases. You need to evaluate if the chance for a better settlement is worth the risk of a deadlock. This depends greatly on circumstances. Do you actually have any options? If you do not make the deal, will you be kicked out of the game in two turns? Will your opponent make a deal with someone else which will greatly reduce your chances for a re-negotiation? Sometimes you can afford to risk, sometimes you cannot. The key point is to that you need to base your decision on a calculated analysis of your position, not on a *predetermined attitude*. Do a lot of talking. It establishes you as someone he can take seriously and, as the talk continues, fosters an investment of his time and energy and makes him more eager to settle on a deal with you.

How to get out of deadlocks

Persistence and creativity are essential when you are seeking to work your way around a deadlock. You can get yourself out of trouble by discussing the details of the deal. For example, suppose you are attempting to convince a player not to attack a certain border. For this, you have given your word to remove your armies elsewhere and not to threaten him. However, he is still concerned that your threat will remain at large. He is not interested in the deal. You can introduce other factors to help the deal. One method is by throwing in a couple of goodies: "I will attack your enemy," or, "I will move away my armies from North Africa so you can get the continent." You can tip the deal over and take it out of a deadlock.

Sometimes, even all the creativity in the world may not help you to break a deadlock. Do not get upset over it, this is not necessarily a failure. Some deals are not meant to be.

And one last tip: Trust your instincts when you negotiate. Your instinct is among the most powerful negotiating assets you have. Relax, go with the flow, enjoy yourself as you negotiate your way toward a better, more rewarding game experience.

7.3 How to Control People

> *"Anybody can become angry - that is easy, but to be angry with the right person and to the right degree and at the right time and for the right purpose, and in the right way - that is not within everybody's power and is not easy."*
>
> *Aristotle*

Did you ever want to be in control? Everyone does. You should be able to control and influence the behaviour of other people and at the same time, stop them from controlling and exploiting you. As usual there are a number of techniques you can utilize to master this art.

7.3.1   Can You Do Me a Favour?

Someone approaches you and asks you for a big favour. You think about it and in the end are not totally sure you can do it. Feeling bad, you apologise and tell him that unfortunately you are unable to do it and that you are so sorry. You genuinely wanted to help, but you could not. A while later, he approaches you again and this time asks for a smaller favour. Now you think this is something you can do and you agree to it, feeling better.

What has he done? He has leveraged the power of your guilt over the bigger favour to get you accept the smaller favour. A job well done!

In this process, he has taken advantage of three main psychological motivations:

- You feel that in contrast to the first request, the smaller one is no big deal.

- You feel bad for not coming through on his original favour, and the smaller favour seems like a fair compromise.

- You do not want to be perceived as unreasonable. A small little favour is not going to kill you.

Always beware of the guy who asks you to do something. Look deeper and more carefully before you commit yourself.

7.3.2   Divide and Conquer

Have you ever been in a situation when a player keeps getting stronger and stronger and no one does anything about it? For example, he has North America and is just about to expand and get South America and everyone seems to be busy with their own little issues. No one seems to feel any strong inclination to do anything to contain him. This is not because people are stupid or do not care. The reason is that the responsibility to act is divided among many players. Nobody does anything since they assume somebody else will. Alternatively, they think that since nobody else is doing anything, it may not be that important. Basically, when there is a division of responsibility, the incentive to act is reduced proportionally.

So, how do you solve this problem? You need to get somebody to do something. You need to increase people's responsibility. The best way to accomplish this is to appeal to one person at a time. Divide and conquer! Pick someone and brainwash him. If you got nowhere with him, do not panic. Move to the next player and appeal to him. At some point you may get enough players to reach a critical mass. After that, just let the ball roll!

Similarly you should always aim to isolate your enemy's power. You should plan to isolate him both geographically and politically. The most effective form of isolation is to separate him from his allies and friends. Instead of confronting the person directly, you can work in the background and turn his allies away from him. Make him look stupid and immoral among his allies until they start to put distance between themselves and him. Your enemy will soon become an isolated player with no one left to turn to. Strike when he has no one and eliminate him.

Du Fu, the famous Chinese poet of the Tang dynasty, states this nicely:

> *"If you draw a bow, draw the strongest. If you use an arrow, use the longest. To shoot a rider, first shoot his horse. To catch a gang of bandits, first capture its leader. Just as a country has its border, so the killing of men has its limits. If the enemy's attack can be stopped [with a bow to the head], why have any more dead and wounded than necessary?"*

7.3.3 Exploit Anger

"A monkey, whilst munching a ripe pear, was pestered by a wasp, who was eager to have a part. The wasp threatened the monkey with his anger. He settled on the fruit. But it was soon knocked off by the monkey. The irritable wasp chose an alternative route. After using the most insulting language, which the other calmly listened to, he so worked himself up to violent passion that, losing all consideration of the penalty, he flew to the face of the monkey. He stung him with such rage that he was unable to extricate his weapon, and was compelled to tear himself away, leaving it in the wound. Thus entailing on himself a lingering death, accompanied by pains much greater than those he had inflicted."

As Jonathan Birch poetically put it in the above passage, anger leads to a cloudy vision. Be the monkey. Accept the little sting, but expect your opponent to destroy himself out of anger.

It is an old trick to escalate a situation when your opponent is angry by making him even angrier. People who are angry will not think rationally and are known to make mistakes. As always, taking advantage of mistakes made by your opponent is your aim.

Sun Tzu states:

> *"If your opponent is of a hot temper, try to irritate him. If he is arrogant try to encourage his egotism … One who is skilled at making the enemy move does so by creating a situation according to which the enemy will act; he entices the enemy with something he is certain to take. He keeps the enemy on the move by holding out bait and then attacks him with picked troops."*

7.3.4   Depend on me

Make others depend on you. If they do not, they may get rid of you at the drop of a hat. Hence, in general you should aim to create a situation where they will end up with a disadvantage without having you on their side. They need to have an incentive other than mere alliance. As you know well, alliances and friendship can be short lived. In this regard, Machiavelli states that:

> *"It is better to be feared than loved. You can control fear, but you can never control love. Friendship can be changeable and can make you insecure if you depend on it. It is better to make others depend on you out of fear of losing you than out of love of your company. Thus a wise prince will think of ways to keep his citizens of every sort*

and under every circumstance dependant on the state and on him; and then they will always be trustworthy."

In Risk, make sure that any alliance is backed by some dependence on you. For example, your alliance can help your ally to fight on one front against his enemy. You can then put your armies in a place where his other front is protected. He can rely on your alliances and use your armies as a protection from the outside world. However, you can use your *intimidating force* to make sure he will not cross you, since if he does, he will be attacked either by you or by someone else when you pull out your armies.

7.3.5   Appeal to self-interest

"The men that have changed the universe have never gotten there by working on leaders, but rather by moving the masses."

Napoleon Bonaparte

If you need to get someone's attention, the quickest and most efficient way is to appeal to their self-interest. Once a player understands how your plan benefits him, he will naturally be all ears. You can deliver a speech and people may listen to you, and you can teach them about a great cause. The problem is that, once the initial excitement dies, everyone starts to ask what is in it for them. Why should they bother at all, if it does not help their lives? However, if you can show them that your cause will *directly* benefit them, they will be supporting you without hesitation.

Robert Greene wisely states that:

> *"People build walls to keep you out; never force your way in, you will find only more walls within walls. There are doors in these walls, doors to the heart and mind, and they have tiny keyholes. Peer through the keyhole, find the key that opens the door and you have access to their will with no ugly signs of forced entry."*

7.3.6   *To Interfere and Not to be Interfered*

When a conversation is underway between you and another player (for example, when negotiating over a deal), you may feel that you do not want any interference from anyone else. Equally, if a deal is taking place in front of you, you may feel that the parties are drawing up to a conclusion that does not suit you. You may want to change the course of the conversation and *interfere*.

Controlling interference (either interfering or stopping it) is also very helpful to use in real life. Practice this as much as you can. The best way to learn, as usual, is by an example.

To interfere

Suppose two people are negotiating, and if their deal is successful, it will be a disaster for you. Once they get allied together, they are most likely to turn against you. You want to stop this deal. If they do not get together, there is a higher probability that they will fight with each other and not with you. Interfering does not have to be an aggressive move. It can be achieved in a subtle and friendly way; Gandhi style.

Here is an example. Suppose you are in Africa and two players want to negotiate (See Figure 7-4). One of the negotiators (Grey) resides in North America while the other (Black) controls South America. They are initiating a discussion on a deal over the Venezuela/Central America border so that they will not fight each other.

You are naturally alarmed. If the deal succeeds, it means only one thing: Black will be fighting you for Africa. He has his back secured and will have nowhere else to go but Africa. Clearly, this will cause all sorts of problems for you. As a result, you need to *interfere* and disrupt the deal. What would you do?

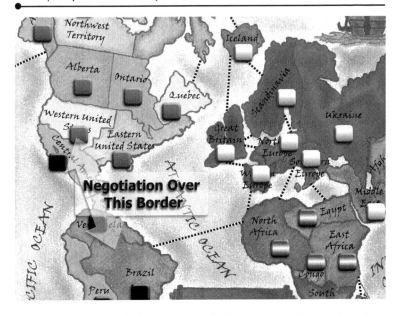

Figure 7-4. Grey and Black are negotiating over the Central American border. You (Stripe) want to stop the deal taking place.

A good approach is to delicately state negative remarks on the argument as it takes place between the two. Every time Grey says something positive about the deal, you can counter it with something negative. The following conversation can take place:

Grey says to Black: "Once we've made this deal, we will both end up with a secure continent and we can focus on somewhere else."

You say to Black, "Look, his continent has five bonus armies, you only get two, he is benefiting a lot more than you are in this deal."

Grey says, "You can then expand to a better continent, conquering North America will be more difficult for you than others."

You say to Black, "He has two borders to expand from, he can go to Europe or Asia, while you no longer have a choice if you make a deal. He is again benefiting more than you do."

Grey says to Black, "Listen, if you aren't sure we can put a time limit on the deal. We can make it last only a few turns. How many do you want? I am flexible."

You say to Black, "Wow, do you really think you can trust him. He gets his deal, he will then grow because of bonuses and he gets more than you every turn. When the deal is expired, he will attack your continent and get it all, while laughing at you. Don't do it."

As you can see, in every step of the way, you are putting a stick in the wheel and preventing a smooth negotiation from taking place. The reality is that even if they try to ignore you, your statements may remind them of something they have not thought of before, and that could be enough to disrupt the deal.

To Stop Interference

If you are subjected to interference, you should respond to such remarks appropriately to defuse them. It is critical that you realise that this is indeed happening to you.

Once you know that you are under verbal attack, you should initiate a counter-counter argument. You should indicate to everyone that you have realised what the interferer is doing and that you will not let him take control of the conversation. For example, you can turn to the interferer and say, "Stop messing about, will you?" and smile. If he keeps interfering, you should also keep repeating your statement or something similar, "Come on now. Let us have a conversation. [Turn to your negotiating party] He is just afraid of this deal for himself. He is trying to mess with us since he knows if we make this deal, it will be bad for him. If we make the deal, we both benefit, and he will end up as the loser."

Now, even if the interfere tries to save himself, he is cast as a person who advises based on his own interests and is not neutral. No one will listen to him anymore (at least you hope) while this particular negotiation is taking place.

Remember to smile when you say your counter-interference statements to indicate that you do not really care. If you carry on with the negotiation without dealing with an interferer, you may very well be doomed. The more you leave it, the deeper you will go into the mud until you sink!

7.3.7 *You are So Good*

You can prevent your opponent disagreeing with you. Too good to be true? Well, here is a way to do it. You start by telling him that he is very clever and nice, and he is highly respected when it comes to *concept X*. You can tell him that he is beyond such earthly features and he is in a class of his own and that he belongs to a group of people who believe in *concept X* strongly. You can then say that such people (the people you just described) would never object to *Point A*.

A while later you can bring *Point A* forward (which is what you wanted to say all along). When you mention *Point A*, he ends up in a dilemma: He cannot simply disagree with *Point A* even if he does not agree with it. If he disagrees, he will risk losing his special status you mentioned earlier. You have prevented him from outright disagreement. Ego is a strong emotion and is easily manipulated.

You need to execute this delicately as not to make it look like you are sucking up to him. If it fails, all that happens is that he will not accept your argument and will not agree with your point, which was the original result anyway.

Let's look at this from a different angle. When people publicly express their beliefs on a particular topic, it is much more difficult for them to change their views, even when it is right to do so. When expressing your opinion, always seek to know how others may react to your view and leave enough space for yourself so that you can get out of it safely. Equally, you can use this technique to put pressure on someone who naively expresses their rigid opinion on something. The more you push them, the more they feel they have to stick to their half-baked belief. Let them sink enough in the mud. When the argument has reached a point when it is relatively obvious it will not work, go for the kill.

7.3.8 Don't Follow the Crowd

People have a tendency to follow the crowd. An action is considered appropriate if others are doing it too. A great example is when people laugh. Is it really that people feel something is funnier if others are laughing? Probably not, nevertheless they do laugh if others laugh. If a bus lane is used by five cars, the chances are very high that another car will follow suit.

People find it difficult to make independent beliefs. In the absence of such belief, they will embrace the view of the group as their own. Another interesting example is the attitude of investors (such as those who carry out share dealing) where there is a *herd following mentality*. Needless to say, if you are following the herd, you are (by definition) always behind. Forward planning and independent belief is the key to success in any competitive environment.

Just because everyone is saying Player A is becoming too powerful and cannot be trusted, it does not mean it is necessarily true. You have to think for yourself and see if there are any benefits for you in joining the crowd and potentially weakening the poor player. His power may actually be to your advantage by shielding you from other more powerful players.

Similarly, you can take advantage of the herd mentality to push the crowd in a particular direction. You need to get another person to follow you, then another, and soon a cascade can occur.

In this section you were introduced to a number of techniques to control conversations and people by using short keywords or just to be aware of the other person's intentions. It is also beneficial to practice physical postures and body language. There is a large body of research on how to spot a liar using a variety of techniques such as body language and analysis of conversations. *Never Be Lied To Again: How to Get the Truth In 5 Minutes Or Less In Any Conversation Or Situation* by David J. Lieberman is a great source of information on this topic.

7.4   *Direct versus Indirect Arguments*

"Contrariwise," continued Tweedledee, "If it was so,
it might be; and if it were so, it would be; but as it
isn't, it ain't. That's logic."

Lewis Carroll (Wisdom and Ignorance)

In Risk, you are generally confronted with two types of players:
Players who are with you and players who are against you. Of
course, everyone wants to win eventually, but in the course of
the game you always tend to have a number of *friends* and a
number of *enemies*. As a result, when you want to initiate an
argument or a deal, you have two main choices:

- *Direct Argument*. States the conclusions first and then
  provides the supporting evidence.

- *Indirect Argument*. Analyses the evidence and then
  moves forward to the statement of conclusions and
  recommendations.

In the game, you always have to make a choice between these
two approaches, which largely depends on the style and
reaction of the player you are trying to argue with. Here is
what you do depending on the player:

- *Friend*. If the player is likely to be sympathetic to your
  cause, a direct style is a safe option.

- *Enemy*. If the player is likely to be negative, or will
  challenge you, you may prefer to build up your case
  and lead him to the conclusion. This build up may take
  place during a number of turns in the game so that you
  can conceal the fact that you are following this
  approach.

As you can imagine, dealing with a *friend* is arguably much
easier than dealing with an enemy, and the direct approach
will get you quickly to the point you are trying to make. It is
usually the indirect approach that needs more work and it is
the skill that needs mastering. The following section provides a
useful and systematic way of constructing an indirect
argument.

7.5   How to AIDA

> *"The worth of money is not in its possession,*
> *but in its use."*
>
> *Fables Aesop*

A person who is not sympathetic to your cause needs to be treated delicately. You need to know how to *sell* an idea and get someone to do something for *you*. Once you sell an idea to a player, you can get an *action* out of him. The marketing industry has been at this for as long as one can remember and the techniques they use are directly applicable to Risk.

A time-tested and very effective formula is known as 'AIDA', which stands for *Attention-Information-Desire-Action*. The idea is to follow this sequence of activities to get the desired behaviour from the target audience. These four concepts are explained below.

7.5.1   Attention

Your first move is to grab the attention of the player you like to engage with so that he starts listening to you.

To get someone's attention, you need to give a *clear and concise statement*. For example, use the following techniques to grab the attention of the other player:

- *Ask:* "Do you like to have access to North America via Europe?"

- *Offer:* "If you don't attack me over this border, I will not attack you either."

- *Past experience:* "I have never broken a treaty with anyone."

- *Information:* "The most powerful player in the game is going to receive armies as much as both of us put together in the next turn."

- *Statement:* "Black's intention is to invade South America because that would be the most ideal move."

All you are trying to achieve here is to get the other player to listen to you. Once you have his attention, you can move on to actually telling them what your offer or request is.

7.5.2 *Information*

Now that you have got the attention of the player, you want to give him enough information so that he develops an interest in your case. Your intention is to persuade him or inform him of your problem.

As a Risk player, one of the best offers you can make is to tell a player that you can make their life easier. People usually like to hear that you can solve their problems and this is equally applicable in Risk. Remember that people are always touched if you give them favours (proportionally of course). They also believe that a deal is fair if both parties benefit from it. As a result, always aim to make your case look like a fair deal. You do not want them to be under the impression that you are exploiting them and forcing them into something they do not like.

In any case, keep them interested at this stage. Let them know it is going to be worthwhile to carry on with the conversation so that you can move towards the next stage.

A few examples are as follows:

- "I am intending to go towards North America from South America. You can therefore go towards Europe if you wish. This is beneficial for both of us since we can free up our armies to use elsewhere."

- "The Australian player only has one option: to expand to Asia. He would then be on your doorstep and can attack your African continent at any moment. You are then at his mercy."

- "The European player is manipulating everyone not to attack him because he tells you that he is not threatening anyone. Meanwhile, he will be receiving more continental bonus than anyone else if he manages to keep control of Europe. We should stop him while we can."

- "Don't listen to these people, they are trying to create a war of attrition to weaken us. They will come to kill us both."

7.5.3 Desire

Now that you have got his attention and managed to persuade him to listen to you, you need to create a desire so that he does what you want him to do. This is the actual concept you are trying to sell. You have to make it so desirable that he would be unable to think of any alternatives, such as going to someone else. As it is well known, it is the *control of desires* that gives you the ultimate power.

To control his desire, you need to know what he wants, what he lacks and how you can help him by your offer or statement. You can even create desires for him. There are a number of ways to generate desires:

- *Give him an incentive.* Make your case appear to be good value for money. "Listen, I am going to attack him from here. He will then become quite weak at this border."

- *Show that you are credible.* Recall your past and demonstrate your honesty. "I have played Risk many times before and anyone who makes an alliance with me always benefits because I am not a backstabber."

- *Demonstrate that you will be minimising his risk if he listens to your case.* "I will not attack your continents from any direction until it is only you and I who are left in the game."

- *Show how you may help him.* "I can attack the large army in the Middle East. Once it is reduced, it will be beneficial to both of us."

- *Show what the future may look like for him.* Picture a world that he will like. "Look, once Europe has been overtaken by me and Africa by you, you can focus on west and perhaps go for South America then North America. You would be getting a lot of bonus for your continents." This way, he would start focusing on the far future assuming that what you just told him is likely to become true. Hence, when you offer him the first steps that would lead to this future, he may listen to you more willingly.

You need to make sure that your offer beats the competition, so that the person you are dealing with will have enough incentive to come to you as opposed to someone else. Ultimately, everyone wants to win. Any offer initiated by anyone tends to be designed to benefit the initiator. People are naturally sceptical unless they are proven otherwise when they are shown that following your suggested route will benefit them and will increase their chances of winning the game.

7.5.4   Action

Now that you have set his desires, get him to act on it and do what you want him to do. If you have got this far, this is the easiest task. In order to make him carry out the action, you can put on a bit of time pressure:

- "Take this deal this turn or leave it."

- "If you don't act now, he will conquer the continent and with his bonus armies we won't get a chance to break through his borders. The time to act is now."

Basically, aim to give him a clear-cut action to follow. If he needs to invade someone, or move his armies, etc. then indicate to him precisely what this action should be. Do not be vague in telling him what he should do. Otherwise all your efforts will be lost. People tend to be more comfortable if you define the problem and the solution for them. Do not expect them to come up with the solution themselves. Once he has a clear action to follow, it will be easier for him to balance it against other factors, and hence he is more likely to follow.

7.5.5   Put it All Together

"I use emotion for the many and reserve reason for the few."

Adolf Hitler

As an example, here is a combined AIDA sequence:

- *Attention:* "Look, you are under pressure from Player A, if you don't get your act together now, he will come knocking on your door with a massive army."

- *Information:* "He is getting armies twice as much as everyone else. He also has four cards, so he is likely to have a combination. You need to sort it out now."

- *Desire:* "I can help you on this. I can attack and reduce his armies at this border for you. It will make it easier to break through his continent."

- *Action:* "You need to remove your armies from here so I can come through. Then start attacking him so when my turn comes, I can get a country of his continent."

Follow the AIDA formula as much as you can when constructing arguments. Since it is systematic, it helps prevent you forgetting a particular, and potentially crucial, step.

Notice that players are usually strong with the *Information* and *Action* concepts. However, they often miss the opportunity to take advantage of the *Desire* or *Feel* concept. Emotions are very powerful in humans and you should always aim to unlock their power. If you can connect with someone emotionally, they will listen to you. If an observer asks them, "Why did you do what he told you to do?" he may simply say, "I don't know, it just *felt* right."

Experience shows that appealing to the player's current beliefs is more likely to be accepted. After all, he already believes what you are saying is true. Would you think that if appealing to his common belief did not get you anywhere, logic would be the next option to use? The answer is: it depends. In direct arguments, where the opponent is on your side, you can use logic. However, in indirect arguments, the player you are dealing with is not usually sympathetic to your cause. Hence, logic is most probably not going to work on him. Thus, the next best thing is to appeal to his emotions. Unfortunately, an appeal to the intellect is least likely to win acceptance in this case.

Interestingly enough, players usually attempt to appeal to the intellect, thinking that it is the best approach as they are setting up a *logical argument*. As practice shows, the game is not an exercise in philosophical theory; players are less interested in being right than in simply winning the game. Make sure that you take advantage of this.

Remember that your choice of *appeal to feel* depends on the mindset of the target audience. The way you put the deal forward can be different if they are *pro-risk* or *risk-averse*.

- *Risk-averse audience.* They are generally conservative in their approach to taking decisions. As a result they prefer to calculate all possibilities and only take routes that have a clear future as far as they can tell. For example, you can appeal to them by saying, "Once you have made a deal with me, you will be able to get the continents as you like. Then you have two options which are both possible and lucrative. You can expand easily from there without increasing the number of your borders. No one will be attacking you without second thoughts. I think it's a fantastic option for you."

- *Pro-risk audience.* These players are generally interested in taking a novel approach to a problem and solving it in a *completely* new way. Consequently, they are willing to take chances. In this case you can say, "You have got to go for it. It will change the game for you. Think about it. It will put us at the top of the world, and it really doesn't cost us much at all. Just imagine, you will get rid of your strongest neighbour in no time."

Notice how both examples are charged with emotional feeling and do not strive to appeal to logic. Instead, they *energise* the player into thinking that in the first case he is secure, and in the second case he has to take a chance.

7.6 How to Deceive

"Men are so simple of mind, and so much dominated by their immediate needs, that a deceitful man will always find plenty who are ready to be deceived."

Niccolo Machiavelli

As indicated earlier, emotions play an extremely important role in the process of decision making. When you enter the emotional land and leave logic behind, you are subject to a variety of factors which may influence your decision. You may end up choosing a sub-optimal option. Powerful emotions such as fear, greed, ego, curiosity, guilt, and intimidation are greatly influential on all of your decisions. One needs to control his emotions to be able to make sound choices. You need to be aware of emotionally charged concepts of exploitations, both not to be deceived and equally to be able to deceive your opponents.

The essence of deception is *distraction*. Being deceptive is an important skill to master. Perhaps one of the great explanations is given by Du Mu on his interpretation of *The Art of War*, that:

> *"A military force is established by deception in the sense that you deceive enemies so that they do not know your real condition, and then can establish supremacy. It is mobilised by gain in the sense that it goes into action when it sees an advantage. Dividing and recombining is done to confuse opponents and observe how they react to you, so that then you can adapt in such a way as to seize victory."*

Sun Tzu himself states that:

> *"A military force has no constant form (i.e. no predictable strategy) just as water has no constant shape. The ability to gain victory by changing and adopting according to the opponent is called genius (Just as the flow of water is determined by the earth)."*

Humans are habitual and like to predict others. Behaviour that seems to have no consistency or is random irritates and intimidates. If used well, you can keep everyone on their toes. After all, nothing is more terrifying than a sudden change for no apparent reason.

What this all means is that you need to use everything at your disposal to make it difficult for your opponent to understand your next moves. The less he knows about your moves, the more chances you have of winning against him.

The following sections explore deceptive and counter-deceptive techniques.

7.6.1 Double-Sided Sentences

"The truth is the same from every angle. A lie always needs to be facing forward."

David J. Lieberman

During the 1960 presidential campaign, Richard Nixon was trying to remind the Americans that his opponent, John F. Kennedy, was in fact a Catholic and not a Protestant. Americans had never had a Catholic president in the past. Nixon thought by revealing the fact that Kennedy was Catholic, people might feel uncomfortable and hence he may end up with an advantage. However, he could not just go and tell people, "Beware, he is a Catholic, do not vote for him." He would look utterly bad. Instead, being Nixon, he sought to deliver the message in a different way. Nixon said: "I don't want anyone not to vote for John Kennedy because he is a Catholic." A double-sided sentence indeed! His intent was obviously not the actual meaning of the message, but the actual information it carried. When someone goes through the trouble of making a point of telling you that he is not doing something, rest assured that it is exactly what he is doing.

An example in Risk is as follows: "I didn't attack Player B because Player C was vulnerable." The usual reply is, "Why is Player C vulnerable?" Aha, now you can explain your fantastic plan, use Player C's vulnerability and tell him what should be done. The original discussion on attacking Player B is lost in the noise.

7.6.2   *Act like an Emperor*

> *"Everyone should be royal after his own fashion. Let all your actions, even though they are not those of a king, be, in their own sphere, worthy of one."*
>
> *Baltasar Gracian*

All the great men have a common feature. They all believe in themselves very strongly. Let's face it. If you do not believe in yourself, how can you expect others to do so? You need to act like an emperor to be treated like one. This is almost like self-deception, though since this may work on you, it may also work on others. You need to be careful not to cross the line to arrogance, as that usually does a lot more harm than good.

To *feel* like an emperor you can follow these rules:

- *Make a bold demand*. Since you are an emperor, you should not back off from your original demand. Aim high.

- *Get the strongest*. Find and compete with the highest authority in your environment. Compete with the strongest player in the game. You will end up at the same level as him and presumably have the same amount of power.

- *Give gifts to higher-ups*. You can demonstrate to them that you are equal if your treat them well.

The more you ask for, the more you will get. The less you ask for, naturally, the less you will get.

7.6.3 Trying Too Hard

> "...Two and two are four. Sometimes, Winston.
> Sometimes they are five. Sometimes they are three.
> Sometimes they are all of them at once. You must try
> harder. It is not easy to become sane."

> **George Orwell, in 1984**

The harder someone tries, the more you should be concerned. Of course there must be a reason for his eagerness. Someone approaches you with a deal which you turn down. He then comes back and this time offers you a deal with more benefits. If he keeps coming back all the time, he must be up to something. It probably means that his initial deal has been so underrated that he wants to better it and hopes to get your attention this time.

Similarly, when something out of ordinary happens and a player does not draw any attention to it, you can be sure that he does not want any attention. As usual, there is always a reason. When your attention is being directed one way, make sure to look the other way to see all the angles.

7.6.4 Appeal to Moral

> **"Morality is the greatest of all tools for leading
> mankind by the nose."**

> **Friedrich Nietzsche**

This is one of the most cunning techniques one can use to deceive someone else. It shows how crafty humans can be in the art of deception. If it does happen to you, you probably will not realise it at the time, and if you use it yourself, well, I hope you sleep well at night and with a clear conscious!

This technique is best described with an example. Suppose you are in North America. Your strategy in the game is to make a deal with your neighbour, South America, so he can then expand to Africa. At some point later in the game, you would like to break the deal (he obviously is not going to like this).

You want to get his continent and practically put him out of the game. He suspects that you might be interested in breaking the deal. You want to reassure him that everything is fine and you have no intention of breaking the deal whatsoever.

If he suspects that you are about to break the deal, he can pull out of the deal before you do, undermining your entire effort. You decide to appeal to moral. You say, "I was once playing in a game and there was this guy, John. Ah! What a player. He said to his neighbour that he was going to move his ten armies out of his continent the next turn. When the next turn came he added another five instead. Outrageous! I could not believe how nasty some people are. I could never do something like that."

Your neighbour is never going to suspect that you, being so upset about such a small act, are ever going to do anything close to stabbing him in the back. The rest of course, is history.

What has happened is that you have presented yourself as a highly moral person (by giving extreme examples) only to deceive the other guy into thinking you are as honest a person as he can get. The problem is of course that he will learn his lesson the hard way.

7.6.5 Give Before You Take

> "Open-hearted gestures of honesty and generosity bring down the guard of even the most suspicious people."
>
> *Robert Greene, 48 Laws of Power*

In ancient China, Duke Wu of Cheng decided to take over the increasingly powerful kingdom of Hu. Without disclosing his plans to anyone, he got his daughter to marry Hu's ruler. He then called his council and asked his ministers, "I am considering a military campaign. Which country should we invade?" As he expected, one of his ministers replied, "We should invade Hu." The Duke said in an angry voice, "Hu is a sister state now. How dare you suggest invading Hu!" He had the minister executed for his naïve remark. The Duke made sure that this incident was leaked to the public. The ruler of Hu heard about this, and considering other tokens of the Duke's honesty and the marriage with his daughter, he took no precaution to defend himself from the Duke. A few weeks later, Duke Cheng's forces invaded Hu's kingdom and conquered the country.

Always aim for a reputation for honesty. Once people take you as honest, it will be difficult to convince them otherwise, and you can then deceive and manipulate them easily. Generosity is a great way of disarming people. It softens people up, ready to be deceived. When it comes to trust, people are usually wary until they are proven otherwise. You can reassure them of your *honesty* by giving something valuable away. This can be some information, a bit of resources, or basically anything else that the other person would classify as valuable. By gaining a reputation for liberality, you win people's admiration while distracting them from your power plays. Remember that generosity needs to be used with a definite strategic goal in mind. Indiscriminate generosity can have the reverse effect. If you are seen as a person who gives to be loved and admired, you can no longer use generosity to control people. After all, if everyone receives, why should anyone feel special?

In Risk, you can help an ally by attacking his enemy or moving your armies out of his way. As another example, suppose a newbie player is about to randomly attack a large army, which you can see is not going to get him anything. You can explain to him (in a very honest way) that, "If you attack him, you will end up losing all your armies and would become very weak. Even I would be able to attack you and get your cards!" You are effectively giving valuable information to him. If you have not told him, he could have been in trouble. Now he starts to trust you more as he thinks you had no reason (other than being a nice guy) to help him on this. Next time, you can be trusted! That is a great position to be in. When it is the right time, cash it in.

It is critical that your opponent takes your actions as favours and gifts. Ultimately everyone in Risk wants to win, so it may not always be easy to convince someone that you mean well. Remember, however, your strategy can backfire. Once you use it on a player and he realises that he was deceived, he may never trust you again, no matter how much you try.

7.6.6 Appeal to Ego

"The nice thing about egotists is that they don't talk about other people."

Lucille S. Harper

Never underestimate the power of appealing to a person's ego. It is a strong emotion and you can easily get a response from anyone. An example is as follows: "I remember your move in the last game we played. You did very well. Respect, man! I learn a lot from you. I don't mind if we make a deal over this border. I am sure you will trust me. After all, you have lots of experience and you can tell what kind of a player I am in a split second."

You can also use ego in a *reverse psychology*. No one likes to be considered as a lesser player in any way, shape or form. If what you say to someone suggests that he is a lesser, he would go a *long way* to prove you otherwise. If that *long way* is to your benefit, you can take advantage of him by exploiting his ego. For example, in Risk you can say, "I don't think you have even a tiny chance in getting a single country of South America, let alone the whole continent." He may then be very much inclined to prove you otherwise, and may go ahead and make an invasion. Of course, this can be to your benefit if you happen to be in Europe. You have got two other players to engage in a war.

Similarly, if you are on the end of this exploitation, do not be tempted to prove yourself. Always look at the bigger picture and predict what people are after. What matters is to get there in the end. Do not let your ego get in the way.

7.6.7 Play as Innocent

"If competent appear incompetent, if effective appear ineffective. When you are going to attack nearby, make it look like you are going a long way; when you are going to attack far away, make it look as if you are going just a short distance."

Sun Tzu

Balance of power is an important element in the game, and you need to think of many potential manoeuvres well in advance. Suppose you have an enemy that you want to weaken. If you can *convince* someone else to do the fighting for you, then you do not have to do it yourself. For this to succeed you need to *shift* the opinion of many players. You need to *create a coalition and make its objective the destruction of 'your' enemy*. Recent history shows that this is indeed a *fashionable* method, and it usually succeeds in getting the war you want. Examples are the Gulf War I, the Kosovo War, and the Gulf War II.

Now, in Risk, suppose you are in control of South America and you need to expand to Africa (see Figure 7-5A). One way to achieve this is to put lots of armies into Brazil and prepare for war. However, you may wish to avoid getting the other player alarmed. Instead of placing your armies into Brazil, reinforce your only other border, which is Venezuela. Brazil is then left with the same balancing armies as North Africa. When you are ready to invade, you can move your armies into Brazil from Venezuela either for back up or as the preparation for invasion.

However, while your armies are in Venezuela, the player in control of North America can get paranoid and start reinforcing Central America to balance power in Venezuela (see Figure 7-5B). Your army in Venezuela acts as *a magnet force*. It forces your opponent to place his armies in a place defined by you, even though he may have needed them elsewhere.

There is, however, a problem. Once you decide to move your armies away to start the African campaign, you will be left with a possible *threat* from the North American *attracted armies* that are no longer balanced by you.

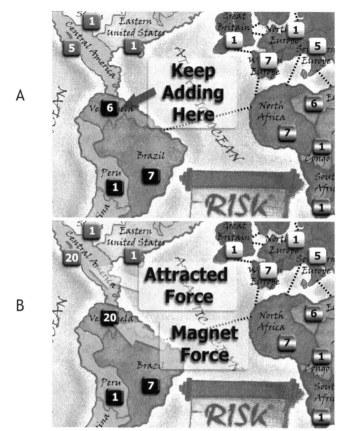

Figure 7-5. *(A) Keep adding to Venezuela instead of Brazil. (B) Armies are balanced with North America.*

A neat solution is to use diplomacy. Before starting the African invasion, make a deal with North America suggesting that, "It is a waste of armies to build up on the Venezuela/Central America border and we don't really want to invade each other. So why not move them away and reduce the balance?" Historically, this is similar to ABM treaty (Anti Ballistic Missile), which was intended to reduce the stockpiles of nuclear weapons. There are two possibilities:

1. If North America agrees, you are free to move your armies and use them in the African campaign as shown in Figure 7-6C&D. If you get this far, it means that

everything went according to plan and you are now effectively conquering a rather valuable continent.

2. If North America does not agree with you, you can turn the whole argument around and make a deal with Africa. Reinforce Venezuela and prepare for war in North America. This will be trickier since the number of armies at stake is high. If you go for a fight with North America, you may win the continent, but you may become very weak temporarily, which may have undesirable consequences.

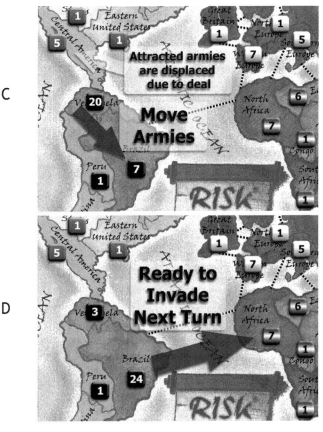

Figure 7-6. *(C) A deal will let North America use attracted armies elsewhere. (D) After a deal with North America, move armies to Brazil for invasion.*

As you can see, performing diplomacy in advance can be advantageous. All you need is to be farsighted.

Remember, if you want to get into a conflict with someone, the crudest method is to invade him at your will. Instead, if you use diplomacy, you may get better results. For example, let him attack you first rather than starting an invasion. This is achieved by weakening one of your borders. If you start the invasion, others may develop a negative view of you, while if you have been invaded by someone else, they will sympathise with you. Let him start the invasion and tell everyone that you have all the rights in the world to defend yourself! Only then deploy your armies (which you have prepared all along for this invasion anyway).

This is in fact a standard practice in diplomacy; to pretend that you are innocent while you are not.

7.6.8 Act Dumb

> *"It is an exceedingly rash thing to let anyone see that you are decidedly superior to them, and to let other people see it too."*

Arthur Schopenhauer

People do not like to be confronted with someone who is more intelligent. Invariably people tend to justify someone's superiority with luck, good fortune or even flatly refusing to admit his superiority.

You need to keep the extent of your abilities unknown. Robert Greene explains this beautifully in *48 Laws of Power*:

> *"What is understandable is not awe inspiring. We tell ourselves we could do as well if we had the money and time. Avoid the temptation of showing how clever you are. It is far more clever to conceal the mechanism of your cleverness."*

When you let others know how you succeed, they may use your own ideas against you. It is an easy temptation to boast about your success and satisfy your vanity. Do not fall for it.

In Risk, if you appear to be too strong, everyone will come after you. Pretend that you are not that clever. Make deliberate mistakes to make them think you are just another amateur player. Other players may drop their guards and you can then have a much easier time. On the other hand, if you show off your superiority or experience, everyone will seek to prove you wrong. The chances are that they will succeed. Do not give them any excuses.

7.6.9 Control Depression

> *"Remember that there is nothing stable in human affairs; therefore avoid undue elation in prosperity, or undue depression in adversity."*
>
> *Socrates*

Depression is usually due to three mental distortions:

- *Permanent*. You feel that the situation will not change.

- *Critical*. You believe that the problem is more significant than it really is.

- *All-consuming*. You think that it will affect everything else in your life.

When any or all of these beliefs are present and magnified, it can dramatically increase your anxiety and hopelessness.

Now, as you can imagine, there are two ways you can deal with depression. One is to understand it and attempt to reduce it. The other is to use it to depress an enemy. By artificially inflating any number of these parameters, you can make your opponent feel anxious and agitated.

As an example, you can make your opponent nervous by saying, "Once he invades you, he won't leave anytime soon [*Permanent*]. His invasion will rob you of your crucial bonus armies [*Critical*]. Once you have got no more armies, you are ultimately doomed [*All-consuming*]."

Similarly, in order not to feel depressed about a situation, you can think of a problem as *temporary*, *isolated*, and *insignificant*, which does not concern you at all. In short, by modifying the parameters either positively or negatively, you can control the amount of depression you or someone else might suffer.

7.6.10 Define the Options

> *"The wounds and every other evil that men inflict upon themselves spontaneously and of their own choice are in the long run less painful than those inflicted by others."*

> *Niccolo Machiavelli*

Henry Kissinger, who was President's Nixon's secretary of state, was considered a clever man who knew how to play the power game. Reportedly, he considered himself as someone who knew a lot and used a trick to control his boss. When he wanted Nixon to make a decision, he would provide him with a number of options. He described the options as if he had a neutral point of view and what would matter is how Nixon would decide. However, in the process, he used to bias his options (or even manufacture them himself) in order to get Nixon do what he thought was best to do. Ultimately, even if the choice turned out to be wrong, Nixon only had himself to blame.

In dealing with your opponent, you can always provide a number of options that no matter what he chooses, he ends up doomed. People like to think that they are free to choose and can easily be deceived into thinking that they are in control. Those who are in the process of choosing always find it difficult to believe that they have been manipulated. For example, put a large army next to your neighbour and later tell him he has three choices: "If you attack me, I have no choice but to attack you. If you don't move your armies to your other front, your other border will soon break. Of course, if you move your armies away, I can also move mine, provided I can trust you. The choice is yours."

7.6.11 Evolve

"Preach change as much as you like, and even enact your reforms, but give them the comforting appearance of older events and traditions."

Niccolo Machiavelli

Christmas day is a day of celebration. Conventional wisdom states that it is the birth of Jesus Christ and hence why people celebrate the event. However, upon examination one might discover a lot more about the history behind this particular day. The Christian Church under Pope Liberius, in A.D. 354, declared that the 25th of December was the birth date of Jesus Christ. This was based on the current tradition. The Romans celebrated the turn of the year with *Saturnalia* or the festival of Saturn, god of the harvest. This was between 17th and 23rd. It was the most cheerful festival of the year. The Germanic people held a festival at the winter solstice celebrating the rebirth of the sun and honoured the great fertility gods. In A.D. 274, Roman Emperor Aurelian established an official cult of the sun god, Mithras. He declared his birthday, 25th of December, as a national holiday. He was in turn worshipped by many Roman soldiers. Mithras was the Persian god, the Sun of Righteousness. Mithras was the mediator between Ahura Mazda and the Earth. Ahura Mazda is the god of Zoroastrian faith, which originated in Persia. Hence, over time, a single day was simply morphed into the flavour of the day, as men of power saw fit to do so. They introduced change without disrupting the tradition.

You can always take advantage of this evolutionary approach to bring change without making it look obvious. If you want others to change, you can let them *evolve*, so that it will not appear that you have managed to change their minds. At the end of the day, you just want results, how you get them is up to you. If you ask someone to change their mind, the chances are that they will not. Most people see this as a sign of weakness. It all goes back to ego. You must accommodate for this. Instead of forcing someone to change his mind, give him more information. Allow him to make a new decision based on the additional information. Politicians use this technique skilfully.

As you probably know, politicians rarely admit to their mistakes. If they find themselves in a situation that needs explaining (i.e. they have made a wrong choice and since have changed their minds), they diffuse the situation by saying, "My position has evolved." Who said politicians were not smart?

A Risk example is as follows: "I can see why you said that then, but now that Player A has conquered Europe [a new piece of information to support your new position], I think we need to rethink our situation and make new decisions." Hence, if he was refusing to cooperate with you before, he may now be more interested in engaging in negotiations given that something new has happened. The information you give must be relatively new. If it is too old, he may think that he should have known about this, and based on his ego, he must have acted on it accordingly. Therefore, your statement is not really adding anything new. He could also become embarrassed not knowing the old fact. Hence, be diligent when you state the facts.

7.6.12 How to Know if Someone is Lying

> *"Who lies for you will lie against you."*
>
> **Bosnian Proverb**

Everyone has dealt with lies at some point. There is one undeniable truth about lying. Everybody does it, but nobody likes it when it is done to them. Ever since the beginning (the very beginning), entities have always tried to deceive each other for gain by telling lies. Lying effectively and detecting them is an arms race that has been ongoing forever. A look at the animal kingdom shows how diverse these strategies can get when it comes to convincing some other animal that you are not what they think you are (so that you will not be eaten alive!).

As for Risk, players compete over resources and inevitably this competition leads to telling lies as well. It is an important skill to know how to lie, to what extent, and how to detect it. Of these three, the first two are easier to understand and learn and are not things that one can seriously encourage others to do. The third one, however, is a well-researched topic and one a person must certainly know. The following summarises some of the founding on how to detect a liar:

- A liar will make little or no eye contact. A person who is lying to you will do everything to avoid making eye contact.

- A liar moves his hand up to nose and ear more often due to extensive thinking.

- There is movement away from his accuser, possibly in the direction of the exit.

- A liar will not point his finger at the person he is trying to convince.

- A liar willingly answers your questions, but asks none of his own.

- In truthful statements a fast no or yes is followed quickly by an explanation. If the person is lying, the rest of the sentence may come more slowly because he needs time to think up an explanation.

- A liar always wants to change the subject. He then appears to be more relaxed. The guilty wants the subject changed; the innocent always wants a further exchange of information.

- A liar offers an introduction in his statement starting with "I don't want you to think that..." Often that is exactly what he wants you to think. Whenever someone makes a point of telling you what they are not doing, you can be sure it is exactly what they are doing. An example: "Not to be annoying or anything,..."

- Numbers are cooked up on the spot. A liar will not have enough time to think through his statement. The numbers in the story end up being created as opposed to remembered.

- If he lies about one thing, everything he says is questionable.

- A liar uses humour or sarcasm to defuse his accuser's concerns rather than responding seriously.

- He uses an obvious fact to support a dubious action. For example, suppose a Risk player is intending to attack someone's continent. The to-be-attacked player upon realising this may say, "I'm not sure you have enough armies to get my entire continent in one go!" The devious player says, "I'm not surprised, not everyone can calculate the correct pace of a Risk game and also keep up with how much potential power I have."

- When something out of the ordinary happens and the person does not draw attention to it, it means that he is trying to draw attention away from it. Similarly, a liar runs off a long list of items in the hope that one will remain unnoticed. For example, you may be negotiating over a deal with someone in Risk. You want to highlight how good you have been to him. You may start with a long list of your actions, "I have been helping you to defend yourself against Player A, I moved my armies out of that continent so you can get it, I never broke an alliance with you in the past,…" The list goes on. However, you might have *forgotten* to mention that you blocked his entrance to South America, which would have been an obvious move for him. Watch out for the guy who justifies something with a list.

If you find it necessary to lie, do not deliver a lie directly! Instead, twist the truth ever so slightly so that you can get to your objective with minimal effort. Sometimes a little lie which is carefully executed can save up hours of pain. It may even make the situation better for everyone. For example, delivering bad news is always one of those situations where you do not want to be outright truthful right from the headline!

7.6.13 We Are on the Same Boat...

"It is surprising what a man can do when he has to, and how little most men will do when they don't have to."

Walter Linn

218 | Chapter 7: The Art of Debate

If you are on a skinning boat with someone, the chances are that you sympathise with each other and understand the pain. If you both know each other, you may develop a sense of camaraderie which is established through the hard time.

The *same boat syndrome* is also known as *Negative Equality Nostalgia* (or *NEN*). This is the positive feeling one gets when knowing a peer is in the same level of trouble as they are.

For example, in a single turn two of you might get attacked by someone who has just broken the treaties with both of you and has left you both in a dreadful situation. You may both feel upset and vulnerable. This can bring you together and may lead you to get allied against the common enemy.

However, the sense of *NEN* is often exploited by those in competition with one another. In the context of the above example, you might say that you feel weak and have no intention of attacking anyone for the foreseeable future. You hope that your new comrade will also follow suit. However, you may be planning to attack everyone in the next turn, and simply want others to think that you have no such intentions, thus feeling superior in the process.

An analogy is doing homework. If you do your homework but tell a classmate that you have not done it, you may feel better. You hope that he will not do his homework either. It leaves you feeling superior since you have done your homework and he has not.

7.6.14 Curiosity

> *"Until you have the courage to lose sight of the shore, you will not know the terror of being forever lost at sea."*
>
> *despair.com*

Sometimes you can take advantage of the curiosity of a player. Tell him that, "Look, it's only a game. You won't know what will happen if you don't give it a try. You can always go back. But if you don't do this now, you may come to regret it later on. The world could have been yours and you missed it because you weren't bold enough. Believe me, even if you fail, it's still worth knowing how this might have worked."

Despite the fact that you have not provided any reasons for him to follow this particular action, you sound almost convincing. He may simply fall for curiosity, so it is always worth a try. What have you got to lose?

7.6.15 Who to Trust?

> *"Trust your enemy, but don't trust your ally."*
>
> *Niccolo Machiavelli*

Paranoia can sometimes help. Be cynical, expect any move and *do not trust anybody*. Risk players usually consider themselves free to do as they like, which means they resort to activities that they may not even consider in real life (or at least that is what you hope!). So be careful. Risk is only a game and within the rules of the game any player should be able to do anything he wishes. All that matters is to win the game and you should do whatever it takes to get there.

However, this does not mean that you can be as nasty as you like. If your aim is to win the game, you will find that achieving your goal may be easier if you do not do any evil! Beware of the psychology of other players. Tacitus famously said:

> *"Men are more ready to repay an injury than a benefit, because gratitude is a burden and revenge a pleasure."*

If you need to *gain people's trust*, do not lie to them. Make them believe that what you tell them is always in their interests. This way, you can convince them to rely on you. Remember, once a player decides that you are *unreliable*, he may never trust you again.

7.6.16 The Promise

> *"Tada yori takai mono wa nai" means "Nothing is more costly than something given free of charge."*
>
> *Japanese Proverb*

Henry was an older man who went store-to-store selling pocket watches. Those in the store, salespeople and shoppers alike knew that he was a peddler and a retired millionaire. He did nothing that was illegal per se. So, how did he become so wealthy selling pocket watches?

Henry would walk into the shop and ask if anyone would like to buy a beautiful handcrafted crystal lamp for thirty-five dollars, hundreds less than what one would expect to pay.

He made the lamps himself and enjoyed giving them away. Since he had only one sample, he needed to take orders. He diligently took down the names and addresses of each eager person and refused to accept any sort of deposit. "You'll pay when you get it and when you're happy with it," he would say, smiling. Henry had now established himself as a trusting person and one who had a beautiful product at a fantastic price. He had their trust and confidence.

Henry also carried a large box with a handle. Invariably someone at some point would ask what was in the box. This is when Henry went to work. He opened the box revealing beautiful sterling silver pocket watches individually wrapped and protected. He would tell his eager audience just about anything he wanted to about the watches. They had no reason to doubt him of their value. He was trustworthy. Henry would sell the pocket watches to most of the nice folks who placed orders for his lamp. Interestingly, nobody ever did get a lamp, just an overpriced pocket watch, sold to them by a nice old man[3].

So how did Henry become rich? It was not because he was selling the watches. It was because he sold an interesting story. To avoid being deceived always look at what you are getting, not what you are promised. You can gain someone's trust by giving them something. Later, when the time comes, cash it all in. You can then get hard at work selling the *real thing*. In Risk, this can be used in two ways: in a single game and between multiple games.

---

[3] The story is taken from *Never Be Lied To Again: How to Get the Truth In 5 Minutes or Less in any Conversation or Situation.*

In a single game tell someone that you will shortly remove your armies from a country. A few turns later remove your armies and let him know that you have honoured your statement. He will now trust you even more. Next you can suggest a deal to him. Since you have developed a trust with him, he will be more inclined to negotiate with you.

As for multiple games, build up a trust in the first few games. Once you have got his confidence, you can make your winning moves, be it honest or dishonest.

7.6.17 Avoid Being Deceived

"And there's that one undeniable truth about lying. Everybody does it, but nobody likes it when it's done to them."

An Aphorism

You can be deceived when getting information from someone. Occasionally people want to tell you the truth when asked, but may find it easier to lie if they have the chance. To avoid being deceived, make it a bit more difficult for them to lie. You can achieve this by hiding your true intention so that the other person will not know where you are heading. The following examples will clarify:

- "Do you like to invade South America?" You can be deceived by this. Instead cover your intention: "Do you feel an invasion is wise at this time?"

- Instead of, "Do you want to attack Player A?" say, "What do you think of Player A?" With the second sentence it is more difficult for the other person to see what you have in mind. If he does not know where you are heading, he will not be able to deceive you.

7.6.18 What Not to Say?

"Never argue. In society nothing must be discussed; give only results."

Benjamin Disraeli

Never boast on your winning abilities. If you tell others that you are invincible, the chances are that they will prove you wrong in this game! However experienced you might be in the game of Risk, you can never win the game by fighting against everyone. Show what you mean by your actions. Words are a dime a dozen. If other players interpret your moves and speech as arrogant, they unconsciously start to dislike you in the game. This only means trouble for you! Always say less than necessary. Before suggesting anything, consider the alliances of other players. Notice which players benefit others based on current strategies and alliances. Only support those that will benefit you. Similarly, disrupt those relationships that are hostile to you, or those that you are not comfortable with. This needs to be carried out delicately; otherwise once they realise what you are up to, they may all become hostile to you simultaneously, which is something you always want to avoid.

In the long run, if a player's disagreement does not matter to you, then do not bother with a demonstration. There may come a time when he will realise your argument through experience. Save your energy and focus on something more important.

7.7 How to Talk

> *"He who causes another to become powerful ruins himself."*
>
> *Niccolo Machiavelli*

Socrates was said to hold knowledge in high esteem. One day an acquaintance met the great philosopher and said, "Socrates, do you know what I just heard about your friend?"

"Pause a moment," Socrates replied. "Before telling me anything I'd like you to pass a little test. It's called the *Triple Filter Test*."

"Triple filter?"

"That's right," Socrates continued. "Before you talk to me about my friend, it might be a good idea to take a moment and filter what you're going to say. The first filter is *Truth*. Have you made absolutely sure that what you are about to tell me is true?"

"No," the man said. "Actually, I just heard about it and..."

"All right," said Socrates. "So you don't really know if it's true or not. Now let's try the second filter, the filter of *Goodness*. Is what you are going to tell me about my friend something good?"

"No, on the contrary..."

"So," Socrates continued. "You want to tell me something bad about him, but you're not certain it's true. You may still pass the test though, because there's one filter left: the filter of *Usefulness*. Is what you want to tell me about my friend going to be useful to me?"

"No, not really."

"Well," concluded Socrates. "If what you want to tell me is neither true nor good nor even useful, why tell it to me at all?"

This is why Socrates was a great philosopher and held in such high esteem[4].

Just as Socrates believed, knowing what to say and when to say it is essential for any successful person who wants to be in control. In any conversation, you need to be able to command the direction of the conversation and to some extent seed it. This usually requires a number of well-placed *keywords* that once said can tilt the conversation slightly to one direction; a direction that you desire. It is essential to spot the right moment to use the right phrase. This is particularly helpful when either you are engaged in a negotiation or when others are discussing global Risk issues and you want to jump in and influence the conversation. This section contains a number of tactics you can use to influence the flow of the conversations. As usual, practice them in Risk and use them in real life.

---

[4] This also explains why he never found out his best friend was having an affair with his wife...!

7.7.1 Getting More Information

To steer the conversation into your desired direction you can use a few short keywords. If used in an efficient way, they can be extremely effective. These words can be used to extract information from any conversation. While the other player is talking, you can say:

- *'Meaning ...'*: This forces him to offer you the reason for his position. He will then give you his view on the larger picture.

- *'And...'*: The most simplistic word you can say, but this can have a huge effect. You will be able to gather additional facts.

- *'So...'*: Let's get to the conclusion. There are many times that a conversation seems to go on forever and you just want to get to the bottom of it. This will give you the bottom line.

- *'Now...'*: If you want actions, use this to force him to formulate what needs to be done after all he has said. He will proceed to tell you *exactly* what he means and how it may apply to you.

Equally well, if you are talking and want to switch gears and move on to a different subject, a number of keywords can help greatly:

- *'Because...'*: This word is usually followed with an explanation and everyone expects it.

- *'Let's...'*: This is a positive word. It suggests to people that you have agreed on something and now you are moving on to the actual detail of carrying it out. Basically, the argument is closed.

- *'Try...'*: You can always give it a try. After all, what is the harm in doing this? When you run out of reasoning and facts, or when someone stubbornly refuses to accept your arguments, use the 'try' keyword and convince him that since there is no harm in doing it, you might as well do it just to be on the safe side. This technique has in fact been used extensively by different religions from around the planet, "Just try this *religious act* (replace it with your own favourite), so you would be on the safe side (and don't end up getting tortured in hell). After all, it's a small thing; it won't cost you much or take too much of your time!"

An interesting example: "Let's give it a try because if it doesn't work we can always go back to the way it was." Clearly you have not explained any reason for this particular action, yet it seems to make sense just the same.

7.7.2   *When to Give Information Away*

Always ask questions to collect information and check its consistency with what you already know. *Never reveal what you know first.* Always look at the big picture. Sometimes it is better not to reveal your position, even if it means that you may suffer great short-term losses. Once he has heard you and knows what you know, he can modify his story to be consistent with yours. You may lose the chance to find critical new information that you have been looking for.

7.7.3   *Interruptions*

Suppose you find yourself in a situation where the other person talks so much that you do not get a chance to speak. He keeps interrupting you all the time. To break the flow, you need to use a few short *keywords*. These play on two susceptible angles of human nature: ego and curiosity.

- "You're a smart person; let me ask you a question."

- "I know that you would want me to ask you this."

- "You're the only person who would know the answer to this."

- "Along those lines..." The other person might be more willing to let you carry on if you resume the conversation with his last thoughts.

7.7.4 Defensive Arguments

When you talk to a person, he will only become defensive if he feels he has been attacked verbally. If you want to get some information out of him or to get him to cooperate with you, you do not attack him. For example, imagine if you say, "Why are you so expansionist? You go around attacking everyone on the map!" The usual response is: "No, I am not an expansionist." He goes defensive straight away. Instead, you can say, "All these invasions you are doing on the map is only going to make you weak. Everyone will come back for revenge. Try to start slowly and invade people one at a time." Notice how this feels more like a kind and wise statement from an ally and a friend. The end result though can still be the same: You want to stop him from attacking you.

Use *let's* and *try* in your sentence to get information or get someone to do something without sounding demanding. Then use the following guidelines:

1. Assume your suspicion as fact. Example: *being expansionist*.

2. State at least two truisms. These are facts that you both agree to be true. Example: *invasion makes you weak*, and *others will fight a weak player*.

3. Switch the focus of your statement from a threat to a request. Example: *try to expand slowly*.

4. Make an easy and reasonable request so he can accept it. Example: *invade one at a time*.

In Risk, there are times that you may have found yourself confronted by another player who is about to invade you or is contemplating the option. You may keep your fingers crossed, wish yourself luck, and hope that he will not invade you. However, there is something you can do. You can tell him something to change his mind. Here are a number of approaches.

A. "If you attack me, I will invade you and hunt you down for the rest of the game!" This approach is terrible, though it may be the most common. Not only do you sound threatening, but you also have reduced his desire to change his position since if he does, he would appear weak.

B. "You are planning to attack me, aren't you?" This is slightly better, since you indicate that you are already aware of his plans. If he says yes, you can then engage in a more civilised conversation. If he says no, he would look bad if he invades you having admitted earlier that he was not going to.

C. "I want to talk to you about your plans to invade me." By this, you are telling your opponent that you are fully aware of his plans for invasion and that you have been anticipating this all along. You have changed the focus from the invasion act to talking. He may reply that he does not want to talk about it though.

D. "I know that you are stockpiling to invade me. You know that I am not going to be happy when you attack me. I just want to tell you that by invading me you will become extremely weak. I am then forced to use my satellite armies to attack you from behind. Besides, Player B may use the opportunity to invade you and you won't have a chance to survive." With this approach you indicate that you not only know about the invasion, but also you do not think of it as a wise move for him. You deliver this as if you do not really care, since if he is going to invade you, it will not make any different anyway. But you are more concerned about what follows and how it may impact him in the future. The future is of course something that he is always interested in.

7.7.5 Truth Suggestions

The technique known as *4-3-2-1* is elegant. You deliver a number of true messages and then immediately follow it with suggestions. The brain accepts the true statements and automatically *thinks* that what follows must also be true. As long as the suggestions are obviously false, the brain will accept them as true.

In order to execute this technique you can use a systematic approach. First deliver four true statements. These can be anything as long as your opponent takes them as true. Then follow this by one suggestion. Your suggestion should be about what you want him to do or feel. Now, repeat the same with three true statements and two suggestions, then two true statements and three suggestions and finally one true statement and four suggestions. By combining the true statements with specific suggestions, you can lead your opponent into accepting your suggestion.

Scenario

You are playing Risk. It is the start of the game and everyone has been allocated a number of random countries. At this stage all players are wondering which continents to claim and hence get a good initial start by getting continent bonuses. At the same time, players try to avoid any major conflicts to preserve their armies. Suppose you have found yourself in North America with another player and you want to claim North America for yourself. Using 4-3-2-1, you can say:

"Look, we are both in North America. You are probably wondering how we are going to divide this between us. You don't want to end up without a continent. You want to get the best for yourself and that would be not to lose too many armies.

I know you have played in the past. And that you ended up without a continent because you hesitated. I am sure you don't want that to happen again. I think we can easily solve this issue this time and we can both end up in a better position.

You know that controlling North America can be difficult since it is surrounded by everyone. I have more armies than you have in North America. I don't think you like to lose any of your armies by fighting me over North America when you need to use them to protect your continent. You may easily get South America or another continent. You can then secure it in no time with all your preserved armies.

It is still early in the game, and relatively easy to move armies. This is your chance to prevent a war of attrition. You still have lots of options as you can control another continent. I can help you by moving my armies out of the way, so you can get out easily. I think you still have a chance to win."

7.7.6   Soft and Direct

When you give an order, expect people to follow it and they will. The best way to get a person's attention is to speak *softly* and *directly*. Not only will people often do what you expect them to do, but they often feel how you suggest they should feel.

A few examples are as follows:

- "You seem to be in revenge mode, attacking anyone who is attacking you."   Then watch him do exactly that.

- "I think you are still upset because of Player A's invasion into your continent." This will make him upset over Player A's behaviour. This is even more effective if he has ended up with a truce and you want to get him to start another war of attrition with Player A.

7.7.7   The Power of Positives

Players buy into positives much better than negatives. If you tell a player, "Do not invade Europe", he will hear "Invade Europe". This is very similar to telling a child: "Do not touch the paint." Most children will probably develop an *urge* to touch the paint!

Hence, emphasising negatives tends to have poor results. Always strive to encourage the player into thinking positively. Instead of pointing out the negative outcomes, suggest the benefits that will be gained (and the risks reduced) as a result of an action. Provide a *carefully selected* number of options of which they can select from.

Here is an example. Suppose a player in South America is considering his options. You are in North America. You can say:

Option 1.   "Please don't invade my North American continent."

Option 2.   "You basically have two options to expand, one is a large continent such as North America and the other is a smaller continent such as Africa. I am going to fight to the bitter end to protect

> my continent and it will cost you to get it and to keep it. It is much cheaper for you to go to Africa."

As you can imagine, the second option is much more effective. It also provides a biased trade-off of options as explained earlier, which can be useful.

7.7.8   Every Argument has Two Sides

When constructing an argument, aim to appeal to the player in such a way as not to make it obvious that you are trying to manipulate him. If you provide only one side of an argument (usually the side that benefits you), he will automatically think that your entire plan is constructed in such a way to benefit you and *exploit* him.

Instead, attempt to provide both sides of the coin. Analyse the situation and let him know the pros and cons of making different decisions and how they may benefit you *and* him. This way you end up with a trade-off analysis of the situation which will then look more methodical and less forceful. He is more likely to accept your argument and follow your suggestion.

Of course, if you want to influence his decision, you need to bias the trade-off analysis slightly so that the argument can be beneficial to you. You can accomplish this by cooking a bit of data (such as how powerful another player is) or exaggerate the pros and cons of a particular situation. If the argument is well structured, and it *feels* right (appeal to emotion), players usually accept it. Experience shows that when people are listening to you, they tend to focus more on the logical structure of your argument than the facts supporting it. In order to manipulate them, keep the logic in place, but twist the supporting data. Better still; just modify the conclusion as if logic and data are only there to support the fake conclusion.

7.7.9   Giving a Speech

Sometimes in Risk, you need to give a speech. This is when you have thought about your strategy and know what you want. For example, you work out that if you can get two players to start a war of attrition, or a player to invade a particular continent, you will greatly benefit from this. Now you want to initiate a talk that eventually leads to this. As you can imagine, if you start with "You guys need to attack Player X", the chances are that they are not going to listen to you.

Instead what you need to do is to start building a consensus. At the end of the day you need to get the people to conform to your idea. That is your goal. All you care about is the end result; how you achieve this does not really matter as long as you get there in the end.

As usual you need to approach it in a systematic way. First, carry out a bit of research:

- What are everyone's goals and motivations?

- What kind of an effect is your speech going to have on their attitude? If they are going to be hostile, you need to persuade them. If they are going to be on your side, can you take advantage of them to spread your ideas?

- What do they need to know? What information do they have that you do not? For example, a player may have the following knowledge that you do not:

  o He has cards ready to cash.

  o He has played with another player previously and can predict his next moves more accurately than you.

  o He is a more experienced than you and knows the most common strategies from this point onwards.

Once you have worked out the problem, you can approach it in a number of ways.

You can go ahead and give a great speech using the AIDA technique. Grab their attention, build up the argument logically, tell them how wonderful your plan can be and finally give them instructions on how they can carry it out. If you have a semi-friendly audience, this may work. However, a hostile crowd would simply dismiss your speech as propaganda.

To deal with a hostile crowd, a better option is to level the field first. You can carry out this process over a few turns. You can give your speech in bits. A remark here and another there will slowly start to mount. You can of course modify your comments as time goes by to reflect the changing circumstances. Over time, you may build a consensus without too obviously having done it. This is gradual propaganda. The problem is that even if it is gradual, people still do not like someone telling them what to do or giving them *good solutions* they have not worked out for themselves. Ego, as always, gets in the way.

The best approach is perhaps to engage them in the process of finding a solution. Instead of giving them the bits and pieces of information, you can give them facts that would lead to the solution, but they come up with an answer *themselves*. All you are doing is focusing their attention on a well-packaged piece of information that they can use to logically conclude what you had in mind. Since they are participating in making up the solution, they will be much more prepared to accept it as well. After all, they think that it was *them* who came up with the idea in the first place. This not only satisfies their ego, but also makes them listen to you more as you provide them good pieces of data. They will not become hostile towards you. Even better, if the solution turns out to be disastrous, they would not hold you responsible for coming up with such a daft idea.

The only downfall is that you cannot take credit for the brilliant solution you came up with. But does that matter? This is why you should not get carried away by *the means*, and only focus on the goal. Give up satisfying your ego if you want to win. It is the price to pay! Imagine yourself as a cool, calculating guy who knew it all along, pulled all the strings and never told anyone that it was all his idea. Give up your own ego and you will succeed!

8 Dynamics of the Game

"Who controls the past controls the future. Who controls the present controls the past."

George Orwell

The previous chapters provided you with a range of guidelines. Now you can take advantage of your strategic position and benefit from the psychology of your opponents.

What you have not seen yet is how a game can actually be modelled and analysed. In fact, there is a large body of research on *Game Theory* which is directly applicable to playing Risk. As with any system, it is desirable to understand the choices of actors (or players) in the course of the game and be able to predict the outcome of the game if possible. The correct method is to create a sufficiently abstract model of the system under observation that captures the *essence* of the underlying system, but is simple enough to understand and make predictions. In this chapter, you will first be introduced to a number of common techniques in Game Theory and later will see how this can relate to Risk. You will find out why certain strategies will not work if you keep playing repeatedly, or if *killing turtles* is wise!

Game theory has its foundations in the theory of *Rational Choice*. It is a branch of applied mathematics which attempts to understand a player's choices and how he can maximise their return by selecting the right choice. It was originally developed to understand economic behaviour. Now it is increasingly used in various disciplines such as political science, sociology, philosophy, biology, computer science and computer games. It is a great tool for analysing power relationships.

The object of this chapter is not to give a comprehensive guide to game theory. Instead it attempts to selectively show the relevant aspects of the theory that can be used in Risk. An interested reader should refer to more dedicated literature on this topic.

Before introducing the general form of game theory, let's analyse a historical example. In order to do this, you first need to know what *Rational Choice Theory* is.

8.1 Rational Choice Theory

"Much that passes as idealism is disguised hatred or disguised love of power."

Bertrand Russell

In rational choice theory, human individuals or groups can be modelled as *actors* who choose from a *choice set* of possible actions in order to try and achieve desired outcomes.

Each actor has an *incentive structure* which consists of the possible choices of actions, their associated costs, and the likelihood that they will lead to desired outcomes.

Each actor is then modelled based on two different categories of power:

- *Outcome power*. This is the ability of an actor to bring about outcomes.

- *Social power*. This is the ability of an actor to change the incentive structures of other actors in order to bring about outcomes.

This model has been used for a wide range of social interactions where actors have the ability to exert power over others. For example, a *powerful* actor can:

- Take options away from another's choice set.

- Change the relative costs of actions.

- Change the likelihood for a given action which leads to a specific outcome.

- Change the other's beliefs about its incentive structure.

With this, you can model a wide variety of systems where agents compete for power. It is a rational model, which attempts to capture the logic of the decision maker. You can also use it as a guide for organising your thoughts when dealing with other players. For example, suppose your opponent wants to attack you:

You can:

- Block him by using someone else's forces. This way he no longer has the option to attack you. Alternatively, you can make a deal with him. Again this will remove a choice (invading you) from his choice set.

- Move a large number of armies to your border near him and reassure him that any invasion will be extremely costly to him. You have changed the relative cost of his actions.

- Show him that his invasion may not reduce your power as much as he thinks. All he will get after expending a large number of armies is to make sure that you do not get two extra bonus armies for your continent on the next turn. You have changed the likelihood of his action leading to profit.

- Show him that invading you is actually not a good idea at all if he wants to win the game. In fact, it might be better for him to get an easier continent which also happens to have less number of borders. Effectively you are trying to change his mind about his choice leading to a particular outcome.

Rational choice theory is very effective in modelling rational behaviour. However, humans are not always rational and this is why it makes them more complex and challenging to analyse. There is always a need to look at humans from many different angles and with many different models.

8.2   The Cuban Missile Crisis

"Generations to come will scarcely believe that such a one as this walked the earth in flesh and blood. I believe that Gandhi's views were the most enlightened of all the political men in our time. We should strive to do things in his spirit: not to use violence in fighting for our cause, but by non-participation in anything you believe is evil."

Albert Einstein

The Cuban missile crisis is a well-studied subject in human history due to its extreme importance and the fact that the world nearly got destroyed! As a result, there have been many researchers who have tried to model the crisis so they can predict the outcome of future conflicts.

The Cuban Missile Crisis was a confrontation during the Cold War between the Soviet Union and the United States regarding the Soviet deployment of nuclear missiles in Cuba. The missiles were apparently placed to protect Cuba from further planned attacks by the United States. This was also rationalised by the Soviets as retaliation for the U.S., who had deployable nuclear warheads in the United Kingdom, Italy, and most significantly, Turkey. The U.S. discovered the missiles using spy planes, which then led to the crisis. In the event of a launch, the U.S. could only retaliate by attacking the Soviet Union and destroying everyone in the process. They wanted the missiles removed. The question though was how to achieve this.

In one of the most famous works, *Essence of Decision*, political scientist Graham T. Allison describes the Cuban Missile Crisis and uses three different models to analyse it. Allison used the crisis as a case study for future studies into governmental decision making. In doing so, he revolutionized the field of international relations.

Allison provides three different viewpoints through which we can analyse the events:

- *The Rational Actor model (Based on Rational Choice Theory)*
- *The Organizational Behaviour model*
- *The Governmental Politics model*

To illustrate the models, Allison posed the following three questions in each section:

1. Why did the Soviet Union decide to place offensive missiles in Cuba?

2. Why did the United States respond to the missile deployment with a blockade?

3. Why did the Soviet Union withdraw the missiles?

Each model attempted to provide an answer to each of these questions.

8.2.1 Rational Actor Model

In this model:

- Governments are treated as the primary actors.

- Each government uses a payoff matrix. They examine a set of goals and score every action accordingly. They would then pick the action that has the highest score.

Under this model, Allison answers the three questions as follows:

1. Since Soviet Union did not have as many ICBMs as they desired, Nikita Khrushchev ordered nuclear missiles with shorter ranges to be installed in Cuba. In a single move, the Soviets bridged the 'missile gap' and scored points in the Cold War. They believed the U.S. would not respond harshly.

2. Kennedy and his advisors evaluated a number of options, ranging from doing nothing to a full invasion of Cuba. A blockade of Cuba was chosen because it would not necessarily escalate into war, and also it would force the Soviets to make the next move.

3. Because of *Mutually Assured Destruction*, the Soviets had no choice but to accept U.S. demands and remove the weapons.

8.2.2   *Organisational Behaviour Model*

In this model, when leaders are faced with a crisis they do not look at it as a whole. Instead, they break it down and assign it according to pre-established organisational lines. The following describes this model:

- Leaders settle on the first proposal that adequately addresses the issue or in a sense is *satisfying*. Due to resource limitations, they will not evaluate all possible courses of action to see which one is most likely to work.

- Leaders emphasise short-term goals with less uncertainty.

- Organisations follow set procedures when taking actions.

Under this theory, the crisis is explained as:

1. Prior to this event, the Soviets had never established nuclear missile bases outside of their country. Placing the missiles in Cuba was handed to established departments, which in turn followed their own set procedures. Unfortunately, their procedures were not thoroughly thought out, and as a result they made mistakes that made the detection of the missiles easier for the U.S.

2. Kennedy and his advisors were almost unanimously in favour of air strikes. However, such attacks were not guaranteed to disable all of the nuclear missiles. An alternative was to use the navy, especially since Kennedy was able to communicate directly with the

fleet's captains. Hence, they really did not consider a large number of options and just chose the most conservative one.

3. The Soviet Union did not have a back-up plan to follow if the U.S. took decisive action against their missiles. They simply had to withdraw.

8.2.3 Governmental Politics

In this model, a nation's actions are best understood as a result of politicking and negotiation by its top leaders. The following statements apply to this model:

- Leaders decide based on many factors, even such as personal interests and background.

- Leaders have different levels of power based on charisma, personality, skills of persuasion, and personal ties to decision makers.

- Due to the possibility of miscommunication, misunderstandings, and downright disagreements, different leaders may take actions that the group as a whole would not approve of.

Based on this theory, Allison concludes that:

1. Kennedy's revelation of the Soviet lack of ICBMs put a lot of pressure on Khrushchev. The Soviet economy was being stretched, and military leaders were unhappy with Khrushchev's decision to cut the size of the army. Placing missiles in Cuba was a cheap way to solve the problem and also secure Khrushchev politically.

2. Kennedy decided on a forceful response rather than a diplomatic one since the Republicans in the U.S. Congress made Cuban policy into a major issue for the upcoming congressional election. He could not ignore this. Kennedy's close advisors favoured a blockade as an option. On the other hand, Air Force General Curtis LeMay strongly supported air strikes, though Kennedy was not fond of his ideas. Kennedy also distrusted the CIA's advice. The result was that he had to make a choice, and he chose blockade.

3. Deals were made behind the doors. These were not known to public until much later. Khrushchev, with his plan in ruins, tried to save face by pointing to American missiles in Turkey, a position similar to Cuba. A deal was made between the two countries. The U.S. was to remove the missiles a few months later (without making it public), while simultaneously promising not to invade Cuba. The Soviet Union in return would remove the missiles, *publicly*.

Of course the above analysis was performed by Allison based on whatever data he could obtain, and he admitted that he did not have access to a lot of data on the Soviet Union's internal affairs. Nevertheless, the above analysis is an interesting study on the conflict.

As you can see, a crisis such as this can be interpreted in many different ways, all of which can be valid and important, and can shed light on the underlying decision-making process.

The above story can inspire a Risk player to understand events from different angles. While decision making in general is a rational process, the actual decisions may be influenced by other factors such as psychological and mental states of the decision makers at the time. This is in fact a key point since understanding the psychology of the opposing leader is as important as understanding the crisis itself. Sometimes, just knowing how the other party will react is a great advantage in reducing your search space and making it easier to converge on an optimal solution.

From this analysis, we can learn that a crisis does not necessarily have to be solved by force and there are always more ways to consider. For example, if you find yourself in a tricky situation where you are stuck between bad and worst, you can pass this decision to someone else, and it will no longer be your problem: 'The ball will be in his court'. The other party has to make a move and you take advantage of any irrational decisions or outright mistakes he may make.

Remember, in this story the actual problem was not to stop a nuclear war. The Cold War was more of a game of balance where both parties were benefiting from the continuation of the conflict (or at least the armies were!). The actual problem was to solve the crisis in such a way so that neither party was humiliated or appeared to be weak. It was all about saving face, and at the same time saving humanity from disaster. Therefore, solving the crisis depended greatly on the emotional and psychological state of the two key decision makers.

A similar situation in Risk is when a player has no choice but to invade you, while he realises that the invasion can get him killed. This is when the range of potential decisions he makes goes from being completely rational to completely emotional and random. After all, who has not heard of a player who suddenly says, "Oh, what the hell, let's just try this. I am going to invade you. Just for fun. Let's see what happens"? And just like that you may find yourself on the receiving end of a suicidal invasion.

Another interesting analogy is that the governmental advisors are like players in Risk. Most of the time, when a crisis takes place and an argument or negotiation follows, everyone jumps in to *advise* the two parties. Usually their involvement can be quite influential. Of course, everyone suggests something that most benefits them. However, their advice can also benefit you. The problem is that they attempt to seed the negotiation with their *preferred* choices. As seen in the organisational behaviour model, the leaders may not consider the full range of possible actions. There is always a limit on the available resources, and in Risk it is perhaps the time you have to complete your turn. As a result, a negotiation would automatically start around the seed and may not go much beyond that. Always be wary of the *audience*. Skill of persuasion, your natural ability to convince others of your ideas and being able to think quickly on your feet while others are contaminating the process are the most important skills a true leader must have.

8.3 How to Stop People Ganging Up Against You

"It takes great talent and skill to conceal one's talent and skill."

La Rochefoucauld

Everyone wants to become powerful. However, power brings about its own problems. Being too powerful in Risk means being the subject of envy, but also the menace of your competitors. Others would do anything to bring you down from your privileged state. Does this mean you should not be powerful? Not at all. In fact you should certainly aim to become as powerful as you can, but without letting others know the extent of your power.

Once other players discover that you are leaving them behind and are stockpiling armies, they may develop an incentive to gang up against you. Repetitive winning is also a great motivation for people to gang up on you. As you already know, you cannot go against the whole world, however powerful or clever you are. Hence, at this stage you need to act cunningly, deceiving them into thinking that you are just as vulnerable as they are.

This is easier said than done. You need to practice a few times and be willing to accept failure. The following are a number of techniques you can use to help the situation:

- *Target the key player.* The crisis often starts with a key player searching for destruction of better players. He is usually quite experienced and sees himself as the potential winner. Once he realises that you are getting out of hand, he starts aggressive propaganda against you, telling everyone that if they do not get rid of you, it is all over for them.

  If this happens, you are in trouble! Other players start to follow suit and sooner or later someone will start attacking you. In a few attacks and in a couple of turns, you will be reduced to the weakest player, and from there you are on your way out. Your best bet to get out of this is to focus on the key player who started it all and take him out of the game as soon as possible.

  Start the diplomatical process even before the game starts. Use propaganda and gang up against the key player. Tell others that he is the biggest threat. Make people believe that as long as he is in the game, they have no chance to win. This kind of player usually talks a lot. You need to be at least as vocal as he is. This can be difficult sometimes, but there is no better way to stop someone from talking than talking yourself. Aim to take him out before you go out and perform this repeatedly over many games until the annoying player learns the lesson.

- *Lose a game.* If you have been repeatedly winning, players start to think that you are invincible. To wipe out this adjective from your reputation, attempt to lose dramatically so that everyone will remember your downfall in the future. Next time, play better. Your intention is not to be labelled as 'unless we gang up against him, he will not lose'.

- *Make Yourself Trustable.* Try to play the game without the annoying player present. You can then gain the reputation of a loyal player by being trustable. Once you have got them to trust you, you can play against the annoying player and hope that others will come to your side.

- *Turn the tables.* If you have been repeatedly ganged up on and kicked out of the game, you play as the victim. Target the key player who starts the crisis and tell others that as long as he is in the game, there is no chance of winning, as you have experienced repeatedly. Get other players to gang up against him.

- *Make an alliance with the weakest player.* You can get allied with the weakest or an amateur player. He can benefit from your advice and survive longer in the game, and you can get him to help you against others. He can cover your back and give you his vote, both of which can be extremely useful against the gang.

- *Silent Allies.* If two players are related (such as friends, couples, etc.), they may naturally assume that they are allies even if they do not talk about it. Logically, they can gang up against you so they both stay in the game longer. To save yourself, target one of them consistently over and over again. In any game you play with them, aim to remove the same person first. Eventually the losing half may start to rethink his position.

An interesting case occurs when a couple are playing in a game. You need to decide which one to target first. This is a classic situation where you can exploit emotions. It turns out that targeting the female partner is more beneficial than the male partner. If the female partner wins consistently, the man will not be too upset. He may convince himself that it was better for her to win (at least she is happy now!). If you target the man, you may not achieve much as they still be relatively happy. On the other hand, if you target the lady, the man may end up winning more often and the woman gets agitated. The man probably does not want the lady to be upset. He starts to rethink his position and will be less motivated to gang up against you. The game becomes more balanced as a result.

There are a number of methods you can use to get out of this dilemma. When a game is played repeatedly, your decision in the previous games can have an impact in the current game. A strategy that can get you to win a single game may no longer be applicable if you want to win more than one game. The ultimate strategy to win all the time is naturally an adaptive and flexible strategy. It should respond to yours and other player's actions throughout the games.

Fortunately, the dynamics of repetitive decision making has been studied in detail by scientists. *Game theory* investigates this in great detail and there has been a huge interest in developing strategies that can overcome this problem.

One of the most interesting concepts in game theory is the *Prisoner's Dilemma*. The following sections describe the relevant parts of this theory and show you how it relates to winning repeatedly in Risk.

8.4 Rational Self-Interest Hurts Everyone

"Success is a lousy teacher. It seduces smart people into thinking they can't lose."

Bill Gates

Imagine that you are in South America and are confronted with another player in North America. You are both wary of each other and you do not know what the other's plans are. You have two choices: To build up armies on the border (Venezuela) or just leave it as it is. Your opponent also has the same choice set. If you do not build up, and your opponent does, you are in big trouble. He can simply invade your defenceless border. The situation is exactly the same if you build up and your opponent does not. It will be a great disadvantage for him. The rational choice is therefore to build up. The problem is that you end up allocating a large number of much-needed armies in a border for no use other than matching your opponent's armies. In reality, you would both be better off if you *cooperated* and did not build up at all.

This phenomenon is known as the *Prisoner's Dilemma*, which is well studied in game theory. Two people have been put into prison. A clever prosecutor tells each one of them: "You can either confess or remain silent. If you confess against the other and he remains silent then you can go free, but I will make sure the other will be put into prison for twelve months. Likewise, if he confesses and you remain silent, you will be the one who stays in prison. If you both confess and I get two convictions, I'll see to it that you both get a maximum of three months in prison. If you both remain silent, I will only keep you in prison for one month. The choice is yours. Have a think, I'll be back in an hour."

Both prisoners, having thought about their dilemma, chose to confess. That way, in the worst-case scenario, they only had to stay in prison for three months. What is interesting is that if they both remain silent, it would be better for both of them.

This puzzle illustrates a conflict between individual and group rationality. A group whose members pursue *rational self-interest* may all end up worse off than a group whose members act cooperatively. Equally, this puzzle suggests that if a group had *not* rationally pursued their goals individually, they may all end up better off.

It is interesting to note that the game of chicken discussed in Section 6.4.2 is also an special case of Prisoner's Dilemma with a different payoff matrix. The difference in the game of chicken is that one will win only as long as he has chosen the opposite of his opponent. If they choose similar to each other, they will both perish.

Prisoner's Dilemma (also known as PD) was created at the Rand Corporation in 1950 by Merrill Flood and Melvin Dresher as part of an effort to study strategies in intercontinental nuclear war. PD is usually represented by a *payoff matrix*. The payoff matrix for the risk example is shown in Table 8-1. Suppose you make a deal with someone over a border. There is always a chance that either you or he will break the deal and become a *backstabber*. Table 8-1 shows the result of different combinations of the two player's decision whether to cooperate (honour the deal) or backstab (break the deal). For example, if both players do not place any armies (row 1, column 1) they both stand to win. On the other hand, if Player A breaks the deal and Player B honours it, Player A ends up with a great advantage since he has surprised the other player with his devastating invasion. Player B is the loser. He is at the receiving end of an invasion from someone he trusted. This is shown as *Surprise Win, Shocked Attack* in the table (Player A's outcome, Player B's outcome).

Similar to the situation found in a game of Risk, the PD scenario is often used in political science to illustrate the problem of two states engaged in an arms race. Both states have two options: to increase military expenditure or to make an agreement to reduce weapons. Neither state can be certain that the other one will keep to such an agreement. Therefore, they both incline towards military expansion. As in PD, the paradox is that both states are acting *rationally*, but end up producing an apparently *irrational* result.

	Player B (Honour Deal)	Player B (Backstab)
Player A (Honour Deal)	Win, Win	Shocked by Attack, Surprise Win
Player A (Backstab)	Surprise Win, Shocked Attack	No Cooperation, No Cooperation

Table 8-1: Payoff matrix for a border build up between two players. The syntax for each item is (Player A Outcome, Player B Outcome).

This puzzle gets even more interesting when it is iterated, i.e. played out a number of times between the parties. This is discussed in the next section.

8.5 Should You Be Nice?

> *"A prince never lacks legitimate reasons to break his promise."*
>
> Niccolo Machiavelli

By now you may think that you have developed enough skills to feel confident enough to win a game of Risk. If it is so, then well done to you! However, that is just the tip of the iceberg. If you want a bigger challenge, read on.

One of the most valued skills any Risk player should have is the ability to win *repeatedly*. Winning once is hard enough, but winning over and over again, especially against the same opponents, is as hard as any game can get. The problem is that many psychological factors come into the equation. A winner is by definition someone to watch out for. The more he wins, the more likely it is that he wins again, and so he will be under attack even more.

The other problem is that each player has a history of activities. Your opponents may remember that, a couple of games ago you took advantage of them and broke an alliance, something they may never forget. Next time you want to make a deal with them, they have no incentive to do so.

This issue can be more systematically analysed. What you want to know is the best strategy to follow, such that you can win the highest number of times when you have played Risk repeatedly. The most important issue is how others will react to you when you move from one game to the next. Consider every Risk game as a PD (Prisoner's Dilemma). In each game you have the choice of *cooperating* with your opponent (making a deal), or *backstabbing* him (breaking the deal). You want to know if it is wise to make or break a deal, given that you will be playing with this opponent in the future. Remember, in this case you can interpret the making or breaking of a deal as you desire. Making a deal is similar to leaving a positive impact on an opponent while backstabbing is similar to leaving a negative impact on him.

The choice of backstabbing over multiple Risk games is similar to *iterated prisoner's dilemma* (IPD). The question in IPD is to find the best strategy that can beat all other strategies and get the highest score.

Robert Axelrod explored IPD in his book, *The Evolution of Cooperation*. He invited academics to submit their best algorithms for a tournament competition. The idea created quite a buzz and attracted a large number of participants. After the competition was held, Axelrod examined the top-scoring strategies and found several conditions necessary for a plan to be successful. He found that the successful strategies should be:

- *Retaliating*. A successful strategy must not be blindly optimistic. It must always retaliate. An example of a non-retaliating strategy is *Always Cooperate*. This is not a particularly good choice as *nasty* strategies will ruthlessly exploit such softies.

- *Forgiving*. A successful strategy must be forgiving. Even if it retaliates, it will fall back to cooperating mode if the opponent does not continue to play defects. This strategy stops cycles of revenge and counter-revenge and ultimately leads to winning more games.

- *Non-envious*. A successful strategy should be non-envious. It should not strive to score more than the opponent.

- *Nice*. The most important condition for a successful strategy is to be *nice*, that is, not to defect before its opponent does. Therefore a purely selfish strategy will never hit its opponent first. A nice strategy is by definition a non-envious one.

Axelrod discovered that when these encounters were repeated over a long period of time with many players, each with a different strategy, *altruistic* strategies did very well over time while *greedy* ones did poorly. Axelrod concluded that: "*Selfish individuals for their own selfish good will tend to be nice and forgiving and non-envious*". Hence, as Richard Dawkins stated in *The Selfish Gene*: *Nice guys finish first*.

This theory also explains why amateur Risk players become more agitated when backstabbed as opposed to those who have more experience. Experienced players are more successful in predicting the backstabbing behaviour and are therefore not so surprised when it takes place. Amateurs on the other hand are affected significantly more when they are confronted with other players' behaviour, in particular when backstabbed. The early exchanges experienced by amateur players are likely to have a greater effect on their future than experienced players. This principle goes part way towards explaining why the formative experiences of young people are so influential and why they are particularly vulnerable to bullying. They can even end up as bullies themselves.

A community of backstabbing Risk players, usually breeds backstabbing strategies where such behaviour is taken as normal. This is sometimes so pronounced that when playing with them for the first time and upon the proposal of a deal, they declare, "We don't usually do deals because we know a deal can always be broken, and it usually is!"

You may now wonder which strategy succeeded in Axelrod's tournament. It turns out, that the best strategy was one of the simplest with only four lines of code. This strategy was *Tit-for-Tat*.

8.6   Tit-for-Tat

"Men ought either to be indulged or utterly destroyed, for if you merely offend them they take vengeance, but if you injure them greatly they are unable to retaliate, so that the injury done to a man ought to be such that vengeance cannot be feared."

Niccolo Machiavelli

So you have been backstabbed. What is the first thing that comes to your mind? Revenge...! Yes..., let it grow. How do you feel now? Probably a lot worse. All you can think of is to show the backstabber what he really deserves. But can you really do anything about it? As a result of backstabbing you have probably lost a great deal of your power. The more you have lost, the angrier you will be, but at the same time the more helpless. Now revenge completely obscures your vision and you get consumed trying to find a way back.

But hold on; is this what you really want? Let's look at the bigger picture. All you want to achieve is to win a maximum number of times. That is your main goal. Hence, it does not really matter if in a game someone stabbed you in the back. As long as you have a fixed long-term strategy that works, receive the knife and smile! Rest assured that your turn will come and you will deal with it swiftly and efficiently at that time.

What is that strategy? In Axelrod's competition, Tit-for-Tat proved to be a highly effective strategy for winning in IPD. It was introduced by Anatol Rapoport. The idea was to retaliate every time your opponent backstabbed you. Here are the rules to follow:

1. If someone stabbed you, stab them in the next game.

2. If no one is bothering you, never stab anyone. Always cooperate.

3. Be quick to forgive an opponent that has stabbed you in the past. Call it cool and move on.

4. For this strategy to work, you need to play with your opponent more than once.

With this strategy, you will be able to respond to anyone who turns his back on you, while at the same time, you do not give anyone any excuse to be hostile towards you. Forgiveness is effective in stopping the cycle of revenge and maximising the profits for both of you. It is as if both parties have learnt from their mistakes. They have come to the conclusion that there is no long-term gain to stabbing each other in the back every time and have decided to cooperate with each other from now on.

Now imagine if this strategy is mixed with other strategies in the game. Tit-for-Tat gains against *Always Cooperate*, since they will always cooperate with each other. Tit-for-Tat against *Always Backstab*, is cooperative originally, and then immediately falls into backstabbing behaviour as not to get caught out and will do just as good as the backstabber. Forgiveness of Tit-for-Tat is advantageous against random strategies since there is always a chance of getting back to cooperative mode.

However, as always, there is a catch. This strategy needs to be carefully applied if the number of games you are going to play with your opponent is known in advance. Suppose you want to play only a single game of Risk with someone. What is the best strategy? Backstab if it means you will win the game (all things being equal). Your opponent will not have a chance to retaliate and you have also prevented him from backstabbing you since you have done it sooner.

This is not suggesting that if you are playing with someone only once, you should be nasty to them; quite the contrary! Your reputation has an effect on other players as well. It is quite likely that you will be playing with other players, in which case your behaviour may be remembered. However, in general, the main point of the analysis is that you should be wary of a player who is only going to play against you once. He can be up to anything, good, or evil. As a result, a defensive position is much safer than an all out cooperative one. Remember, you have been warned!

Logically you can take this principle one step further. Suppose you know that you are going to play only two games with your opponent. Again backstabbing is to your advantage since you may lose the chance to retaliate if he backstabs. Hence, there is an additional fifth rule for Tit-for-Tat to be effective:

5. The number of games you are about to play should not be known in advance.

The effectiveness of this rule depends greatly on the correct prediction on the number of games you will ever play with your opponents. As you become more and more uncertain and realise that there might be yet another opportunity in the future that you will meet again, it pays off to play cooperatively. As the likelihood of playing against an opponent is reduced, you should be more inclined to use the backstabbing strategy (or at least play defensively). If while playing the board game or an online game, you realise that you are playing against a set of strangers that you are *sure* you will never play again, you should choose to backstab them all and break their deals. This is why, historically, a rouge stranger entering a community for a short time is feared and not trusted until proven otherwise. A short-term stranger with no potential future contact is the most feared individual you will ever come across.

8.7 Turtles

> *"The world is a dangerous place to live in; not because of the people who are evil, but because of the people who don't do anything about it."*
>
> *Albert Einstein*

One of the most interesting concepts in Risk is that strategies can evolve over time. Depending on who you play against, you may adopt different strategies. As a group of people continue to play against each other, certain new *fashionable* strategies may emerge. Counter strategies are then developed and the cycle continues.

However, certain collections of strategies make the game more enjoyable and players feel more satisfied. Other strategies may bring the game down and ultimately make it boring or even unplayable.

This is not a new concept. Risk is about competition for resources. Any resource can be extremely useful. If all players attempt to exhaust it at once, the resource can become useless to everyone.

An example will shed light on this. An interesting strategy for survival is known as 'The Turtle Strategy'. This is very simple. Just stay put, do nothing and grow. The idea is to become big enough so you cannot be taken out, but also avoid conflicts to retain your armies. Do not worry about continents or maximising the number of countries you own. The name is inspired by the fact that it is slow and big. The defence mechanism for this strategy is that if someone attacks you, you will snap back to kill the offending player. However, do not forget that a turtle, by definition, should not put its own existence in danger. Card collection is optional. A turtle with cards, despite potential bonuses, may become more vulnerable. It can become a more lucrative target as the number of cards approach five.

The turtle strategy can be used when:

- You are badly damaged, your only chance for survival is to stay put and isolate yourself.

- You are left with no continent because it was taken by all others.

- You think you can exploit everyone and get away with it.

As you can imagine, the first two are considered moral by most players, while the last approach usually raises eyebrows. The problem is that in a population of non-turtling players, a turtle can have an advantage since he is exploiting the inability of others to kill him. Anyone who wants to kill the turtle will become a subject of attack himself. Therefore, no one volunteers to kill the turtle. Meanwhile, he grows and becomes even more annoying.

The problem becomes deeper when players start to adopt this strategy as a winning strategy and not as a temporary resolution due to the circumstances they experienced in the game. If all players turtle, the game comes to a halt as no one attempts to attack anyone else and a long marathon starts. The game becomes boring!

Naturally, most players are not interested in a boring game. Hence, there is always certain resentment when a player adopts the turtle strategy. In the Risk community, turtling is a controversial subject. There are basically two camps: *Turtle Believers* and *Turtle Killers*[5]. First, you need to know how many different ways a turtle can die!

8.7.1   How a Turtle Dies

There are basically three ways a turtle can die:

---

[5] No turtles were harmed or killed in the making of this book.

1. Turtle dies while killing an aggressor. He may decide to *snap back* at someone without being able to recover from the aftermath.

2. A player who might be excessively strong, stupid, brave, or highly altruist decides to kill the turtle.

3. Everyone in the game (or at least a sizable number of players) realise that the turtle is a growing threat and decide to end his life for the good of all.

Now, let's see what the two camps believe in.

8.7.2   Turtle Believers

Some believe that turtling is just another strategy, like all others. It is a strategy you choose to use when you need to, such as when you have just been attacked and have no choice but to resort to any means so you can to survive. They believe that there is no shame in adopting this strategy.

They even go so far as to think that turtles are actually helping other players! For example, they argue that since they have been left without continents at the beginning of the game, they are helping others to get their continents by not competing with them. They ask why they should deserve to be the primary target, even though they have stopped competing with others over the main resources, i.e., the continents. Turtles may stop obtaining cards and just stay idle, hoping to reduce the incentive of others to attack them for cards.

Interestingly enough, turtles do not mind other turtles, until of course there are enough of them to kill the game.

8.7.3   Turtle Killers

This camp believes that turtles should be removed swiftly and systematically. They think that the existence of a turtle in the game hurts everyone, and ultimately, if no one does anything about it, the turtle wins.

Hence, this camp strongly resents the turtles. They usually resort to a common doctrine of some sort to get everyone to gang up against them. They may even go as far as banning anyone who does not follow their *house style*.

8.7.4 The Tragedy of the Commons

Upon examination of the real issue, you may realise that the problem is not the turtles themselves. It is the reaction of others to this strategy that makes the difference.

There is no doubt that if a turtle is left on its own, it can eventually come back to haunt everyone. The issue lies with the behaviour of the players who support the turtle or have a tendency to become one themselves.

This problem is known as the *tragedy of the commons*. This was popularised and extended by Garrett Hardin in his 1968 science essay of similar title.

The problem is best described by an example. Hardin stated that suppose you have a community with access to a common land for the grazing of animals. Since the resource is limited, it is to everyone's benefit to add more and more animals to the land to take advantage of the resource. There is a large incentive for people to act selfishly. The problem is that the pasture is slightly degraded by each additional animal. If everyone keeps adding animals, it will eventually exhaust the resource and ruin everyone. As Hardin stated:

> "*Therein is the tragedy. Each man is locked into a system that compels him to increase his herd without limit, in a world that is limited. Ruin is the destination toward which all men rush, each pursuing his own best interest in a society that believes in the freedom of the commons. Freedom in a commons brings ruin to all.*"

The crucial fact is that each individual gains all the advantages, but the disadvantage is shared between all the individuals using the resource.

Hence, everyone keeps exploiting the resource until no one can benefit from it anymore. 'Free rider' is sometimes used as the terminology to describe the behaviour of such exploiting individuals. Free riders are people who consume more than their fair share of a resource, or shoulder less than a fair share of the costs of its production.

Hardin argued against the reliance on conscience as a means of policing the resource. He suggested that relying on morality favours selfish individuals over those that are more farsighted.

As you might have guessed, herein lies the moral dilemma!

8.7.5 *The Moral Dilemma*

Let's explore this dilemma with a thought experiment. Suppose there are four players in a game with the following characteristics:

- Player A: Turtle player with one card.

- Player B: Player who has a combination. Not so strong.

- Player C: Another player who also has a combination. Not so strong.

- Player D: The strongest player who has a combination with the potential to win.

If you are playing as player D, what would you do? You have got two general options:

- *Cash cards and attack the turtle, player A.* The Turtle Killers believe that the turtle should be killed first. They expect Player D to attack Player A no matter what. Turtle Killers will support this player wholeheartedly and will slap him on his back for being such a sportsman. The problem is that Player D is almost giving up winning the game by weakening himself greatly and letting Player B or C win an easy game. Amazingly, they were the people who slapped him on his back! A rational player will probably not choose this option.

- *Cash cards, attack Player B or C and get their cards, cash them and be in the same strong position.* Followers of *Turtle Killer Strategy* will be annoyed, especially if Player B or C happen to believe in that doctrine. They will probably swear that this was a stupid move. The problem does not end there though. Once player B is removed, Player D is again confronted with a choice between A and C: "Shall I kill the turtle or not?"

The moral choice is to kill the turtle, since that will help three people and annoy only one ineffective player. But of course, Player D has all the incentives in the world to do otherwise. His rational decision will lead to marathons, less interesting games, and not to mention a couple of really angry losers.

8.7.6 The Doctrine

The tragedy of the commons has been researched extensively throughout the ages and as the world has become more complex, so have the solutions to resource-sharing problems. In the middle ages, the problem was how to share land and farms. Today the problem is how to share wireless frequency spectrums, traffic management, global needs over population needs, and Internet domain names.

Although the problem is known, the solution is far from obvious and solved. The majority of the solutions converge on adding community-defined rules to resolve the problems.

As an example, consider the following. The inhabitants of a four-story building would like to install a lift in their apartment block. The shaft was placed when the building was constructed with an option to add the lift if residents wished for it. There are eight flats in this building. In order to buy the lift everyone must pay their fair share. However, one or two may refuse to pay, knowing that they can still use the lift without paying for it. Others will have no choice but to go ahead with the purchase, otherwise no one will have a lift. The free riders have an incentive to exploit the others, but the danger is that the lift will not be purchased and everyone will end up as a loser.

A solution to this problem is to gather the eight participants and make them behave like one, so the decision is reduced from eight independent decisions to one. A vote can be taken, but if the answer is yes, everyone will be forced to pay regardless of their individual decision. Basically, the solution involves the use of an authority (an outside agency or an entity selected by the individuals) to moderate the management of the resource for the benefit of the community.

This way, instead of relying on individuals' morals and expecting them to follow suit, we can rely on a predefined set of rules and have an authority to implement those rules.

Various doctrines have been proposed. The details of such doctrines are trivial and are not important. The key is how to impose them on players. This requires a *system* that can achieve two aims:

1. Identify a free rider. To successfully detect when someone has adopted a Turtle strategy.

2. Force all other players to deal with the offending free rider.

Remember, the idea is not to punish people who adopt a certain strategy. The goal is to prevent the game coming to a dead end, which does not suit anyone. For example, a host can be selected as the authority. The players then agree to abide by the rules of the authority. Everyone therefore knows in advance what they are expected to do or not to do. A doctrine can be adopted as the set of guidelines to be used throughout the game. Anyone who does not follow the doctrine is subject to the authority's will. An example of a doctrine is as follows:

Turtle Killing by Group

Upon detection of a turtle, *a single player* must start the attack.

1. All other players must follow suit. If they delay their attack, the turtle may snap back at the original attacker.

2. Everyone must allocate a certain number of *volunteer* armies to attack the turtle. This depends on the size of the armies of each player (P_k) and the total number of armies of turtle (T). Each player therefore has to balance the volunteer armies based on their own size. A simple calculation will result in the following formula. A_k is the number of armies required to attack the turtle by player k, assuming there are n players.

$$A_k = \frac{P_k(T+L)}{\sum_{i=0}^{n} P_i}$$

L is the number of armies lost as a result of bad luck with the dice. n is the total number of players (apart from the turtle). A_k needs to be rounded up to the ceiling just to make sure the turtle is removed after the attacks. For example, suppose there are 3 players that are ganging up against the turtle. They have 20, 30 and 40 armies respectively. The turtle has 30 armies. Taking the Turtle out for anyone is a costly business. Suppose you want to allocate 1.5 times more than T to make sure you will remove the turtle, irrespective of bad luck (See Section 4.4 for an analysis of how many armies you may need). This means L = 15. Hence, the total armies to be allocated will be $T + L$ = 45. Solving the equation, the players need to allocate 10, 15 and 20 armies respectively. The proportional armies are much easier to provide.

3. Of course, depending on dice, it may be necessary to have more armies to finish the job. This can be accounted for by increasing L to reflect this. Keep attacking until the turtle is removed.

The doctrine requires players to police the game themselves, by following predefined rules. If a player is seen as selfish, others need to deal with him, just like the turtle. For example, if a player did not participate and spend his share of armies on the turtle, other players in the next turn can treat the offending player with the same doctrine. Just calculate how many armies he should have spent on turtle (set it as T), divide it proportionally between the participating players (find A_k), and attack him until he has lost what he should have spent. Of course this needs to be clearly mentioned to make an example of what would happen if someone does not participate.

There remains two main problems with this doctrine: who will start first, and how will players decide who is turtling in an immoral way? This is left to the consensus, is subject to debate, and is left as an open question for the interested reader. You can discuss this with others on the dedicated website for this book.

8.8   House Style

> *"For a long time I have not said what I believed, nor do I ever believe what I say, and if indeed sometimes I do happen to tell the truth, I hide it among so many lies that it is hard to find."*
>
> *Niccolo Machiavelli*

You have seen a number of different strategies so far in this book. An interesting question is: how do they fuse together? Suppose some players want to play repeatedly with each other. What would happen if you had a number of different strategies over time? Two different parameters are continuously affecting the gameplay: the actual strategy used and what players learn from the use of their strategy. After a while, players may switch to more successful strategies (as they have been inspired in previous games) and attempt to adopt it as their own. As more and more games are played, new strategies may be introduced and eventually two different possibilities exist: The population converges onto a dominant strategy or that the population is unstable and subject to attack from new strategies.

For example, as a general guideline, one can use *continents-first* as a good strategy to gain armies in the early parts of the game. However, a different strategy such as *Turtle* may suggest that instead of getting continents, it is better to collect armies and avoid any fighting. A third plan could be to invade anyone who gets a continent. In this game, anyone that successfully acquires a continent is subject to an invasion by someone else. Some people start fighting with each other straight away, while others may have a more patient approach.

As the game is iterated, certain strategies may prevail and eventually all players may adopt a particular one thinking that it is the best all-around plan. At this point an *evolutionary stable strategy* has been reached. This is ESS as defined by John Maynard Smith:

> *"An evolutionary stable strategy or ESS is defined as a strategy which, if most members of a population adopt it, cannot be bettered by an alternative strategy."*

In the context of Risk, an ESS is a strategy with the property that, once virtually all players use it, no *rational* alternative exists that can beat them. In essence, an *evolutionarily stable state* is a dynamical property of a game that any new strategy will be resisted by the current one employed by the players. Hence, a new strategy will find it difficult to perturb the current state of the game.

ESS was originally investigated in evolutionary biology to understand the dynamics of evolution on populations of animal and to show how new generations with new strategies can come to dominate that population.

In order to find an ESS, you can run it as a *thought experiment*. Consider the situation where players have an option of cooperating or backstabbing. This is similar to *multiplayer prisoner's dilemma*. Suppose all players are playing with the strategy to always cooperate. Let's call this AC. Now suppose a backstabber (BS) enters the game. This can be a player switching between strategies or simply a new fresh player. The ACers now do not have a chance. BS will make deals, break them and win while laughing at the other players. Hence, the population is *vulnerable* to BSers. A population of ACers is therefore *not stable*.

Now, suppose you have a population of BSers who continuously break each other's deals. No one can trust anyone. It means that although they do not get surprised when attacked by someone else, they cannot take advantage of cooperation. The population survives (players carry on winning), though as a whole the games will look a lot nastier than those of ACers. Suppose an ACer enters this population. He will soon be kicked out as no one cooperates. In such a population, an ACer has a disadvantage. Hence, a population of BSers is *stable* against ACers. Does this mean that BS is an evolutionary stable strategy? It turns out that, as you have seen already, there is a strategy that can be at least as good as BSers and with an advantage.

Consider now that a Tit-for-Tat player (TT) enters a community of BSers. As soon as a BS has backstabbed a TT, the TT will retaliate. Remember that TT always responded like-for-like. Hence, TT will have as much chance as a BS of winning a game. Basically, a TT can anticipate the backstabbing behaviour of

BSers. For a sufficiently large number of games, TT and BS will win similar number of games. Hence, a population of BSers is *neutral* against the invasion of a TT.

Since, TT and BS can coexist, one can easily imagine that a small number of players may, over time, adopt the TT strategy. This can even be a random switch, or new TT players entering the game.

Now you have a number of BSers who continuously stab each other and stab TTers. However, TTers will act differently when confronted with BSers or their likeminded TTers. Against BSers, they will retaliate, against TTers they will cooperate. Players who cooperate can always gain against those who do not since they do not have to spend a large amount of resources for fighting. The environment (i.e. the Risk game) now actively favours the TTers over the BSers.

Overtime, the TTers will win more of the games until the population will only consist of TTers. As you can see, although the BSers are originally neutral against the TTers, they become unstable once small amounts of TTers enter the population. A community of TTers does not get affected by Bsers, nor does it get affected by ACers. In fact it is hard to find any strategy that can gain against a community of TTs. TT is therefore an evolutionary stable strategy.

TT is also a *collectively evolutionary strategy* as it can collectively share an environment with other *nice* strategies. The interested reader should refer to *The Selfish Gene*, by Richard Dawkins, for an excellent introduction to the concept of ESS. On this topic, Dawkins states that:

> "Group selection theory would therefore predict a tendency to evolve towards an all-dove conspiracy... But the trouble with conspiracies, even those that are to everybody's advantage in the long run, is that they are open to abuse. It is true that everybody does better in an all-dove group than he would in an ESS group. But unfortunately, in conspiracies of doves, a single hawk does so extremely well that nothing could stop the evolution of hawks. The conspiracy is therefore bound to be broken by treachery from within. An ESS is stable, not because it is particularly

good for the individuals participating in it, but simply because it is immune to treachery from within."

Equally well, an environment consisting entirely of backstabbers can still be *invaded* and *converted* by cooperative and forgiving players. Never lose hope...

9 *Online Strategies*

"Entrepreneurs are simply those who understand that there is little difference between obstacle and opportunity and are able to turn both to their advantage."

Niccolo Machiavelli

In recent years, the rise of the Internet has led to a whole range of new online Risk games. These games attempt to capture the board game and make it more accessible. One of the major issues for those interested in playing Risk has always been finding other players. The Internet has solved this by bringing players from around the globe into one common virtual place. You can visit the book's website for a number of online Risk game software applications and examples.

As always, every new approach brings new issues as well. Online games differ from the board game due to their real-time nature. To start with, there can always be a mix of artificial intelligence (AI) and human players. If a player drops out, he is usually replaced by an AI. This way, the game can go on without interruptions. Most of the games are played with six players, irrespective of the number of humans in the game.

Turn times vary greatly in online games. You may have a limited amount of time to play, or you may have as long as twenty-four hours to make your move. This is usually set by a host. For example, in some games you have only thirty seconds to make your entire move. This introduces a faster game in comparison with the board game, where turn times are in order of minutes. In this case, a player has to think, act and respond very quickly, which can be stressful at times. Combine this with anonymity and what you get is a roller-coaster ride. You will also get lots of swear words! Just filter it out.

In order to be agile, you need to practice and learn how to think ahead. Online strategies are not very different from the strategies used in the main board game. However, communication between players is no longer as easy to carry out as it is when playing with a board game. Usually, games provide a text chat box. You can type to other players about your intentions and negotiate over deals.

Communication via text is more compact and does not contain any body language signals. Lack of effective communication, mix of newbie and experienced players, potential loss of game connection, and anonymous identities make online games different from a game you play with friends on a Sunday afternoon.

To give you a head start, the following are a number of tips for successful online gameplay.

9.1 Guidelines for Online Strategies

"Manipulate opponents' perception of what is orthodox and what is unorthodox, then attack unexpectedly, combining both strategies into one."

Emperor Taizong of the Tang dynasty

The strategies used online are not very different from those used in the Risk board game. However, as described above, the pace of the game demands new strategies. The following are a number of tips for online Risk games.

- Lack of effective communications leads to reduced diplomacy and propaganda. As a result, most of your focus should be on the strategic and tactical levels.

- Diplomacy is carried out by text chatting. The most common types of diplomacy fall under the following categories:

    o *Demand that someone leaves a continent.* If someone has a large army in your continent, you can peacefully ask them to leave. This saves you a costly fight and they can get a chance to flee before getting kicked out.

    o *Dispute over continent ownership.* In the initial part of the game, everyone is desperately trying to find a home continent. If players have started from random locations, they have no choice but to accept the distribution of their armies. However, sometimes disputes can happen as a result of unclear division of armies in continents. Similarly, some players may be interested in conquering a particular continent at all costs. This leads to diplomatical debates where players try to come to terms with each other. Keep calm when negotiating.

    o *Ask someone to get out of your way.* You may realise that there is no hope for you in a particular part of the map and you decide to leave. However, you realise that a large army is blocking you. Instead of fighting your way through and losing some of your army along the way, you can *kindly* ask the blocking player to shift his armies.

    o *Forge a treaty or an alliance.* An all out alliance is quite rare. Even treaties are usually made in an informal way. For example: "I am going for Africa." "Ok, let me move my troops to South America first." This suggests that both understand which continents they want and do not intend to interfere with each other's plans.

- Do not feel indebted if someone asks for a favour. Quite often, in the early stages of a game, a player may ask you to delay your attacks so that he can leave your continent. If you agree, you may end up at his mercy. He will then take his time to slowly remove his armies from your continent. This means that you will not have enough freedom to rearrange your armies and are constantly annoyed by his armies. However, there is not much you can do. Since you believe the armies are about to leave, you have no desire to waste your own armies to getting rid of them. At the same time, the other player has no incentive to make it easier for you. Experience shows that a small delay such as this in the early stages of the game can lead to a weaker position in later stages. Watch out for those who casually ask for a favour.

- Online games can introduce custom rules. For example, card bonuses can be set to grow with different sequences. Continent bonuses may be increased throughout the game by a set percentage. Know the rules, so that you can use them to your advantage.

- You need to be patient. Build up slowly and surely to stay alive.

- Cards are extremely important. Sometimes the term *Card Farming* is used to describe the concept of focusing only on getting cards.

- Aim not to attack more than one person at a time. You need to start attacking the weakest players first. The usual practice (though a bit harsh) is to attack a newbie. House style usually dictates the elimination of AI players first before any humans are killed. Some hosts enforce this rule and expect players to follow certain etiquette. Make sure you have read and understood the guidelines.

- Use the *Vulture Strategy*. A Risk online game is all about timing. Time your move well and you will have a great advantage, though this is easier said than done. Wait for two players to fight with each other. When they have become weaker, move in and take one of them out to cash the prize. The prize can be anything:

a continent, an important strategic location or best of all his cards.

- Artificial Intelligence (AI) players can be predictable. Predict and exploit them. They will not mind!

- Beware of players who commit *suicide*. Suicide is usually strongly discouraged in online games since, as the theory goes, it introduces randomness into the game. It is believed that the game becomes unfair for some players. A suicider suddenly decides to go for a kill or expand beyond sustainability. This can be harsh for a neighbouring player. On the other hand, *intimidating* someone with an act of suicide can be incredibly powerful in paralysing their strategy.

- You need to play efficiently and know the software graphical user interface. The pace of the game is usually faster than a board game. For initial short turns this is not an issue. Later stages of the game become more demanding. If you need to execute a blitzkrieg, you need to plan ahead before your turn comes. You need to use keyboard shortcuts to accelerate your gameplay. Use your time thinking and not fiddling with controls.

- Do not get intimidated by other players. If you are a new player, the chances are that someone is going to discover this and comment on it. Once they notice, you may be treated as a weak player and subject to elimination. You need to talk yourself out of this by saying you are here to enjoy the game and that it is only fair if you are given a similar chance to others to compete.

- Keep an eye on the statistics. The more you know about your opponents the better. Parameters such as the total number of armies, the total countries, income earned in the next turn, and the current number of cards each player holds can give you a tremendous insight into how the game is progressing.

It is great to know what to do on paper, though as always you need to practice to master the art. The next section contains a number of walkthrough examples that explore strategies used in online games.

9.2   Online Game Walkthroughs

"Those who are skilled in attack, their opponents do not know where to defend. Those skilled in defence, their opponents do not know where to attack."

Sun Tzu

One of the best ways to analyse the dynamics of online games is to record them and examine them in detail. When you are part of the action, you are way too busy to understand what is going on in the game. Online games can be very fast. A recorded game, however, can be analysed on two fronts:

- The actual tactics used by players to get hold of valuable strategic locations.

- The overall strategy used by players and to understand how players get killed in the early part of the game.

To research this topic, a number of online games were analysed over a specific period and were then examined in detail. These types of games vary greatly in style and pace. Some are quick games with short turn times, while others may have turn times as long as a day! A variety of online styles were considered as part of this research. Eventually, a subset of observed games[6] was selected for presentation in this chapter.

The initial examination of a large number of games showed that the vast majority of players get kicked out of the game due to bad timing of their attacks. After a few turns, players invariably decided to make a *bold move*. The move was sometimes out of boredom and other times due to inexperience. In general those who stayed out of conflicts and had a consistent strategy over the course of the game had a greater chance of winning than those who did not. In this section a number of representative games are shown.

---

[6] Some of the games illustrated here were captured from Lux Delux produced by sillysoft.net.

9.2.1 Bold Move Sequence Graph

To capture the essence of a game, a novel method has been used. Instead of recording and showing exactly how many armies each player uses over the course of the game, it is possible to look only at the major events occurring over time.

Bold Move Sequence graph, or BOMS, is a graph that captures only the players' bold moves used through a Risk game (or any game for that reason). In any strategy game, players may have to deal with small incursions, tactically reposition their armies, gather resources and so on. These, as important as they are, may only confuse an analyst in understanding what exactly is taking place in a game. It is much better if a game is viewed based on major moves made by the players; the so-called 'Bold Moves'.

A *Bold Move* is defined as:

> *"A move by a player that significantly changes the nature of the game and demands a response from other players."*

BOMS graph attempts to capture the bold moves. A series of consecutive BOMS graphs show how a game develops over time and how players expand their empires. Notice that it is not essential to show every move made by every player. If a player cannot respond to a bold move (i.e. he only makes a small defensive army placement), his move is skipped and the next major move is shown.

Figure 9-1 shows the key to the BOMS graph. Each arrow represents a major move made by a specific player towards another. Each player is represented by a letter. The placement of each letter on the map shows that the player owns all or most of that particular area or continent.

The font size represents the relative strength of a player's foothold. A mixture of players in an area is represented by *MIX*. An X shown on an arrow represents a move made by an attacking player that eventually killed the attacked player. All the bold moves by a player in a single turn must be shown in a single BOMS graph.

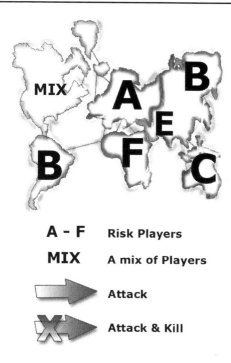

A - F	**Risk Players**
MIX	**A mix of Players**
	Attack
	Attack & Kill

Figure 9-1. Key to Bold Move Sequence (BOMS) graph.

9.2.2   Game 1: Patience is a Virtue

This game illustrates the importance of timing. The players start from randomly place locations. The sequence for cashing cards in this game is set at 4,6,8,10,15,20,... and continent bonus increase every turn by 20%. This encourages players to bias their strategy towards owning continents and not to rely too much on cards.

The game is shown in Figure 9-2 and Figure 9-3. In step 1, Player C attacks Player A. In step 2, Player A attacks the mixture of smaller players in North America and expands into that continent. Remember, each move has an impact on the resources of a player who has made a bold move. It is quite likely that at the end of a move, Player A will be weaker than he desires. This may be enough incentive for others to attack him immediately. As you may expect, this is very common. BOMS graph captures this phenomenon very nicely. In this game Player B takes advantage of Player A's weakness in step 3. Player A's bold move has led to his death! In step 4, Player C follows suit and attacks Player B, who is naturally slightly weaker.

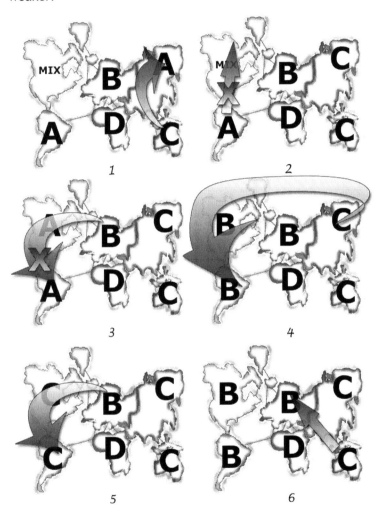

Figure 9-2. Game 1. Steps 1-6.

This moment is critical. B has to make a decision. He can respond to C or get D involved in a conflict. While everyone has been fighting, D has been peacefully stockpiling armies. In step 5, B decides to respond to C instead. This, as it will be seen, is the beginning of the end. In step 6, C retaliates. At this point, B and C are engaged in a war of attrition. Timing it well, in step 7, D decides to show the world what it means to be patient. He invades both B and C, reducing their power. He does not kill anyone in particular, but manages to make C very weak. In step 8, B (again out of revenge or some other emotional feeling) decides to kill C and then attack D. Unfortunately, it is already too late. B is no match for D. Eventually Player D emerges as the world conquer.

In this game Player B and C ignored the existence of Player D for a long time and carried on with their retaliating moves. This

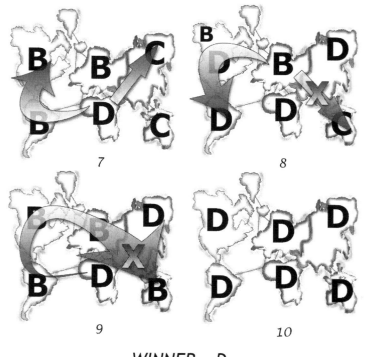

WINNER = D

Figure 9-3. Game 1. Steps 7-10.

cost them their lives. Player D was smart enough to attack both players. If he attacked only one, he could have easily initiated a war of attrition with that particular player and let the third player grow. That could have been fatal.

This example clearly shows that the player who fights less, wins in the end.

9.2.3   Game 2: Save it Up and Spend it Wisely

The rules for this game are similar to the previous game except that the continents grow by 10% every turn. The game is shown in Figure 9-4 to Figure 9-6.

Initially the game is very crowded, though soon a number of major players emerge. In step 1, Player C kills Player B. In step 2, E conquers Australia and eliminates C's foothold. In the next major move, C decides to kill F in step 3. This proves to be fatal. C has been constantly making major moves and is now weak. A takes advantage of this opportunity and invades C in step 4. Meanwhile, D has been collecting armies without getting into major conflicts.

He makes his move and invades E and captures Australia in step 5. C is now paying the price of making too many bold moves too quickly. E goes for the kill in step 6 and C is eliminated. E then attacks D. However, this is not going to save E. He is too weak to compete with others. A attacks E in step 7 followed by D's attack in step 8 which leads to E's elimination.

Now, the battle is between A and D. So far, A has resided in three continents and is expanding to the forth. D, however, started from a corner of Asia and only recently managed to get Australia. Although Player D has been following a non-violence strategy, he has been slow to prepare for the end-game scenario. He has saved himself from getting into conflicts, but has been unable to find a good source from which to acquire armies. Player A on the other hand has been successful in doing just that. In general there are two ways to collect armies: by not spending them or by acquiring them. Correct execution of a balanced strategy is the real challenge. Armies are just like money. The trick is to get the balance right, just as one tries to in real life.

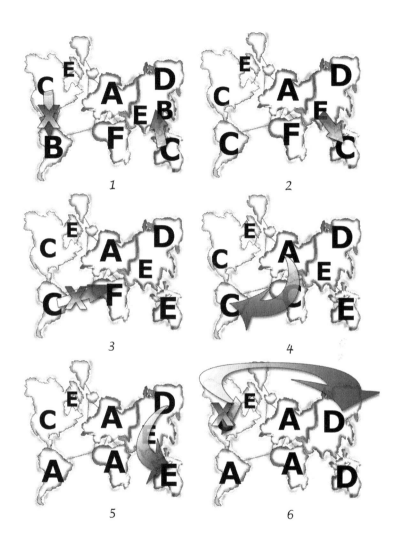

Figure 9-4. *Game 2. Steps 1-6.*

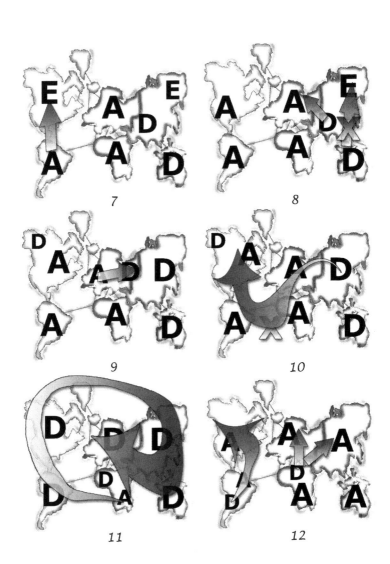

Figure 9-5. Game 2. Steps 7-12.

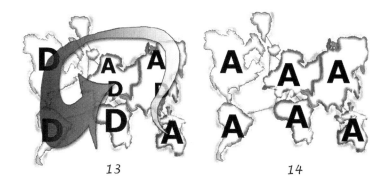

13   14

WINNER = A

Figure 9-6. Game 2. Steps 13-14.

9.2.4   Game 3: Gently Does It

In online games, from time to time, a political battle sets the pace of the game. These particular games are extremely exciting to watch, let along to play. Currently, communication in online Risk games is carried out via a chatbox, which means players talk to each other with short text messages, similar to SMS. Each particular online community has its own vocabulary set and in-house acronyms. Knowing them is critical for anyone who desires to avoid bad form and wants to evade being named a newbie!

Political battles take place over a number of short sentences and are sometime easy to miss, especially considering all the textual noise that is communicated over the course of a game. When political negotiations take place, you can almost guess the course of the game from that point onwards and predict which player is going to win. The following game is a typical example of a political situation.

The game is shown in Figure 9-7 to Figure 9-9. The rules for this game are similar to Game 1.

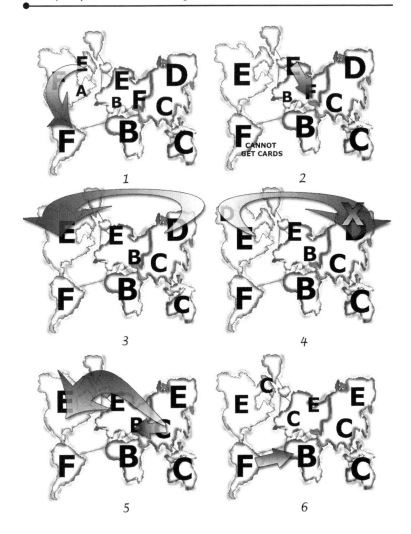

Figure 9-7. Game 3. Steps 1-6.

As before, the game is initially a crowded place. In step 1, E attempts to clean up his North American continent from other players. After a few turns of insignificant moves, E makes a very interesting move. As it can be seen on the map, F has South America and a foothold in Europe. E attacks this foothold in step 2, and effectively eliminates F's armies outside of South

America. F is now in deep trouble. He is surrounded by two continents, both of which want to protect their home continents at all costs. He can no longer get cards without major battles. F is effectively *card locked*. Although he might be doomed himself, his decision can have a huge impact on the rest of the game.

In step 3, D attacks E. In step 4, E retaliates and kills D. Influenced by some unknown desire, C suddenly decides to attack both B and E simultaneously in step 5. He goes all the way from Australia to North America!

E has become weaker. F is glad that E is no longer a strong threat. He takes this as an opportunity and attacks B in step 6. He uses his hard-earned cards to heavily fortify his only two borders. In step 7, E attempts to get back his continent from C. In step 8, B retaliates and gets his continent back from F.

The four-player game has gone into a cycle where each pair are engaged in a war of attrition. The game is slowed down and players are starting to get restless. They reckon that Player F's inability to expand and make bold moves is the cause. He is also heavily fortified which makes it costly for others to make bold moves against him. Everyone feels vulnerable.

At this point a political debate ensues which is very amusing. First, a number of players start to complain about the pace of the game. They want results after all. Everyone wants to win and they always want to win quickly. After a few exchanges, players collectively decide that this must be Player F's fault. Poor Player F tries to convince them that he has no other choice. Other players increase the pressure. Eventually, all other players decide that Player F must make a move and attack. Unfortunately, this forces F to make a decision between attacking E or B. All other players are now heavily engaged in suggesting who he should attack. Of course E and B want to save their own neck. It all comes down to the fourth player: C. C thinks an attack on B is beneficial to him. Upon discovery of this, E encourages C in his thoughts! The end result is that two players are aggressively encouraging F to attack B as opposed to E.

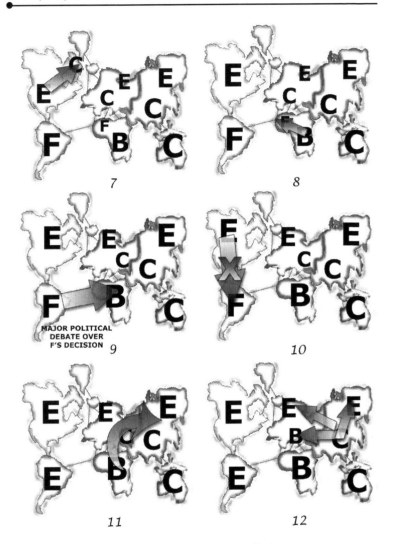

Figure 9-8. Game 3. Steps 7-12.

Eventually F gives in under the huge pressure. He chooses to invade B in step 9. At this point everyone's fate is sealed, though having been in the heat of the action, they may not have realised it themselves.

After F's move, without hesitation, Player E attacks Player F, who is now vulnerable on two fronts. Player F is killed in step 10.

B, in an inefficient move attacks C and E in step 11. He does not achieve much by doing this. C takes advantage of the situation and attacks B and E in step 12. E responds in step 13. B gets killed in step 14 by C. Despite the reward, this proves too costly for C, who eventually gets eliminated in step 15 by all conquering E.

C's insistence on F's choice was his own downfall. B proved to be incapable of making a difference. If F had invaded E, C could have won the game. Therefore, C could have won the game by politics and not by force.

Player E, on the other hand played a great diplomatical game. He initiated the whole crisis by limiting Player F's access to the rest of the world. By doing this he prepared the scene for his next move. A few turns later, when the pressure was on his victim, he managed to encourage another player to indirectly help him, almost at his own expense. This is a classic confirmation of Sun Tzu's wisdom: *"Every battle has been won before it has been fought"*. It is *literally* true in this case.

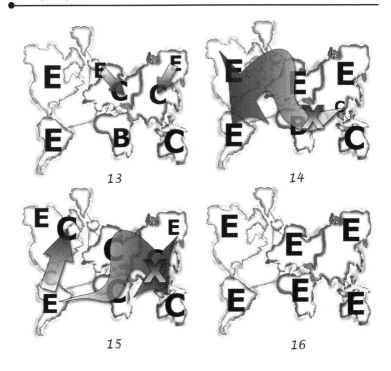

WINNER = E

Figure 9-9. Game 3. Steps 13-16.

10 Scenarios and solutions

"History will be kind to me for I intend to write it."

Winston Churchill

The purpose of this chapter is to show you a number of scenarios and various winning strategies when confronted with different situations. Learning by example is always very effective.

The scenarios presented here have been carefully designed to reflect different aspects of the game, especially in those situations where many solutions may lead to victory. They also reflect common situations in a typical game of Risk. For each scenario a number of popular solutions are given. Some of these solutions are inspired from the Risk community who kindly contributed on the dedicated website for this book.

Each scenario is numbered and each solution is tagged with the following syntax:

[Scenario Number]. [Solution Number]

Hence, *1.B* is solution *B* to scenario *1*.

For all of these scenarios assume that cards will be cashed at 4,6,8,10,12,... and that continent bonuses stay constant during the game. Figure 10-1 shows the key to the names of players used in this chapter.

Figure 10-1. Scenario 1. Playing as White.

10.1 Scenario 1: Playing as Europe

The History

Suppose you are *White* and it is your turn. The map is shown in Figure 10-2 and the history of the game is shown in Table 10-1.

There is a treaty between White and Black. White will not attack North Africa, Egypt and East Africa from Southern Europe, Eastern Europe and Middle East, and in return Black will not attack Southern Europe, Eastern Europe and the Ukraine. This treaty lasts until only White and Black are left in the game.

Your Options

Considering that Grey is next and that he might have a combination of cards, and that Stripe is getting very powerful, what would be the best strategy for White to follow? What sort of diplomacy would you try? Would you attempt to make a treaty with Grey for Greenland? Alternatively, would you attack Grey while he is weak, but withstand his subsequent move next turn?

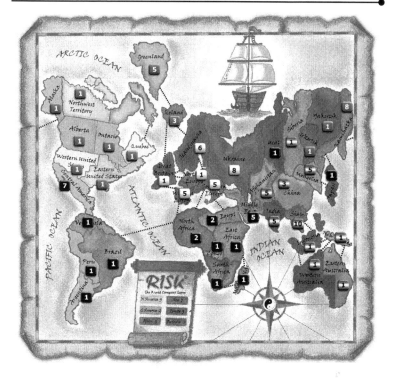

Figure 10-2. *Scenario 1. Playing as White.*

	Turns			
	1	**2**	**3**	**4**
Player	Grey	Black	Stripe	White (To play)
Cashing	Didn't cash	Cashed cards: Got 6	Cashed cards: Got 8	Gets 10 if cashed
Cards Left	4	1	1	4 and has a combination

Table 10-1. *History of Scenario 1. Each turn is a column.*

10.1.1 Analysis of Scenario 1

As you may recall, in order to systematically analyse a problem, you can follow the five P's rule described in Section 3.3. You start with understating your *Position* and your *Problem* and then explore your *Possibilities*. Then you select your *Proposal* based on its *Price*, which means you select an option that is most promising to you. The following analysis is based on this principle.

Situation Analysis (Position and Problem):

Here are the risks:

- Direct threat from Grey. However, he is more interested in getting his continent.

- Black may break the treaty and attack you (Very unlikely at this point).

- Stripe may attack you, just for the sake of stopping you from getting the bonus and becoming more powerful than him over time.

- Should avoid two fronts at all costs.

Stripe seems to be an isolationist. Black seems to be an expansionist. It is difficult to predict Grey's strategy.

Possibilities:

Now that you have identified your position and the risks, a number of possibilities exist:

- *Invade Grey.* South is secure due to the treaty with Africa. Asia is a hard-to-get continent. Attacking Grey is a suitable option.

- *Invade Stripe.* Stripe is getting more powerful every turn. Something should be done about this before it is too late.

- *Invade Black.* Black has two continents already. He is on his way to conquering North America. His success in North America will lead him to global victory. This should be avoided at all costs. The treaty with Black may have to be broken.

- *Slow Growth.* The treaty with Black should be honoured. The only options left are to expand to Asia or North America. Conquering the entire continent of Asia is almost impossible, though getting as many countries there as possible is desirable. North America seems to be a good option too.

These *possibilities* are explored in detail below.

10.1.2 Solution 1.A: Invade Grey

The solution is shown in Figure 10-3. First you can attempt to make a treaty with Stripe for your eastern border. Thus, Stripe will not attack the Ukraine or Southern Europe and you will not attack Ural, Afghanistan or the Middle East. This effectively lets Stripe conquer Asia. So you are giving something in return for the treaty. Grey does not have much power to be threatening, so no one will listen to him and his propaganda will not work.

Equally, Black cannot brainwash Stripe since the offer for Stripe is lucrative. If he accepts your offer, he might have to invade Africa anyway. Black does not want that to happen at all. Hence, your offer will most likely be accepted by Stripe.

Your southern and eastern borders are now protected. You can shift your focus to North America. Meanwhile, Black is also attempting to expand to North America too. This leads to two players fighting against one: Grey will have no chance! Eventually he will be wiped out, though it is difficult to predict who is going to get the cards.

On the other side of map, Stripe will be busy conquering Asia. Black knows that he has to prevent this or he will lose. Stripe can always attempt to get the Middle East and threaten two African territories from only one. This is bad news for Black: he has to balance the border and place armies in two territories. Over time Stripe will be able to break into Africa. Thus, if Black is smart, he should never let go of the Middle East or it will be the end of him.

Therefore, there will be a conflict based around the Middle East between Stripe and Black. This will put you in a great position since Black has two fronts against Stripe and Grey. You will be more successful in the battle of North America in comparison with Black or Stripe. Eventually Black will collapse. Once Black is gone, you can easily expand to South America and end up with a 5 + 5 + 2 = 12 bonus for continents in comparison with the 2 + 7 = 9 bonus that Stripe might get.

It is always difficult to guess the end-game scenario as cards play a very important role (even more important than continents). However, given the current course of the game, generally speaking, this seems to be a very good move to make.

Figure 10-3. Scenario 1, Solution A.

10.1.3 Solution 1.B: Invade Stripe

This solution is shown in Figure 10-4. You can negotiate with Grey to get Iceland and then make a ceasefire on that border. At this point you have secured Europe, which gets you five extra armies. Grey will be interested in this ceasefire since he can focus on getting his continent sorted and focus on Central America. Grey can cash his cards in on the next turn and use a single front to build up against South America.

Figure 10-4. Scenario 1, Solution B.

Now that your back is secure, you can focus on Stripe. You would *honour* the treaty with Black. Thus, your focus would be on Asia. You put all of your troops in the Ukraine and begin the slow process of weakening Stripe. You get five bonus armies, he gets two.

The Grey threat in Asia is likely to disappear. Grey will be busy with his continent and his best move is to expand into South America. If Grey decides not to leave, he will be confronted with you and Stripe simultaneously. Since he already has a front with Black in South America, it will be difficult for him to sustain his position.

10.1.4 Solution 1.C: Invade Black

This solution is shown in Figure 10-5. The key to a good move in Risk is to make everyone think they are in a good position, while at the same time you slowly build up your forces, unnoticed. You can get Black and Grey into a war of attrition by propaganda and diplomatic efforts. While they become weaker, you can slowly grow, and at the right time, take them all.

Similar to the previous option, you will agree to a treaty with Grey over Greenland. You will cash your cards and reinforce. You would slowly accumulate armies. When you are ready, you initiate a diplomatic move by encouraging Stripe to attack Grey in Kamchatka and potentially North America. You argue that Grey's power should be controlled before it gets out of hand.

Figure 10-5. Scenario 1, Solution C.

In short, this is the situation: Black and Grey are engaged in a war. Grey is under attack from Stripe and ends up with two fronts. If you start a new front with Black, they would both have two fronts. After a while they will certainly collapse, which leaves you and Stripe in the game. Make sure to have an advantage over Stripe to win the game.

To get there, you need to *break* the treaty with Black! (Things you have to do in Risk!). The fight with Black will be slow and could cost you. Your aim is to get his continent and eventually his cards. Just make sure that Stripe does not ruin your plans by an attack when you are at your weakest.

People who choose this move usually believe that alliances should only be used when convenient! Whether this is wise is yet to be seen.

10.1.5 Solution 1.D: Slow Growth

This solution is shown in Figure 10-6. Similar to the previous options, you secure Iceland by engaging with Grey.

You will cash in the cards and divide them between your borders. At this point Black is busy fighting with Grey. However, Stripe is in desperate need of additional continents. His best choice is to go for Africa since it is small and easily reachable. A few turns later, Stripe may invade the Middle East (probably winning) and move his troops to that conflict area. You can then *slowly* grow in Asia getting one country after the other. You will make sure that Stripe does not get too upset, so he can carry on his assault on Black and leave you alone. In fact you will passively encourage him to do so. The problem is you cannot actively talk about it as it could upset Black.

Black will end up with two fronts and will eventually collapse as a result. At this point the situation is as follows:

- *Stripe* gets Africa and may go for South America as well, either for the continent or for Black's cards.

- *Grey* owns North America, and would probably like to get South America as Stripe's troops are most probably very thin there.

- *Black* is eliminated.

Figure 10-6. Scenario 1, Solution D.

At this moment, both Grey and Stripe are probably exhausted as a result of a long war with Black. They must both be vulnerable and thin. *This is the chance you have been waiting for!* You will attack Grey from Kamchatka and Iceland and aim to kill Grey in one swift move. If you succeeded and get his cards, you may end up in a much better situation than Stripe.

10.1.6 Your Choice

Position, Problem, and *Possibilities* have now been explored. With a trade-off analysis one can choose the best option. Every time you assume that Player A will do X at a specific moment, you introduce an unknown probability. Your guess and instinct can be extremely helpful in deciding which option to choose. Remember that sometimes you just cannot take the risk because if it backfires, it could be disastrous for you. Always consider what can go wrong, and whether you can handle it or not.

These solutions were presented to the Risk community for a vote on the best option. Figure 10-7 shows the results at the time of publication. In this scenario, solution 1.A was the most popular choice.

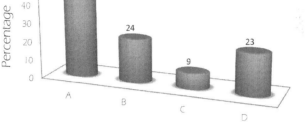

Popular Solution for Scenario 1

Figure 10-7. *Votes collected for different solutions for Scenario 1. Based on 378 votes.*

10.2 Scenario 2: Playing as Australia

In this scenario (shown in Figure 10-8) you are playing as *White* and your objective is to expand and conquer the world. You have Australia under your belt and feel that you are in a very good position as no one can threaten you. Hence, you are playing the classic *isolationist strategy* of *slow build-up*. In this turn you need to decide which direction you want to go and how you want to influence the game. You have also been lucky as you have a combination with your three cards. Table 10-2 shows the card distribution.

No one has made any treaties in this game. Everyone wants to protect his own continent. However, the situation is unstable as players will start expanding soon. Cards are yet to be cashed. The number of armies entering the game is anyone's guess.

If Grey succeeds in getting America, he will end up in a strong position, something you may not like! Grey and Stripe are most likely to collide. Black is already the most powerful and gets more than everyone else every turn. He is also practically your neighbour. What would you do?

Figure 10-8. Scenario 2. Playing as White.

	Turns			
	1	*2*	*3*	*4*
Player	Grey	Stripe	Black	White (To play)
Cashing	Didn't cash	Didn't cash	Didn't cash	Gets 10 if cashed
Cards Left	3	3	3	3 and has a combination

Table 10-2. History of Scenario 2. Each turn is a column.

10.2.1 Analysis of Scenario 2

Situation Analysis (Position and Problem):

Players may have the following thoughts:

- *Stripe.* Stripe is in trouble. Making a truce with Black at the North Africa/Brazil border seems unlikely. Black does not have any reason to cooperate. Stripe's best bet is to make a truce with Grey at the Central America/Venezuela border. This allows him to concentrate on Europe. For Stripe, South America might be a lost cause with strong opponents on both borders, but it might hold long enough before he can establish a new stronghold in Europe.

- *Grey.* Grey will focus on North America initially. It is doubtful that he will have any interest in expanding to Asia. Thus, he is left with either expanding to Europe or South America. They both belong to Stripe. He has a choice of agreeing to a truce with Stripe at the Central America/Venezuela border, but that will only last as long as it benefits Grey. Even if he makes a successful treaty with Stripe, once a fight breaks out (say in Europe), the chances are that Grey and Stripe will go into a *full-scale war* with each other soon.

- *Black.* Black also sees Stripe at every border and the two are going to fight it out sooner rather than later.

The Black player may engage in diplomacy with Grey over the situation once Stripe has been eliminated (Stripe may not like this conversation at all however!).

Possibilities:

Your options are:

- *Invade Europe.* Since Stripe and Black may be fighting each other, Europe is left undefended as they both become too weak to hold anything. Europe is therefore an interesting choice.

- *Slow expansion to Asia.* Black and Stripe will be busy fighting each other. Grey will be busy defending his continent. He might be interested in expanding to Europe or South America. Either way, no one will be interested in Asia and it will be yours to claim.

- *Invade Africa.* This might seem like a naïve idea. The purpose of the fight between Black and Stripe is to get the continents. By entering this conflict, you only get to be attacked, with no immediate hope of actually securing the continent. Both of them will be fighting to the death and it will be much better to stay out of their way. This is not a wise option to consider.

10.2.2 Solution 2.A: Invade Europe

This solution is shown in Figure 10-9. Grey will be busy with North America, taking Greenland, and building up forces to the south, as Asia is currently unconquerable.

Stripe prefers to avoid a corrosive war over Europe. Stripe is unlikely to win Europe as both Grey and Black will have all the motivation to prevent it. Thus, Stripe may get into a long conflict with Grey over the North and South American continents and is basically in a perilous position.

Black will see little value in attacking you since there is nothing to gain. You also have large defensive armies, which is another deterrent. Black can also attack Stripe as he is becoming the weakest target with most reward.

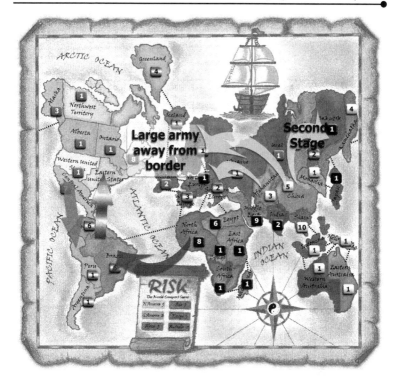

Figure 10-9. Scenario 2, Solution A.

To make sure Grey will not become a threat, you can initiate a war of attrition between Grey and Stripe. This conflict is far away from you and will keep Grey's armies busy. As a result, Stripe may end up with two fronts. If you invade Europe while Stripe is in a conflict with Grey and Black, he will not be able to respond to your invasion.

Hopefully, you would appear dangerous enough to confront but not enough of a threat, hence best avoided.

Thus, in this round you need to solidify your situation. Aim to appear weak whilst halting Stripe's ambitions in Europe. You can wait for the next turn to cash in as you are in no immediate danger, and it is beneficial to appear weaker. While invading Europe, make sure that you do not expand too quickly. However, by refusing to cash the cards, and ending up with four cards in the next round, you would look *dangerous enough*.

If all goes according to plan, Europe should be relatively low on peoples' agendas and shy on armies. Most of the focus will be on South America and a conflict should have broken out, heavily weakening Stripe, Grey, and potentially Black. Meanwhile you will be relatively unharmed, maybe minus a few easily conquerable territories.

Depending on the outcome of this conflict, you can either decide to hold Europe and conquer Asia or hold Africa. Even if you have conquered Europe, you are still better off if you leave it for Asia. The reason is that if you get Australia and Europe, no one is left with any territories to fight over except those that are White! Not nice at all. Leaving Europe instead gives them something worth chasing after (the carrot) whilst you can still limit access routes and play a significant political role in the game.

10.2.3 Solution 2.B: Slow Expansion

This solution is shown in Figure 10-10. Considering that Stripe and Black find each other everywhere they look, a conflict is likely. The same situation could happen with Stripe and Grey. Stripe could be eliminated if he ends up fighting two enemies at once. Once he is out, Grey and Black may make a deal not to attack each other at the Iceland/Greenland border and/or the North Africa/Brazil border. This is bad news for you as it means they will divert their armies directly in your direction.

Hence, *you should be politically active* to make sure this does not take place, even though you have adapted an isolationist strategy. To defuse the crisis you can say, "It is unfair to decide how you want to divide the world once Stripe is eliminated. You (Grey and Black) should just get on with the fight and then deal with this later." Of course, you hope that by that time a fight has broken between them. You hope to get them to turn on each other.

Thus, your aim is to get Grey and Black to start a war of attrition. While they are at war, you should grow enough to become a world superpower with access to almost all continents and a strong political voice.

Figure 10-10. Scenario 2, Solution B.

You start your move by expanding in Asia, but your aim is not to take hold of it straight away. Instead you want to be in a position of power, so when the time comes (such as when Stripe is eliminated), make a move to secure your place in Asia. Meanwhile having large armies next to Grey and Black's continents means that you mean trouble and that you should not be underestimated.

In any case, you should avoid getting into war with both Black and Grey once Stripe is gone.

10.2.4 Your Choice

These two options are both very interesting and have a high chance of success if executed correctly. The votes given for the solution by the Risk community are shown in Figure 10-11. It is a close call!

Popular Solution for Scenario 2

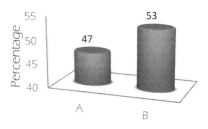

Figure 10-11. Votes collected for different solutions for Scenario 2. Based on 194 votes.

10.3 Scenario 3: Playing as South America

In this scenario (shown in Figure 10-12) you are playing as *Black*. This is the early stage of a five-player game. Players have selected their continents and are ready to start the battle. Everyone is at risk. Unfortunately, Black was the last player and was left to choose South America. At this point in time, everyone has the same number of armies.

What you already know:

- The Edge player is very experienced, and looks at the long-term scenario. He is a *Negotiator*.

- The Stripe player is new to the game and may make mistakes later on (at least that is what you hope for). He is an *Amateur*.

- The White player intends to grow slowly. He is an *Isolationist*.

- The Grey player is aggressive and unpredictable. He is known to have stabbed people in the back in previous games. He is an *Expansionist*.

Figure 10-12. Scenario 3. Playing as Black.

No one has any cards. What would be your overall strategy? What sort of tactics would you choose to survive in the short term? What sort of diplomacy or alliances would you like to have, given the profile of your opponents?

10.3.1 Analysis of Scenario 3

Situation Analysis (Position and Problem):

The map shows that:

- *White.* He will start to grow slowly over Asia. At any rate he will not be a threat until the latter stages of the game.

- *Edge.* He has two main choices: To go for Europe, or South America. He is an experienced player. He will think hard before initiating an attack. Since he is a negotiator, he may listen to your offers of treaties. There is a possibility of getting a treaty over the Brazil border.

- *Stripe*. Initially he will be interested in conquering Europe. Once he has achieved this, he may not have enough experience to know what to do next. Edge may have to keep an eye on him as he would not want a strong neighbour next door.

- *Grey*. Since he is unpredictable, there is no chance of making an agreement with him over Central America. Hence, there will inevitably be a war taking place between you and Grey. Controlling Grey seems to be the key to success.

Possibilities:

Your options are:

- *Eliminate Grey*. Due to Grey's unpredictability, his elimination is an attractive option. Getting North America is also to your benefit. Dealing with Edge remains an issue.

- *Invade Edge*. Instead of focusing on Grey, invade Africa since it is a smaller continent. The problem is that even if this is carried out successfully, Grey is still untamed. As long as it is not dealt with properly, he will remain a threat. Edge is also experienced and can get everyone to attack you. This is not a good option.

- *Growth in Asia or Europe*. Secure South America and do not fight Edge or Grey. Instead focus on Asia or Europe. The problem is that since your empire is divided in half, supporting South America becomes a difficult task if it is suddenly invaded. It is too high a risk to take.

10.3.2 Solution 3.A: Eliminate Grey

Killing Grey is your main aim (shown in Figure 10-13). Once he is gone, you have a much more stable region. However, you do not necessarily want to fight him alone. First, you need to engage in a diplomatic exchange with Edge over the Brazil border. You would make an attempt to have a treaty there. Edge could be interested since he could simply focus on a bigger prize such as Europe.

Once your African border is secure you can concentrate your entire army on one front. Grey will be in trouble. He does not have a continent and has three borders to protect as he has yet to claim the continent. Your expansion in North America can continue until you get the whole continent. You would then be in a very good position to lead the game.

There is always a risk associated with any deal. Putting some deterrent armies in Brazil can offset Edge's temptation to break the treaty.

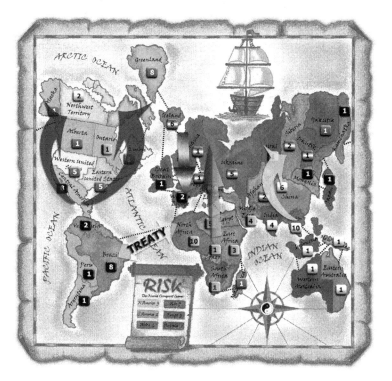

Figure 10-13. Scenario 3, Solution A.

Getting North America can weaken your position. This is a critical moment. You need to offset any potential attack with propaganda since that is all you have. Just hope that Stripe and Edge will be fighting each other and will be busy enough to ignore you. You can always *advise* Stripe on his moves, so he becomes a stronger opponent to Edge. However, this needs to be executed in a delicate way so as not to upset Edge.

If Edge starts to become a problem, put your armies in Iceland instead of Greenland. This does not cost you much, but you have *nailed* Europe. Furthermore you can always go and nail North Africa if Edge starts a full-scale war with you.

Do not forget about White though. If White decides to attack you, use diplomacy to bring his evil actions to the attention of other world leaders so he can be dealt with.

10.3.3 Solution 3.B: Growth in Asia or Europe

Another strategy (shown in Figure 10-14) is to secure South America and then concentrate elsewhere. You may still go ahead and make a treaty with Edge, as a viable treaty with Grey is unlikely. So you can leave a large number of armies in Central America and then start building up in Europe.

The problem, however, is that your armies in Europe can put you in direct conflict with Edge, something you would like to avoid. This could also destabilise your treaty.

If you end up in a war with Edge, Grey may decide to attack you (since he is expansionist). As your continent is very lucrative to him, he will always be interested in it.

Considering the above, it seems that the risks are too high to adopt such a strategy.

Figure 10-14. Scenario 3, Solution B.

10.3.4 The Choice

In view of the choices presented here, it seems that elimination of Grey is the key factor for your success and more important than any other factor. Solution A is the preferred option.

10.4 Scenario 4: Avoid Being the Strongest!

In this scenario (shown in Figure 10-15) you are playing as *Black* against other *experienced* players. You have worked hard to get to a position of power and are now the most powerful nation in the world. You have been getting fruits of your effort and as a result have ended up with a well-fortified continent.

You made an early decision about your overall strategy and decided to expand through South America. As a result you approached Stripe and made a treaty over the Greenland/Iceland border. Stripe proved to be hard to negotiate with. He forced you to accept a time limit on the treaty. The contract says that you would not attack each other for five turns over that border.

You think:

- Stripe seems to be interested in expanding to Africa

Figure 10-15. *Scenario 4. Playing as Black.*

- White has a very good strategic point in the Middle East and can threaten both Africa and Europe from one country. Hence, both Stripe and Grey are nervous about this situation.

- Grey is constantly under pressure from you and does not feel comfortable.

You carried on accumulating armies for the invasion of South America. You are also in possession of cards as shown in Table 10-3.

Hence, this is your chance to take advantage of your early rise to power. The world order is about to change very soon as others start to cash in their cards. You have an important decision to make: To attack South America in this turn or not. If you cash in and invade, you can probably conquer South America easily and end up with a large army at your border. However, can you withstand the backlash? You need to make sure not to end up as the absolute most powerful because other players may all suddenly gang up against you. This can lead to your elimination, and you obviously want to avoid this at all costs.

	Turns			
	1	*2*	*3*	*4*
Player	Grey	Stripe	White	Black (To play)
Cashing	Didn't cash	Didn't cash	Didn't cash	Gets 6 if cashed
Cards Left	4	4	4	3 and has a combination

Table 10-3. History of Scenario 4. Each turn is a column.

What kind of diplomacy would you use to deceive them? Would you wait a bit longer? In this case how do you think the new world order will shape up? Can you assure them that they will not be the next victims? Can you count on Stripe not to break the treaty? How can you prevent others making treaties against you?

10.4.1 Analysis of Scenario 4

Situation Analysis (Position and Problem):

As it can be seen from the map:

- *Grey.* Has just got two continents and probably will be interested in securing them before he expands further. He wants to take North America, but has to watch out for White in the Middle East.

- *White.* Fortress Australia is working well, though he is in desperate need of expansion. Apart from slow expansion in Asia, Africa seems to be a good choice, but that depends on Europe's move.

- *Stripe.* Getting as powerful as you, he has his back secure against Iceland (at least for a while). Africa is a very good choice for expansion. If he can get that far, he can expand to South America too.

In the next turn, all other players may cash cards. This will introduce a large number of armies into the game. If any attack is initiated now, the cards will be used to counter it. Otherwise the chances are that Grey will use his cards to fortify, Stripe will prepare for an invasion and White will simply invade Africa.

Possibilities:

Your options are:

- *Slow expansion in Asia.* Fortify the current position without cashing cards as you are already powerful. Then start to expand slowly in Asia by getting more countries.

- *Invade Europe.* Break the treaty with Europe and invade him. Considering all the effort that went into securing at least one border, it is almost pointless to break the treaty now. There is nothing to gain. Stripe is powerful. This is not a good option.

- *Invade South America.* Do this before the time limit on the contract is over. Grey is vulnerable now, but will use the cards and you could end up in a war of attrition.

10.4.2 Solution 4.A: Expansion in Asia

This solution (shown in Figure 10-16) is a conservative approach. Since everyone might collect extra armies, you have the chance to wait and cash in after them. You are already powerful and do not want to appear too strong.

Expand slowly in Asia. Meanwhile, others consolidate their armies and secure their positions. Your aim is to wait for the opportunity to invade South America. Wait for the trigger which can happen if someone attacks Grey. Your South American invasion will create two fronts for Grey and put him in big trouble. Hopefully, this trigger happens in two turns, so

Figure 10-16. Scenario 4, Solution A.

you can cash your cards with the maximum number of armies and use them in the invasion.

Make sure you get the continent in a single turn and leave enough armies at the border to handle the counterattack. The good news is that you do not increase the number of your borders after the invasion.

Watch out for Stripe as he could break the treaty. One way to de-risk this is to eliminate Grey (if possible) and immediately reinforce the Greenland border with potential new armies collected from Grey's cards (if you get any). You do not have to necessarily attack Europe at this time. Just a deterrent, so he does not get any ideas. In any case, avoid ending up with two fronts. Alternatively, leave Africa for White so he can get his prize for getting rid of Grey. You can then focus on either Asia or Europe. If Europe proves to be a difficult and unpredictable opponent, do not hesitate. Once you have your borders relatively secure, invade him (by then, the five turns limit is probably long over). Keep the initiate to yourself. Attack is the best form of defence.

10.4.3 Solution 4.B: Invade South America

Instead of invading South America a few turn later to get the whole continent, the other option is to invade immediately as shown in Figure 10-17. However, even though you can have a total of eighteen armies in Central America before the invasion, you may still be unable to withstand the counterattack from Brazil. In particular, if Grey cashes his cards, he will be even stronger. If he does not have a combination with his cards in the next turn after your invasion, it will be your lucky day! You can reinforce yourself to even contain his attack with his cards a turn later.

However, you cannot count on his lack of luck! A safe option is to break him. Instead of getting the South American continent, get Venezuela, then Brazil and North Africa to rob him of bonuses. Next turn, you have two choices:

- If he has cards, he will certainly use them against you. All you need to do is to not let him enter North America.

- If he does not have cards, get the remaining countries of South America and seal it!

You should aim to encourage others to attack Grey so he ends up with two fronts. Stripe in particular will be interested in Africa. However, you need to make sure you can contain Stripe once you have eliminated Grey. Use diplomacy to get White and Stripe to engage in a war so that you will end up as the most powerful.

Figure 10-17. Scenario 4, Solution B.

10.4.4 The Choice

Your choice depends greatly on how much you can trust Stripe. If you know he will not break the deal, an immediate invasion (Solution B) seems to be your best choice. You have the initiative and the choice to carry out your plan in smaller steps.

This is a calculated risk. If your opponent does not have a card combination, your move will greatly benefit you.

Waiting for a few turns only makes it more difficult as everyone may fortify, though it lets you fortify against Stripe as well. If Stripe has a history of backstabbing, fortifying against him is the preferred move (Solution A).

If you have never played with Stripe before, or you cannot guess his move, take the risk and choose Solution B. Fingers crossed, it may all work out in the end!

10.5 Scenario 5: Stuck in Asia!

In this scenario (shown in Figure 10-18) you are playing as *Black*. The card distribution is shown in Table 10-4.

Figure 10-18. Scenario 5. Playing as Black.

This scenario is slightly different from the previous one. The challenge is to examine the problem from all angles and find every player's optimum move.

History

You were originally in Africa, but decided that it has become too competitive. Thinking that by residing in Africa you would get squeezed between Grey and White, you left hoping to get lucky elsewhere.

You went to Asia and adopted a strategy of slow, concentrated growth. All you wanted was not to get kicked out of the game.

Meanwhile, everyone was busy getting their continents secure. Edge just managed to get his continent. Stripe plans to get Europe in one turn. White and Grey already have their continents and are aggressively competing over Africa.

Grey made a clever move earlier on by making a treaty with Edge over Central America. They agreed not to attack each other over that border. He has since counted on this deal and has moved all his armies to a single front, which is helping him greatly to fight in Africa.

All players are quite experienced.

	Turns				
	1	*2*	*3*	*4*	*5*
Player	Edge	Stripe	White	Grey	Black
Cashing	Didn't cash	Didn't cash	Didn't cash	Didn't cash	Gets 6 if cashed
Cards Left	3	3	3	3	3, but has no combination

Table 10-4. History of Scenario 5. Each turn is a column.

To thoroughly analyse this scenario it is best if the game is played out from everybody's point of view. Once everyone's best moves are known, it is possible to work out how the game will progress.

Questions

- *Playing as Black.* Edge's move may have a significant effect on the game. Can you predict what he will do? What would you do about it as Black? Would you carry on growing, or initiate an attack to control the game? How do you keep them divided?

- *Playing as Edge.* Would you attack South America? What would you do about Black?

- *Playing as Stripe.* Who to make a deal with? What to do? Where to go? How about Black?

- *Playing as White.* Where to expand? Should you fight to the death to get Africa or give it up? What about the Black forces?

- *Playing as Grey.* Can you count on Edge? Is it worth it? Is it taking too much risk?

10.5.1 Analysis of Scenario 5

Situation Analysis (Position and Problem):

- *Edge.* Having secured his continents, he is interested in expanding and needs to decide where to expand. In the next turn, if he cashes cards, will end up with a large number of armies to place on the map. Should he break the deal (an immoral act) to get South America in one go, especially since Grey is already fighting White and his armies are busy elsewhere? Is Edge able to sleep at night with a clear conscience if he breaks the deal?

- *Stripe.* Is looking to get a deal with anyone, as he is in the middle of the world and is squeezed from every direction. Since Edge already has a deal with Black, he may be reluctant to make a new deal, especially if he plans to break the current one. No one owns Africa yet, so it is impossible to approach a clear owner.

- *White*. Is the most powerful and in a good defensive position. He needs to expand. His choices are: Africa, Europe, or Asia.

- *Grey*. Has counted too much on Edge, and feels vulnerable. At the same time he sees Africa as being within his grasp.

- *Black*. Is threatening everyone with the largest concentrated army on the map. Everyone could be a target. They all know that if Black grows, it will be a big problem in the future. No one is willing to do anything about it though. It is too costly for them to attack Black for no potential gain. In short they are all doomed. You, as Black, are exploiting this and slowly growing. There is only one problem. If they gang up against you, you will be out of the game in no time. You have to be sure to keep them divided indefinitely.

10.5.2 Solutions

Possibilities for each player are as follows:

Edge:

Edge's action depends greatly on his morals and whether he has a combination. It also depends on Black's move in his turn. Edge has the following choices:

1. *Break the deal.* With nineteen extra armies entering the game, Edge can easily conquer South America and withstand Grey's counterattack. It is also likely that Grey will simply give up South America to focus on Africa. Edge will be most vulnerable when South America is conquered. To reduce the chance of a backlash, he can offer a ceasefire to Grey after his attack and suggest a deal. However, Grey, having been stabbed in the back, may not be amused!

2. *Honour the deal.* Grey will be busy fighting with White. Edge can honour the deal and make it known to Grey

that despite the fact that he could have taken advantage of it, he has not. Hence, he is such a gentleman! Hoping that Grey will honour the deal too, Edge can concentrate on his other borders and fortify them knowing that he is accumulating armies more than anyone else and does not need to make a bold move yet. Eventually he can expand to Asia and slowly grow, and meanwhile watch Europe closely.

Stripe:

At this point in the game, Stripe's best choice seems to be getting Europe, securing it and slowly growing. It would be too early to engage with others. Making a deal with Edge (if it succeeds) is to his advantage, though Edge, who already has a deal with someone else, may benefit a lot more. Hence, in the long run, making a deal is not a wise move. Stripe should fortify against Black as much as he can. He should cash his cards if he has a combination.

White:

White is in a very strong position. His move depends on Edge's move. He has got two options:

1. If Edge attacks Grey, White can also enter the conflict and initiate a new front for Grey. Grey will eventually collapse and White is well placed to get Africa.

2. If Edge does not attack Grey, White can concentrate on fortifying his own position. Black is a direct threat which White should fortify against. He can move back his African armies to help with the Siam front against Black's threat.

Grey:

He has already made a decision to go for Africa while counting on Edge's morality. There is no going back. Based on Edge's move he has two options:

1. *If attacked by Edge.* In this case Grey is doomed. He can show the world how he despises Edge, but that will

not solve his problems. If Grey chooses revenge, he will be only weakening himself by fighting. It will be suicide. Instead, Grey can focus on Africa. In this case, he will end up competing with Edge, who has two continents. Edge is receiving more than twice the continental bonuses. Grey will soon be confronted with Edge again.

2. *Not attacked by Edge*. In this case, Grey can conquer Africa, especially if Black has already attacked White. He also needs to put a deterrent in Venezuela as a precaution.

Black:

Black is becoming an extreme threat. All other players are wary of him. Most vulnerable are White and Stripe. Black has four choices:

1. *Invade Europe*. In this case, Black can establish himself in Europe for good and plan to get a decent continent. However, Stripe will be fighting him to death. Unfortunately Black is not big enough to eliminate Stripe in one turn.

2. *Invade White*. Black can attack White and conquer Australia and have armies left to defend it. White will be squeezed between Grey and Black, though Black would need to expand from Australia when everyone else has secured larger continents. This move may be interesting initially, but may prove limiting as the game progresses.

3. *Grow even further*. Black can simply carry on with his current strategy and grow even more to become a larger threat. He can delay his bold move until after Edge has his chance to make a move and the world had settled into a more stable state.

4. *Wait and then Invade Africa*. Black also has an opportunity to wait one turn. If Grey had been invaded by Edge, Black can also enter Africa.

The preferred option for each player depends a lot on other player's choices. Black needs to lead the game as it is his move. This is his chance to get a continent. It will never be easy again to get Australia. Considering unknown issues in the game, it seems that his best choice is to take the risk and invade Australia. Then, it depends greatly on Edge's decision. Hopefully, it will all work out well in the end.

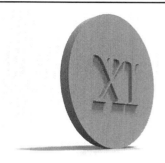

11 Final Remarks

"If you don't think little things make a difference, then you haven't shared a bed with a mosquito."

Michelle Walker

It is all about the detail. Get it right, and you will be successful. Get it wrong, and you will have endless issues to deal with. This book intends to cover the *details* and hopefully help you to achieve not only more in Risk, but also in life. Risk is a game with an infinite number of possibilities. It is abstract and enjoyable without complicated rules, while simultaneously letting you step into the mind of an emperor.

With Risk, you can learn a great deal about people and understand the mechanism of their behaviour. You can experiment with new skills in the game with peace of mind. If it goes wrong, it is not the end of the world. It is only a game after all. Thus, you can be more adventurous.

In any case, negotiation and knowing how to deal with other people is a crucial skill to master. William Glasser captures this concept very nicely with the following statement.

We Learn ...

10% ... of What We Read

20% ... of What We Hear

30% ... of What We See

50% ... of What We See and Hear

70% ... of What We Discuss With Others

80% ... of What We Experience Personally

95% ... of What We Teach Others

Your best bet is to keep practicing these skills on something until you get them right every time. Like many other skills such as driving or riding a bike, what you learn should eventually become second nature. Once you have stored these skills in your cerebrum, you can use them much more effectively when needed and apply them to the real world. Remember, what matters is to know the process of gaining skills. Once you know how to acquire key skills, you can always practice to get better at them. Albert Einstein beautifully illustrates this with:

> *"Education is what remains after one has forgotten what one has learned in school."*

Keep playing Risk or similar strategy games while considering the psychological aspects of human nature at all times. As a Risk player, you will be exposed to many issues found in everyday life in the course of a single game. Observe, respond, and learn. Analyse your moves to find out why the move you made did not quite go according to plan. Self-reflection is the key to success. Be honest with yourself and accept your weakness. Only then can you overcome your limitations and improve your *human-handling* techniques. Take responsibility for everything in life rather than blaming other people, players, obstacles, and luck. In short,

> *If you do not think you are the one who is responsible for the outcome of your actions, you will never learn anything new.*

And finally, there are only two rules for a successful Risk player:

1. Do not tell them everything you know.

2.

Ehsan Honary
May, 2007

Appendix A: Dice Odds

One of the most interesting aspects of Risk is that it incorporates chance. This makes the game much more realistic in comparison with predictable games such as chess. It demands strategies that can deal with the *concept of chance*, hence, the name of the game.

As you may know from the rules, attackers and defenders can choose how many dice they can throw. The number of dice used has an impact on the likelihood of winning as well as the potential number of armies put at risk. The question is how many dice one should throw and whether it is better to attack or defend. To answer this, you need to know the probability of each combination of dice throwing.

Table **A-1** shows these probabilities.

Major conclusions derived from the table are as follows:

- The more dice the attacker throws the more chances he has got of winning. This is similar for the defender too. Of course, more armies are at risk as well, though in the long run it is always beneficial to throw more dice. Hence, throw as many dice as you can.

- Considering the above, the majority of the battles are fought with the attacker throwing three dice and the defender throwing two dice. The table shows that the attacker has a 37% chance of winning against the defender when killing two armies. The defender has only a 29% of winning. Thus, the attacker has a slight advantage over the defender.

The moral conclusion: *take the initiative and attack*. If you know a battle is due, attempt to start it yourself. You will have control over the direction of the attack as well as a slightly biased dice combination. The gods of luck will be on your side!

The Odds		Attacker		
Defender		41.67 % ATTACKER WINS	57.87 % ATTACKER WINS	65.97 % ATTACKER WINS
		58.33 % DEFENDER WINS	42.13 % DEFENDER WINS	34.03 % DEFENDER WINS
		25.46 % ATTACKER WINS	22.76 % ATTACKER WINS	37.17 % ATTACKER WINS
		74.54 % DEFENDER WINS	44.83 % DEFENDER WINS	29.26 % DEFENDER WINS
		N/A	32.41 % BOTH WIN	33.58 % BOTH WIN

Table A-1. Dice odds in Risk.

Reference Table

This section provides you a reference of the most important concepts in the game and where you can find them in the book.

Concepts	
If you want to know ...	Located on these pages
what to think about in each turn	32
about mind mapping	32
how to profile players	40
how to have a large presence	50,52
if isolation is any good	46,60
If it is good to show that I am powerful	64, 241

What to do?	
If you want to know ...	Located on these pages
who is an aggressive/expansionist	41
who is a conservative/isolationist	42
who is a deal maker/negotiator	43
who is strategy-less/amateur	45
what an isolationist thinks of others	46
what a negotiator thinks of others	46
what an expansionist thinks of others	46
what an amateur thinks of others	47

What to do?

If you want to know ...	Located on these pages
what happens if I expand too rapidly	66
how to deal with a surrounded army	68
how to exploit impatience of others	83
how to make sure I will get the cards of a weak player when he is eliminated	81
what is the difference between a treaty and an alliance	101
how should I initiate an alliance	102
is it really possible to get a country without direct use of force	95
how to respond to an offer of alliance	103
how to use propaganda	114,118
how to deal with an intimidator	124
how to escalate a situation	130
how to create a conflict	136
how to defend myself in a conflict	137
what can I learn from cold war confrontations	138
how can I resolve a conflict	135
what are Risk player's incentives	141
is it really possible to get a country without direct use of force	95
how can I make a player do I want him to do	151
about deception	201
how can I improve my talking	222,230
should I kill a turtle	253,254,256,257
what should be my limits when negotiating	163
how can I improve my negotiation skills	167,171,173,183

What to do?	
If you want to know ...	**Located on these pages**
what should I do if I become weak	86
how should I plan for a negotiation	171
a few good tactics when negotiating with a Risk player	173, 183
how to control people	184
how can I stop someone from interfering with my plans	189
what is the difference between direct and indirect argument and how should I use them	194
stop losing my power	241
what should I do if no one is doing anything about the turtle	257
is breaking a deal any good	260
is it better to defend or attack	323
if online strategies are any different	265
about a few Risk scenarios	283
how can I stop people ganging up against me	241
how can I stop a couple to gang up against me	243

Definitions	
If you want to know ...	**Located on these pages**
the definition of tactics, strategy and diplomacy	27
about 5 'P's rule	32
how can I use 20-70-10 rule	47
what does 4,6,8,10,15,20, ... mean	62

Definitions	
If you want to know ...	**Located on these pages**
what does 5% continent growth mean	63
what is an exchange country	69
what is a buffer country	68
what is an intersection ground	70
what does Total War mean	76
how does Taoism relate to Risk	77
what is principle of least effort	78
what is 20-80 rule	80
what is a treaty	101
what is an alliance	101
what is argumentum ad nauseam	114
what are talking points	115
what is black/white/grey propaganda	116
what is doublespeak	121
what is nailing	84
what is LAS and MSP	163
what is brinkmanship	130,134
what is slippery slope	131
what is AIDA	195
what is Prisoner's Dilemma	245
what should I do if I am stabbed in the back	247,249
what does it mean to be nice	248,260
what is tit-for-tat	249
what is iterated prisoner's dilemma	247
what is turtle strategy	252
what is the rational choice theory	236

Definitions	
If you want to know …	**Located on these pages**
what is tragedy of the commons	255
what is an evolutionary stable strategy	260
what are dice odds	323
what is a BOMS (Bold Move Sequence) graph	270
what is card locking	279
what is card farming	69
what is vulture strategy	267
what does it mean to suicide	138, 268
what does Total Diplomacy mean	77

Advice and Examples	
If you want to know …	**Located on these pages**
which continent is the best	56
how many armies should I use when I want to attack	64
should I go for continents or cards	61
how many armies should I leave in my borders	66
how many players cheat in Risk	147
is it really possible to get a country without direct use of force	95
about a few online walkthrough examples	269
a few examples of treaties	104,106,108
how many players cheat in Risk	147
a historical example on crisis management	88,90

Acknowledgments

The book you are holding is a result of many games played over the years with a variety of friends. I am thankful to all of those who lost with humility and also those who tried to teach me a lesson by kicking me out of the game. I decided to put all those lessons into this book and hope to reduce the suffering of others. I would like to thank H. Bakhshayesh, Will Pearson, Shahram Zamani, Oliver Bittner, Christian Wager, Sean McLellan, Xavier Fosse, Anthony Yeung and many others.

I like to thank Sara Honary for the design of the Risk map used in this book and also Farhang Afshar for his inputs and support.

I would like to thank the online Risk communities for providing endless discussions on online Risk games and variants.

To make this book a reality, I had to research a large number of topics and put together a bit of everything. In order to achieve this, I had to stand on the shoulders of giants. The references contain a number of sources that I used in writing this book. I am grateful for their hard work and I have thoroughly enjoyed reading and researching them. If you find their quotes or ideas interesting, please refer to the corresponding sources for further detail.

And most important of all, I would like to thank my lovely wife, Matin, for her great support and feedback during the writing and production of this book. Without her encouragement, this book would not have become a reality.

References

Axelrod, R. (1984). *The Evolution of Cooperation*. Basic Books.

Carl von Clausewitz (1832) *On War*.

Clearly, T., (1988) *The Art of War Sun Tzu*, Shambhala Publications.

Fadiman, C., (1985) *The Little, Brown Book of Anecdotes*, Little Brown & Co.

Greene, R, (1998) *48 Laws of Power*, Profile Books.

Levitt, S.D., Stephen, J. Dubner (2005) *Freakonomics: A Rogue Economist Explores the Hidden Side of Everything*, William Morrow.

Lieberman, D.J., (1998) *Never Be Lied to Again: How to Get the Truth In 5 Minutes Or Less In Any Conversation Or Situation*. St. Martin's Press.

Machiaveli, N., (1513) *The prince*.

Maynard Smith, J. (1982). *Evolution and the theory of games*. Cambridge: Cambridge University Press.

Mind Gym, (2005) The Mind Gym: Wake Your Mind Up. Time Warner Books.

Robins, A., (1992) *Awaken the Giant Within*. Free Press.

Reynolds, Paul (2006) *Suez: End of empire*. BBC article published in ww.bbc.co.uk.

Schatzki, M., (1981) *Negotiation: The Art of Getting What You Want*.

Schopenhauer, A., (2005) *The art of always being right*, Gibson Square Books.

Shirer, W.L., (1960) *The rise and fall of the third Reich*, Arrow Books.

Dawkins, R., (1976) *Selfish Gene*, Oxford University Press.

Other Sources

Journey to the West (also known as His-yu chi or Xiyou ji) which is one of the Four Classical Novels of Chinese literature originally published anonymously in the 1590s.

Index

Printed in Great Britain
by Amazon

53637353R00203